Edwin Muir

Edwin Muir

An introduction to his work

Roger Knight

Longman
London and New York

Longman Group Limited London

*Associated companies, branches and representatives
throughout the world*

*Published in the United States of America
by Longman Inc., New York*

© Longman Group Limited 1980

First published 1980

British Library Cataloguing in Publication Data

Knight, Roger
    Edwin Muir.
    1. Muir, Edwin – Criticism and interpretation
    821′.9′12   PR6025.U6Z/   79–42832

    ISBN 0–582–48901–6
    ISBN 0–582–48906–7 Pbk

Set in 10/11pt Comp/Set Times Roman
Printed in Great Britain by
Richard Clay (The Chaucer Press) Ltd, Bungay, Suffolk

For GSJ

Contents

Acknowledgements

All quotations from Muir's poems are taken from *Collected Poems* (1963)

Parts of Chapter 1, 'The Story and the Fable', have appeared in *The Use of English*.

The publishers are grateful to the following for permission to reproduce copyright material:

the author, P. H. Butter and Gavin Muir for an extract from *Edwin Muir: Man and Poet* by P. H. Butter, published by Oliver and Boyd, 1966; Faber and Faber Ltd and Oxford University Press Inc for the complete poems 'The Return', 'The Enchanted Knight', 'The Poet', 'The City', 'Then', 'The Ring', 'The Face', 'The Question', 'Comfort in Self-Despite' and 'Too Much'; extracts from the poems 'October at Hellbrunn', 'The Hill', 'Merlin', 'Troy', 'The Human Fold', 'The Letter', 'The Prize', 'The Confirmation', 'The Commemoration', 'The Myth', 'In Love for Long', 'The Bridge of Dread', 'The Labyrinth', 'The Transfiguration', 'One Foot in Eden' and 'Orpheus' Dream' all from *The Collected Poems of Edwin Muir* copyright © 1960 by Willa Muir. Reprinted by permission of Faber and Faber Ltd and Oxford University Press Inc; The Hogarth Press Ltd for extracts from *Selected Letters of Edwin Muir* edited by P. H. Butter; *Essays on Literature and Society* by Edwin Muir, Second Edition 1965; *Transition* by Edwin Muir, 1926; *An Autobiography* by Edwin Muir, 1954 and *Belonging* by Edwin Muir, 1968; The Hogarth Press Ltd and Harvard University Press for extracts from *The Estate of Poetry* by Edwin Muir, 1962.

In the end the only events in my life worth telling
are those when the imperishable world irrupted into this transitory one.

(Jung, *Memories, Dreams, Reflections*)

Hold the hye wey, and lat thy gost thee lede:
And trouthe shall delivere, hit is no drede.

(Chaucer, *Truth*)

I think that if any of us examines his life, he will find that most good has come to
him from a few loyalties, and a few discoveries made many generations before he
was born, which must always be made anew. These too may sometimes appear
to come by chance, but in the infinite web of things and events chance must be
something different from what we think it to be. To comprehend that is not given
to us, and to think of it is to recognize a mystery, and to acknowledge the
necessity of faith. As I look back on the part of the mystery which is my own life,
my own fable, what I am most aware of is that we receive more than we can ever
give; we receive it from the past, on which we draw with every breath, but also –
and this is a point of faith – from the Source of the mystery itself, by the means
which religious people call Grace.

(Edwin Muir, *An Autobiography*)

Introduction

Writing to a friend in 1925, Edwin Muir said, 'I feel art is for me the only way of growing, of becoming myself more purely; and I value it for myself, I know it is my own *good*, the only real good for me, and the personal feeling, the personal integration seems to me more and more the thing that really matters.'[1] The growth of which Muir speaks is of a kind that his best prose work, *An Autobiography*,[2] both records and beautifully exemplifies. That book is no ordinary story of a life; it is one of the most intimate, instructive and wise bodies of insights into the growth of a poet's mind that our own century has to offer. Deeply and necessarily personal though the origins of the book are, in following the growth of that mind and listening to the witness of the poetry we are simultaneously in the country of the historian of culture, the philosopher of art and the visionary. In an article written soon after Muir's death, Michael Hamburger said that in his poetry 'a truthful and thoroughgoing subjectivity turns into its opposite'.[3] That is true of *An Autobiography* too. Muir decided to undertake his autobiography in the first place in an attempt to 'find out what a human being is in this extraordinary age that depersonalises everything' (17 May 1938). But, as the phrase 'a human being' suggests, the result was not a celebration of his own individuality. 'The Eternal Man', he said, 'has possessed me during most of the time I have been writing my autobiography and has possessed me too in much of my poetry.'[4] He tells his 'story' in order 'to save from the miscellaneous dross of experience a few glints of immortality', to get at the 'fable' underlying the multifariousness of ordinary life. There will be much to say about the fable in the course of this book; it is enough to say here that it signifies that common ground – the 'changeless ground' of his poem, *The Window*, on which all men are united but which they can only rarely glimpse. It is to the discovery and celebration of this ground that, in Muir's view, men address themselves in art, myth and religion. If he is true to the main impulse of Muir's work his critic or biographer must become part of that endeavour; in his turn try to reveal something of the relation between the 'transitory' and the 'imperishable' world as it was experienced in Muir's life and expressed in his poetry. In doing that he will, like Muir himself, be striving to interpret the story of an individual in ways that display its connection with that 'changeless ground' and thus with all men at any time. And this has certain implications for the selection and ordering of the material available to anyone describing Muir's work. Muir himself is the guide: correctly he entitles his book *'An' Autobiography* – there could be others. In writing it, his object was not to give an exhaustive account of occasions, people and places, but to reveal the pattern of his life, to discover something of the relations between present and past and, overall, to meditate on the three mysteries with which 'our minds are possessed': 'where we came from, where we are going, and, since we are not alone, but members of a countless family, how we should live with one another' (p. 56). All men are in some degree naturally fascinated by these mysteries but in Muir the first – 'where we came from' – seemed if anything to grow more urgent and complex as he grew older. From his first poems recollecting his childhood, through *An Autobiography* itself, to his great poem *The Journey Back* (written when he was past sixty), his preoccupation with his origins is constant. Its continuing urgency has to be attributed at least in part to the quite extraordinary outward shape of his life. A glance at the circumstantial outline is enough to show that.

Born in the Orkneys in 1887 into what he described as 'a culture made up of legend, folk-song, and the poetry and prose of the Bible', he was abruptly translated to the chaos of industrial Glasgow at the age of fourteen. Four of his immediate family died there within two years of this move. Over a period of eighteen years, in Scotland and elsewhere, he held a series of clerical jobs, some of them tedious and enervating, one of them (a job in a bone factory) having the contours of a nightmare that might have come from Kafka – whose stories Muir and his wife eventually translated. In his late fifties he became Director of the British Council Institute in Prague, knew a Communist regime at first hand, leaving Czechoslovakia soon after the putsch of 1948. The outward chronology is startling enough; what of the inner scale on which Muir felt himself to have lived? In 1938 he wrote in his diary:

I was born before the Industrial Revolution and am now about two hundred years old. But I have skipped a hundred and fifty years of them. . . . All my life since I have been trying to overhaul this invisible leeway. No wonder I am obsessed with time.[5]

Later he was to see in Czechoslovakia 'a whole people lost by one of the cruel turns of history, and exiled from themselves in the heart of their own country' (p. 280). This last is a phrase we might with equal justice apply to his own case. Through his poetry and his autobiography he explored his own way back from exile, to a sense of his authentic self. It was an arduous homecoming, its record without equal in modern English literature.

Muir's description of himself as obsessed with time leads us directly to the centre of his work. And yet, obsessions are artistically worthless. The truth is that what with him begins as an obsession, limiting and sometimes enfeebling the poetry, is eventually brought under impressive imaginative control. Muir's mature work displays a depth of insight and a power to give that insight imaginative life for which, in my view, the only conceivable parallel in twentieth-century English literature is to be found in the later poems of T. S. Eliot. It is the journey between these two points – between obsession and mature poetry – that I wish to follow in this book. Not even Eliot, I think, was possessed of the mystery of time and eternity in the intense – and intensely natural way – that was Muir's. In Muir, to know the 'still point of the turning world' is the constant aspiration; his deepest conviction that the 'lifetime burning in every moment' can be known only in remembrance and contemplation. Muir could have said with Traherne: 'The first light which shined in my Infancy in its primitive and innocent clarity was totally eclipsed insomuch that I was fain to learn all again.'[6] Muir's, though, was the incomparable disadvantage of a religious sensibility in an irreligious age. What gives his story so exemplary a force is that against terrifying odds his 'spontaneous piety' – the phrase he used of his father – survived as the basis of his own salvation and some of the finest religious poetry of the age. The clue for him as for Traherne was 'to learn all again'. In describing his childhood in *An Autobiography* it is the sense of timelessness that survives to be recalled. He had known it once; now, through memory and through the creative imagination in poetry, it could be known again. He would have agreed absolutely with Eliot that

> We had the experience but missed the meaning,
> And approach to the meaning restores the experience
> In a different form.[7]

'Our memories', says Muir, 'are real in a different way from the real things we try to resuscitate.' But the 'restoring' of his early days on the Orkney island of Wyre was for him of the utmost significance: it was the foundation of his poetry and of a growth into faith which the poetry both assists and celebrates.

One way of following that growth is through a chronological account of the poetry alone, but that is not the way I have chosen here. Muir's work is a unity. His work as a critic and *par excellence*, as his own biographer, are intimately related to his development as a poet. Many times in the course of this study I have found a phrase from Kathleen Raine's fine essay on Muir coming to mind as if to stress that fact: 'The world of ideas for him was not a doctrine but an experience.' It is a phrase that casts a strong light on the nature of the integrity of Muir's work. The toughness and authority of his mature writing, whether in verse or prose, are in a large degree due to their freedom from mere 'ideas': no modern writer is less given to abstraction, none more instinctively concerned that his judgements shall remain in touch with his intuitions. It is on the one hand what makes him an outstanding critic; on the other, this wholeness belongs with that intimate understanding of the language of myth, legend and emblem so characteristic of his verse. 'My childhood all a myth/Enacted in a distant isle', he was to write (*The Myth*) and we must understand the word 'myth' in its full informing power: Muir no more held to his view of childhood as an 'idea' than did Traherne. Immortality came for him to mean not a concept for the mind to wrestle with but a condition already known. Both men are free of sentimentality; childhood as each remembers it has a secure objectivity. 'My knowledge was divine', says Traherne. 'I knew by intuition those things which since my Apostasy I collected again by highest reason.'[8] The concern of both writers is to re-collect those days when knowledge was all intuition, to testify to its truthfulness in the light of 'highest reason'.

Just as in Traherne's *Centuries* the occasional poems endorse and amplify the prose meditations, so in Muir's poetry and autobiography we may find a comparable unity. There is, obviously enough, a place for the criticism of poetry that makes no mention of the life of the artist. But, on the evidence purely of his own writing, Muir's is of a kind to invite the reconstruction of his life, or, at least of those stages in it that were of most importance to him as a poet. In the early 1920s he tells us, 'I realized that I must live over again the years which I had lived wrongly, and that every one should live his life twice for the first attempt is always blind' (p. 192). His poetry could begin only through a fairly deliberate act of remembering and any adequate description of those beginnings must show what it meant for him. Hence the first chapter of this book is an extended consideration of *An Autobiography*, not itself the outcome of that first act of remembering but demonstrably the culmination of many such acts that assisted Muir's development as an artist. (It is part of my purpose, too, to do justice to the book as in itself a splendid achievement.) And just as *An Autobiography* is concerned not with the 'dross' of circumstantial detail but with the enduring meaning that it obscures, so in describing Muir's beginnings I shall be sparing in talk of places, people and events. I intend this book to be *a* biography in the sense of showing something of the nature of that growth which Muir said was for him the only real good, with the necessary limitation that he implied in his own title.

Accordingly, my later chapters make scant reference to the outward events of Muir's life, with the exception of his experience of Prague in the late 1940s and of Rome a little later. In this they reflect the balance of his own interests in the composition of *An Autobiography*. In general, the chapters he added in the 1950s lack the intensity of those that originally appeared as *The Story and the Fable*. The 1940 version was the culmination of that remembering begun in the 1920s through which he had felt he was 'discovering life for the first time'. By the 1950s he had in a sense 'arrived': the poetry of his maturity reflects an increasingly sure and clear understanding of the nature of the past and its relation to the present. It is thus much more important in the reading of his work that we should know something of his young manhood in Glasgow than that we should know anything of his period in the 1950s as Warden of Newbattle Abbey in Scotland.

Muir's object in writing his autobiography was in one sense identical to what he saw as the proper aim of literary criticism: 'If the poem, having been submitted to analysis, does not assume a new and natural shape, what remains is merely the analysis with its own internal interest; and the poem has been replaced by the criticism.'[9] He had strong things to say about modern 'practical criticism' when it forgot its main object and betrayed an admiration for its own ingenuity. The most useful function of criticism as he saw it was 'to be a helpful intermediary between literature and the reader'. The critics who did this best were those with

a capacity for admiration, that indispensable virtue. If we turn to the romantic critics – Lamb, Hazlitt and Coleridge – that is what we find, and we recognize it as springing from a largeness of soul, a capacity to delight in all that is great. A good critic in this style is one who apprehends by a natural affinity the virtues of a work of imagination and rejoices in them.[10]

There is nothing vague or elusive in this view; Muir's own literary criticism is proof enough that vigour and good judgement are quite compatible with it. The essay from which it comes was written towards the end of his life; but while it owes much to mature reflection, like much else in the work of his maturity it shows the influence of his very earliest experience of oral poetry. Later I shall want to consider more closely the importance to him of a community in which *Sir Patrick Spens*, *Thomas the Rhymer*, *The Demon Lover* and *The Wife of Usher's Well* were still sung around the Orkney farms in a living ballad tradition. To the point here is the naturalness with which oral poetry entered his imagination as far back as he could remember: 'What did we think of poetry? We did not *think* of it at all.' That it had for him personally been first known as 'a natural thing, an exercise of the heart and the imagination' made him suspicious of approaches to poetry that threatened to convert it into the wrong kind of mystery.

The directive to the critic of Muir's own work is clear: if it does not exercise his 'capacity for admiration', he had better leave it alone. And if it does, then he must try to see it whole. He must endeavour to see the relations between individual works, to understand the way they illuminate one another and in turn the order of which they are a part – in short, to give that order 'a new and natural shape'. Only thus far will analysis of individual poems be justified. I hope to reveal that shape as the form of Muir's 'way of growing, of becoming myself more purely'. Naturally that entails judgement as to which works are the real growing points. The critic's task is to suggest and show why we should look here rather than there, at this work rather than that, if we wish to reveal the shape that growth takes. I shall thus not be attempting an exhaustive and comprehensive account of all the poetry Muir wrote. When T. S. Eliot introduced his selection of the poems in 1965 he warned the reader against assuming that it was the best of Muir. The general standard was so high, he said, that inevitably many excellent poems had had to be excluded. That was a generous and just recognition. But, as with any other writer, there are barren stretches in Muir's work and these I have either not drawn attention to at all or have indicated my reasons for quickly passing over them. Muir himself is to a certain extent the guide in this respect too. He wished to see only nine of *First Poems* (1925) printed in *Collected Poems 1921–1958* and he did not wish to include his early long poem, *Chorus of the Newly Dead* (1926) at all. In these judgements I think he was right. I have therefore not discussed them here. Neither have I given much attention to *Variations on a Time Theme* (1934), which is included in *Collected Poems*: it offers ample exercise for a certain kind of interpretative scrutiny, but I do not feel that it repays the endeavour its obliqueness and frequent obscurity calls for. It can be turned up by the interested reader, but just because there is so much else that is worth close attention, I have been guided by what my judgement tells me is both intrinsically good and illuminating in the telling of Muir's story.

I have discussed or referred to Muir's prose works on the same principle: that is, to whatever extent seemed warranted in an account of the poetry. In practice this means that, *An Autobiography* apart, I have made only passing reference to his novels, little more than that to his books about Scotland, *Scottish Journey* (1935), *Scott and Scotland* (1936), most to the four collections of literary criticism: *Latitudes* (1924); *Transition* (1926); *Essays on Literature and Society* (1956) and *The Estate of Poetry* (published posthumously, 1962). The 1956 volume is perhaps tolerably familiar but there is a limited amount of writing from the earlier work, long out of print, that should be better known. Such essays as those on the Scottish ballads in *Latitudes* and on modern writers in *Transition* are valuable not simply to a better understanding of Muir's poetic development but also in their own right. I am indebted, too, to P.H. Butter's *Selected Letters of Edwin Muir* (1974), a source unavailable to most previous commentators. The letters provide much valuable insight into the nature of Muir's art, his conception of the artist and the difficulties he faces in the present age. Muir's first body of original work is to be found in the 1930s and his letters can help us to see more clearly the features of that decade that made it – except for truly original talent – so hostile to the poetic imagination. The nature of his achievement is, I think, more readily appreciated if we see how significantly it departs from, is almost completely unaffected by, the characteristic poetry of the decade. Muir was fully alive to the crises of the age, industrial and political. *Scottish Journey* is a clearsighted and sympathetic account of modern Scotland and the consequences of industrialism and present unemployment, while there is ample evidence from the autobiography, his correspondence and the poems themselves that he was acutely aware of the nature of modern Communism and its theoretical appeal to those living at a safe distance from its realities. His imaginative and intellectual clarity at such a time enabled him to produce poetry that we can now see to have been a deeper, more intelligent response to the times than the representative poems we can find in anthologies of verse of the 1930s.

We will not normally find Muir in those anthologies but he does appear in anthologies of Scottish verse. And yet, just as in the early 1930s he lived in Hampstead without being essentially part of it (the young poets with whom he and his wife were friendly 'seemed to be more real than their poetry') so he never felt fully *of* Scotland. This was not merely a matter of his ancestry. He might say that 'I'm an Orkneyman, a good Scandinavian, and my country is Norway, or Denmark, or Iceland or some place like that' (14 May 1927), but his reasons for not thinking of himself as a Scottish writer are more complex. He was intrigued and saddened by Scotland's history and its literature, but though he occasionally expressed sympathy for Scottish nationalism and the idea of 'an indigenous school of literature', it did not represent his most consistent view. His conclusion in *Scott and Scotland* was that 'Scotland can only create a national literature by writing in English'. In that book he developed the view that Scotland had not had a 'homogeneous language' since before the Reformation. In his reading of Scottish history, the possession of a language that would be adequate for 'expressing the response of a whole people, emotional and intellectual, to a specific body of experience peculiar to it alone, on all levels of thought from discursive reason to poetry' had been lacking 'since some time in the sixteenth century'.[11] It was a conclusion that provoked furious charges from Hugh MacDiarmid that Muir had betrayed the ideals of the contemporary Scottish 'renaissance' in poetry. But Muir felt that the notion of such a renaissance was misconceived and that, much as he admired him, 'MacDiarmid will become a figure like Burns – an exceptional case, that is to say – an arbitrary apparition of the national genius, robbed of his legitimate effect because there will be no literary tradition to perpetuate it'. As he saw it, the Scottish genius had 'gone mainly into international forms of activity: finance, engineering, philosophy, science, to the neglect of poetry, literature, art in general . . . the forms in which a nation survives'. However just Muir's analysis, he felt that 'the really awful phase is the present one: we are neither quite alive nor quite dead; we are neither quite Scottish nor are we quite delivered from our Scottishness, and free to integrate ourselves in a culture of our choice' (10 September 1931).

It can be shown, I think, that even Muir's last poems here and there draw strength from the Scottish ballad tradition that he had once known at first hand. But that is a fact of native inheritance rather than deliberate acquisition. After some early experiments in the writing of Scots ballads, he struck out in quite different directions. More than most writers he resists 'placing'; we cannot with any confidence attach him to any school, movement or tradition. Though he was to be profoundly grateful for his Orkney boyhood his was not the kind of imagination that would be satisfied to resuscitate the mythologies of the islands; neither could it find satisfaction in a Scotland where since 'national unity is lost the past is lost too, for the connection between the present and the past is broken'.[12] His imagination found no echo in the declining tradition of Victorian English poetry – he could never have been a Georgian – nor could he for a long time sympathize with the iconoclasts and innovators among the American and English modernists. (His appreciation of Eliot came late.) His independence of the main streams of English poetry can perhaps be suggested by the fact that we come across more admiring references to von Hofmannsthal and Hölderlin than to any other poets. To Kafka as well Muir came alive as to a kindred imagination. Somehow, while remaining in touch with – indeed, strengthening his hold on – his roots, Muir's mature poetry incorporates a European sensibility. We may see Muir's journey – the key metaphor in his poetry – as an unending search for his beginnings not only in the straightforward sense of understanding what he owed to 'kinsmen and kinswomen, ancestors and friends' (*'I have been taught'*), though that is a necessary step, but of discovering his spiritual masters: writers and artists with whose help he might learn through his own creation to 'gather an image whole' (*Reading in Wartime*) or, in T. S. Eliot's words, 'to arrive where we started/And know the place for the first time'.[13] The nature of that journey is my theme in this book.

Chapter 1

The Story and the Fable

How shall I seek the origin? Where find
Faith in the marvellous things which then I felt?
Oft in these moments such a holy calm
Would overspread my soul, that bodily eyes
Were utterly forgotten, and what I saw
Appeared like something in myself, a dream,
A prospect in the mind.

(William Wordsworth[1])

When in later years Muir asked himself what had most deeply influenced him in the writing of poetry, he could 'only think of the years of child-hood ... and the beauty I apprehended then, before I knew there was beauty' (p. 206). In the first chapter of *An Autobiography*, 'Wyre', Muir contemplates that beauty through the recollection of the events and images of his earliest years. It is the finest chapter of the book and the most important. For the beauty has nothing of the picturesque or pretty about it: what is recalled and described with such clarity is a profound sense of the fitness of all things in the unchanging Orkney landscape, a fitness that for ever after was to figure for Muir as an image of wholeness, an intimation of immortality and the aspiration of his adult life. It is the world of Traherne: 'But all things abided eternally as they were in their proper places. Eternity in the light of day, and something infinite behind everything appeared.'[2] Orkney gave him, 'an image of life more complete' than any he was to know again. His achievement in this book is to persuade us of the authenticity of the child's vision and, almost incidentally, to disclose the springs of his own eventual development as a poet. 'The vast, boundless calm' of his early days breathes again in these pages as he recalls a 'stationary' immemorial world, 'the changed, unchanging reign' of his poem, *The Recurrence*.

While Muir's was undoubtedly an exceptional sensibility, the nature of his attention to experience does not directly invite the reader to think of it in such terms. In a way he seems to play down whatever might have been distinctive in his boyhood; we become convinced that what we are reading is the story of a boy – any normally sensitive boy – brought up in an environment that favoured the development of a sensibility to which most modern societies are now hostile. Partly our conviction is a matter of the style; though the experiences he recounts are frequently intense and clearly of enduring significance in his emotional and intellectual development, there is no rapture. There is, rather, a meticulous and disciplined attention to detail which gradually yields the story of a childhood exceptional only in the depth at which its most characteristic experiences have been absorbed and become a part of a mature and unusual adult personality. It is a prose that demands to be read slowly, with the same thoughtful attention to what is being said that its spare and deliberate character reflects. There is no heightening, nothing of that seductive patina of romance that can and does so often attach itself to remembered childhood. Nostalgia for what is undeniably a lost world is quite absent. Without condescension, for example, Muir straightforwardly reports the Orkney people's belief in 'fantastic feats of strength' and in the fairies that populated their imagination. 'Fairies, or "fairicks", as they were called, were encountered dancing on the sands on moonlight nights. From people's talk they were small graceful creatures about the size of leprechauns, but pretty, not grotesque. There was no harm in them.' This mere 'reporting', however, the apparent acceptance of fact suggested by 'were encountered' and 'were small', is actually an acceptance of the meaning of these things in the people's lives. They were part of a pattern, not a whimsical indulgence; of his father's stories, he says 'they were drawn mostly from an earlier age . . . but in his own time he had known several witches'. Though Muir afterwards heard these stories in later versions and though he says that 'these obviously come from the store of legends that gathered when witch-burning was common in Scotland', the phrase 'he had known' is not accidental. He does not patronize his father: the stuff of these tales was real enough for him, for 'the Orkney I was born into was a place where there was no great distinction between the ordinary and the fabulous; the lives of living men turned into legend'. 'All these things', he says, 'have vanished from Orkney in the last fifty years under the pressure of compulsory education', and he writes about them from the point of view of a poet who knows the meaning of the fabulous: that the body of traditional lore and legend gave to the lives of the people an imaginative order different in quality but not different in kind from that of the poet himself. In this part of the book, indeed, Muir does not simply record all that he can remember of his childhood. It is, we remember, the growth of a poet's mind we are looking back on. What was most significant for him was just this never-to-be-doubted intertwining of the material and the immaterial, the ordinary and the fabulous. For Muir, as I wish later to show, such an intertwining – not the possession of childhood alone, but a common inheritance – nourished his adult poetic vision in some very important ways.

Something of the character of that inheritance may be gathered from his description of family life, and particularly of the place of music and singing within the home. The 'evening filled with talk, stories, games, music and lamplight' could be the introduction to a nostalgic idyll, a conscious re-creation of old and better times. But it is not so. The picture has a detail that leaves us in no doubt about its authenticity. The ballads he sang and heard sung in his own home were part of an active oral tradition; how much so we may judge from his ability to quote from those his mother used to sing but that are now neither to be heard nor found in print. His mother might sing of 'Sir James the Rose/The knight 'o mickle fame' – 'I have never come across it since' – but the repertoire included eighteenth-century broadsheet ballads which, simply in being printed, were an omen of deep cultural change. In remembering this, Muir is able to make a distinction of major significance in the imaginative life of the islanders and in his own development as a poet:

> There was a great difference between the earlier and the later songs. The ballads about James V and Sir James the Rose had probably been handed down orally for hundreds of years; they were consequently sure of themselves and were sung with your full voice, as if you had always been entitled to sing them; but the later ones were chanted in a sort of literary way, in honour of the print in which they had originally come, every syllable of the English text carefully pronounced, as if it were an exercise. These old songs, rooted for so long in the life of the people, are now almost dead (p. 30).

To speak of these songs as 'having been sure of themselves' is to capture the truth of a tradition: it is at once a communal possession, an impersonal guarantor of meaning and beauty, depending on no individual for its life, yet one of the main ways in which individual men and women can know the meaning of their lives. The loss, now that the old songs are dead, is mourned in the late poem, *Complaint of the Dying Peasantry*. The sons of the peasants are now 'newspapermen', music and ceremony have vanished, the 'singing tragedies' 'nailed down in print'; the book of ballads now silently records what was once part of a vital spiritual life:

> Sir Patrick Spens shut in a book,
> Burd Helen stretched across a page:
> A few readers look
> There at the effigy of our age.
>
> The singing and the harping fled
> Into the silent library;
> But we are with Helen dead
> And with Sir Patrick lost at sea.

Towards the end of his life Muir said that 'we begin to die when we stop remembering'. The peasants of his poem remember enough to know that they are dying. They are, it may be said, dying into a new kind of life. And that is true. Muir is no sentimentalist. Indeed, in his book *A Scottish Journey* (1935), he insists that modern Orkneymen probably have the best of both worlds, the pre- and post-industrial. He was always a very sober observer and thus the more reliable in his report on the cultural changes he lived through and describes. The strength and accuracy of his insight in both the prose passages and the poems are those of a writer who knows the facts at first hand. Muir's insights are informed insights. His comments on the quality of the islanders' lives are those of an educated European with a powerful sense of the losses and gains that being educated entails. A people's traditions are intimately a matter of the language in which they are transmitted; when the language changes the traditions change too, are modified or dissolved, and vice versa. Muir's father was obviously a good storyteller; he drew on a store of legends and his skill was such that his children were afraid to go to their beds when he told them his witch stories. But, equally important, he had the support of a language that in the way it had come to be spoken, supplied 'a splendid voice for telling stories in':

It still keeps some of the quality of a chant, and I feel that in its early stages a language is always chanted, since it is new enough still to be cherished as an almost miraculous thing. The strangeness fades, and language becomes workable and commonplace (p. 62).

Muir's comment is, I think, more than a speculation about the evolution of language; it is about a change that he had lived through in his own lifetime. In both idiom and syntax ('The syntactical feeling is much stronger than in ordinary urban or educated speech, and has most resemblance to that of the seventeenth century') the language had its own genius and it gave a distinctive life to the imagination of the people. But that genius was being inexorably smothered by the spread of compulsory education – and, incidentally, the likelihood of good new poets much reduced. ('Most of the local poets who appear in Orkney write in an English laboriously derived from the grammar books.') It is important to realize Muir's sensitivity to this rapid change. He was, we remember, a child at a time when the traditions of the language (a mixture of Norse, Scots and Irish) were, though under threat, nonetheless fairly healthy; when speech, song and story were a distinctive inheritance, a natural stabilizing possession. It became crucial to his later development as a poet that he should recover his sense of what this inheritance counted for in his early life. It is described in these pages and it is active in the way he describes it. To convey the quality of the feeling for language is not easy. Perhaps Willa Muir's comment on her husband's hostility to abstract political systems is helpful: his old-fashioned socialism, she says in *Belonging*, 'was anything but abstract, being rooted in love and hope, words which he was able to use naturally, without self-consciousness'.[3] That lack of self-consciousness – the absence of irony or of defensiveness, of that peculiarly modern watchfulness not to be caught off one's guard – makes *An Autobiography* an unusual piece of modern writing. And Muir's reflections on the language of the Orkneys help to explain the 'naturalness' of his poetic language. I hope to do justice to the positive outcome in detailed discussion of the poems later; enough to note here that behind much of Muir's poetic work there is a faith in the continuing power of the word. Unlike many modern poets who know that they write within a beaten-down language, that they must reanimate a shopsoiled currency, surprising us into awareness – unlike these, Muir seems usually to take words for granted, trusts them to carry a continuous charge; in this sense is, as R. P. Blackmur says, singularly little in love with words.[4] 'The islands', says Muir, concluding his discussion of the Orkneymen's speech, 'produce a terrible number of professors. But simple, uneducated people here and there still speak a beautiful language and know where to set a word in a sentence.' Muir is not among the professors.

This faith in the integrity of language goes back to a childhood when there was very little to challenge it. The point is easily taken if we think of a child in a modern urban culture (and 'urban' may now describe an entire country such as our own), his early experience of language and the uses to which men put it. Modern abuses of language in the interests of politics, commerce and war are sufficiently well documented to need no illustration here. What is more difficult to take in is the change that such widespread abuse has worked and continues to work in the 'very culture of the feelings'.[5] Constant exposure to language as the instrument of some usually unknown agency's design upon us must surely (even, perhaps, though we are generally aware of it) tend to destroy our sense of the power of words to render what is good, true and beautiful, and thus our power to believe in the existence of these values. The language that Muir recalls was one which for the most part people could trust, in the way that children trust language. The important fact is that in a culture such as he describes, that unconscious faith in language as a carrier of unquestioned truths survives childhood, whereas in our society children are from a very early age deprived of such a faith.

That trust which the boy Muir inherited and lived by was part of a larger confidence: 'A child could not grow up in a better place than a farm; for at the heart of human civilization is the byre, the barn, and the midden.' It was a deeply secure world, its rituals and observances affirming continuities of value and belief that are at risk in 'a world of objects that are more and more impermanent'. Most important, it was a setting packed with visual and sensible meaning. Muir's most perceptive critics have commented on the pictorial immediacy of some of his best poetic conceptions – 'icons', John Holloway has called them, 'which rivet the attention and at their most powerful stamp themselves indelibly upon the mind'.[6] Blackmur says of Muir's poem, *The Return of Odysseus*, that it invites no comment other than the 'comment of intimacy'.[7] The pictorial immediacy of *An Autobiography* summons back the intimate contemplations of his childhood, the roots, one sees, of the adult poems that call for these descriptions.

'Our memories are real in a different way from the real things we try to resuscitate.' The dangers that surround any attempt to recall the events of childhood are obvious. If he is to avoid sentimentality – the falsification of the original event and what it meant to him – a man's recollections must be controlled by his knowledge that time and maturity place that event forever out of his reach. The only thing that can be of interest now is the present significance of what is remembered, its place in the way we read the meaning of our lives. Muir avoids the dangers, is indeed disciplined to avoid them by the nature of his interest in writing about his childhood. There is no straining to *evoke* a portion of lost time; the imagination is not at work to supply what strict recollection cannot. The memories described are those that stay in his mind through what is most permanent in them:

… there is one composite one which may conceivably go back to the house where I was born, it brings such a sense of timelessness with it. I was lying in some room watching a beam of slanting light in which dusty, bright motes slowly danced and turned, while a low murmuring went on somewhere, possibly the humming of flies. My mother was in the room, but where I do not know; I was merely conscious of her as a vague, environing presence. This picture is clear and yet indefinite, attached to one summer day at the Bu, and at the same time to so many others that it may go back to the day when I first watched a beam of light as I lay in my cradle. The quiet murmuring, the slow, unending dance of the motes, the sense of deep and solid peace, have come back to me since only in dreams. This memory has a different quality from any other memory in my life. It was as if, while I lay watching that beam of light, time had not yet begun (p. 18).

The most important word in that passage is 'sense' – 'it brings such a sense of timelessness', the 'sense of deep and solid peace'. That sense is still with him; he carries forward into adult life the knowledge that there was a time when it was 'as if time had not yet begun'.

From adolescence on, his entire life was in one way or another to be a search for the 'timeless in time' for 'a deep and solid peace' that would absorb the best and the worst that life could offer. For him now, looking back, that very early memory is an intimation of the reality he seeks. By the time he came to write *An Autobiography*, Muir had come to a faith in the intuitive workings of the psyche, in the wisdom of memory and dream, in their real if inscrutable relation to our conscious life. That faith is the organizing principle of the book. It is why he includes an anecdote about the way in which, after an interval of sixty years, he suddenly remembered a sailor suit he had worn as a child. That memory 'returned by a curious road': 'the fact that after being buried for all these years it should come back now by such a tortuous and yet purposive road struck me as very strange.' The strangeness is part of that mystery within which, but never to the solution of which, all 'roads' in Muir's work run. His imagination came to be deeply possessed of the imagery of roads and journeys, to the point indeed where he felt the existence of 'some deep archetypal image in our minds of which we become conscious only at the rare moments when we realize that our own life is a journey'.

What is summoned back in the early chapters of *An Autobiography* is the unconditional quality that the mystery of existence possessed in childhood, the fact of the natural world drawing the young mind into itself, leaving no room for doubt or reflection. Of the insects:

I could never bear to touch any of these creatures, though I watched them so closely that I seemed to be taking part in their life. . . . The gavelocks and forkytails were my first intimation of evil, and associations of evil still cling round them for me, as, I fancy, for most people: popular imagery shows it. We cannot tell how much our minds are influenced for life by the fact that we see the world first at a range of two or three feet (p. 21).

It may be normal for a small child to have this experience of taking part in the life of things. For Muir, though, the experience must have been the more intense and lasting in its effect for taking place in such a community. In a land where the ordinary and the fabulous intertwined, where adults could be seen and felt to share in the mystery and the magic, there would not be the normal sobering check on the childish imagination. From his mother he learnt which flowers 'could be relied upon', and we don't doubt that she would know, deeply, why 'after I picked a dandelion one day and found it writhing with little, angry, many-legged insects, the faces of the flowers took on a faithless look'.

There is in these early pages a magnificent passage describing an experience of horses on the farm that makes us see in a direct way why Muir stressed that he was born two hundred years ago. The power of the description is supported by a conviction about the natural world that for most of us now is a very remote matter indeed. Here, perhaps more than anywhere else in the book, we feel we are at the source of Muir's knowledge of the mystery. And he writes now in recollection and full adult acceptance of the meaning of the horses; when he describes them fighting, 'rearing at each other like steeds on a shield', it is no handy phrase but a summation of the meanings they carry for him. The 'stationary terror and delight', the fear and the longing, 'added up to worship in the Old Testament sense' – 'so that I loved and dreaded them as an explorer loves and dreads a strange country which he has not yet entered'. From that country would come 'the horses' of Muir's late poem of that name; the latterday world of the artist's imagination would reach down into that first world of childhood for the image of its perceptions, the memory having stayed, as Muir might put it, in answer to a question that had not been asked:

Everything about them, the steam rising from their soft, leathery nostrils, the sweat staining their hides, their ponderous, irresistible motion, the distant rolling of their eyes, which was like the revolution of rock-crystal suns, the waterfall sweep of their manes, the ruthless flick of their cropped tails, the plunge of their iron-shod hoofs striking fire from the flagstones, filled me with a stationary terror and delight for which I could get no relief (p. 22).

'Stationary' (one of Muir's key words) confirms the fusion of the child's emotions and the scene possessing him. 'The eye made quick with harmony' – in Wordsworth's phrase – saw insects 'as if they were magnets drawing me with palpable power'. The pictures – a word Muir uses throughout the book for moments of intense recollection and perception – convey the strength of that seeing and the mystery within it. Describing the lambs in spring, everything looking 'soft and new', he says they kept 'turning their heads with sudden gentle movements which belonged to some other place'. There is a persistent fascination with that 'other place'; his mother 'had always been with me in a region which could never be known again'; the horses 'belonged to a strange country'. It was not, though, an experience of being outside, denied understanding; it was simultaneously a knowledge of belonging and mystery, of deep familiarity and of awe. (Muir's description keeps the farm horses before our eyes but transfers them to an immemorial world.) When towards the end of his life he discovered the profuse Christian iconography of Rome, it was just such a duality that he recognized. It is celebrated in *The Annunciation*, an image at once close to our daily selves, yet mysterious, beyond them; the angel and the girl are here, but they are *there* too, in a strange country that we cannot understand yet that is our birthright and our goal:

> See, they have come together, see,
> While the destroying minutes flow,
> Each reflects the other's face
> Till heaven in hers and earth in his
> Shine steady there. He's come to her
> From far beyond the farthest star,
> Feathered through time. Immediacy
> Of strangest strangeness is the bliss
> That from their limbs all movement takes.
> Yet the increasing rapture brings
> So great a wonder that it makes
> Each feather tremble on his wings.

An Autobiography proves Muir wonderfully sensitive in evoking the physical feel of things and it is, with hindsight, totally convincing that he should irresistibly have come alive to 'that wealth of beautiful forms in painting and stone' that met his eye in Rome. That was a world in which the material and the spiritual flowed endlessly through each other in a natural harmony analogous to that of his childhood vision.

'The child has the original vision of the world.' Muir was eventually convinced that the harmony the child knows before the full weight of the world disrupts it prefigures a permanent spiritual condition, a condition that, transmuted, must forever be sought in adult life. *An Autobiography* records that seeking: the appalling obstacles and frustrations, the false turnings, the eventual arrival. It is often a pitiful story, the more painful and moving for being told without a trace of self-pity or false sentiment. To be flung from the emotional security of the Orkneys into the squalor of Glasgow was to be pressed into Time's service with signal brutality. It would be a mistake, though, to see the move to Glasgow as a sudden lurch from Eden into Purgatory. Division entered the boy's world well before that, but the move confirmed in a very brutal way the loss of his 'first clear vision of the world'. The second chapter of the book is largely concerned with the years spent at Garth, the family's last, unsuccessful, farm before Glasgow, and it was there that the vision began naturally to fade. It was as if 'time had suddenly spoken aloud within' him. In Wyre time had stood still; now all was changing. The family had begun to break up, his brothers and sister leaving home to work in Kirkwall, Edinburgh and Glasgow. He was beginning to feel 'that need to become at once like grown-up people which tortures growing boys'. Much of this change was, as he saw, normal; and while in Orkney he was to a large extent protected against the insecurity and uncertainty that change naturally brings. This was the traditional strength of the environment. The diary Muir kept in the late 1930s and that was included in *The Story and the Fable* concludes with the words: 'I would not for any price have missed my knowledge of that first pre-industrial order; for it taught me something which is inherent in every good order.' The original vision had to fade but, we remember, a child could continue to grow up in no 'better place than a farm; for at the heart of civilization is the byre, the barn, and the midden'. The paragraph of *An Autobiography* from which this sentence is taken says much about the nature of the security that such a background provided. The leading of the bull to serve the cow was 'a ritual act of the tradition in which we have lived for thousands of years, possessing the obviousness of a long dream from which there is no awaking'. The use of the word 'dream' here is not fortuitous; in Muir's own terms, tradition and ritual, independent of men yet unthinkable without them, are intimations of the 'fable', running like a saving thread through innumerable individual lives and communities, giving them meaning, holding back chaos. In this case 'there was a necessity in the copulation and the killing which took away the sin, or at least, by the ritual act, transformed it into a sad, sanctioned duty'. One is reminded of the poems *The Prize* and *The Question* (to be found in the 1943 volume, *The Narrow Place*), both of which are concerned with the distractions that prevent our knowing the more enduring meaning of our lives. The 'dream' is in life; only rarely do we become aware that this is so; there is a life in things waiting for us to see into it:

> We hurried here for some such thing and now
> Wander the countless roads to seek our prize,
> That far within the maze serenely lies,
> While all around each trivial shape exclaims:
> 'Here is your jewel; this is your longed-for day'.
> And we forget, lost in the countless names.

The Prize is an inspiring poem, alive with the conviction that a spiritual reality exists, that the conditions of human life put it forever within a 'maze' towards which the only possible attitude we can take up is one of hope and faith.

That conviction was hard-won. How hard-won we can see from Muir's description of the years in Glasgow, when events seemed to conspire to destroy his image of humanity and deride the 'spontaneous piety' he had inherited from his father. It is the achievement of *An Autobiography* to make us feel the brutality of the change, to show us the cause of Muir's obsession with time. In Glasgow he could see, could hear, smell and touch the savagery of Time's work, everywhere a wasteland in which the traditional virtues had been inverted. This may seem strong, even overblown language; it is not: the evidence is the work itself. In the Orkneys the Muirs had been 'virtually self-supporting', had lived the virtues of cooperation with their neighbours in a 'good order'. Here, on the other hand, it was man against his neighbour, everyone for himself in an unprecedentedly ugly environment. The dislocation was total. Indeed, *An Autobiography* must be one of the last possible testimonies in our culture to the experience of such dislocation. (Its natural company is such books as Lawrence's *The Rainbow* and George Sturt's *Change in the Village*.) 'The first few years after we came to Glasgow were so stupidly wretched, such a meaningless waste of inherited virtue, that I cannot write of them even now without grief and anger' (p. 93). It is a moving and natural statement. 'Virtue' – almost a dead word, it seems, a memorial to lapsed certainties; but it shines out from Muir's sentence, rich with the meanings of the first chapters. We know, having read those chapters, that if we can know what 'virtue' meant and might mean it will be through a quality of living such as is there remembered with such fidelity. The authenticity of that picture earns Muir the right to use language with a resonance that in other hands might easily draw criticisms of sentimentality and overstatement:

These journeys [in Glasgow] filled me with a sense of degradation: the crumbling houses, the twisted faces, the obscene words casually heard in passing, the ancient, haunting stench of pollution and decay, the arrogant women, the mean men, the terrible children, daunted me, and at last filled me with an immense, blind dejection. I had seen only ordinary people before; but on some of the faces that I passed every day now there seemed to be things written which only a fantastic imagination could have created, and I shrank from reading them and quickly learned not to see (pp. 91–2).

The contours of Hell itself. Learning not to see was spiritual death. In the Orkneys the order within which men lived embraced the physical world, was known through its rhythms and those rituals 'possessing the obviousness of a long dream from which there is no awaking'. To be in that order was to gain a sense of oneself, silently to know the answer to the question Muir says urgently confronts the autobiographer: 'How can he know himself?' Glasgow held no answers, stilled all voices, dammed up the sources of vision, in short, laid waste the 'inherited virtue'. Coleridge would have recognized Muir's picture. He knew that

> Inanimate cold world allowed
> To the poor, loveless, ever-anxious crowd.[8]

Muir's description of his encounter with that 'inanimate' world has a rare authenticity. For writers and artists in the nineteenth and twentieth centuries, the rapid urbanization of rural communities is probably *the* central crisis – social, moral, spiritual. It is difficult for any of us to escape some consciousness of loss, or at least of a profound difference in the way we feel and relate to each other. But for most artists, as for most educated people today, that consciousness has rarely been acquired in the deep, direct and unavoidable way in which it came to Muir. Most of us cannot have the direct experience of the kind of expulsion he suffered; sentimentality and distortion are thus ready dangers. On the one hand, plenty of secondrate writers are ready to peddle warm and hazy versions of vanished pastoral ease; on the other, there are those who deride any description of what has been lost through urbanization as the invention of selfconsciously disinherited intellectuals. Muir's credentials being so impeccable, his descriptions have a quite unusually strong claim upon our attention.

That is true of *An Autobiography* and it is true of *Scottish Journey*, the book he wrote after a tour of Scotland in 1934 and that presents the same kind of account of urban life as we find in the later book. Both books contain painful descriptions of the Scottish urban wasteland seen against the background of Orkney life: the alienation of a man from his neighbour, the pervasive competitiveness and adulation of success, the self-induced anaesthetizing of the senses in an ugly environment, the spiritual starvation – all struck Muir directly, not as the constructions of a cultural theory, but as a ghastly affront to the values by which he had lived until his arrival in Glasgow and that he had found no reason basically to question. The traditional values had been inverted indeed to the point where the inversion was unselfconsciously celebrated as a triumph:

> The main ideal was respectability or rising in the world. In such people the wish to get on was not merely a natural desire, but the chief article in an exalted mystical faith . . . one's neighbour was one's worst enemy. . . . In the islands it was considered contemptible to steal a march on your neighbour and tasteless to push yourself forward; but I found that here these things were not only permissible but a mark of virtue.[9]

This inversion of values had for Muir a terrifying outward embodiment in the squalor in which these 'sad and incomprehensible distortions of nature' lived. Reconcilement to ugliness and dirt was possible only by a gradual determination to become insensitive to them, so that eventually 'all one's surroundings there drive the senses in upon themselves and blind them to one thing after another until they perform a utilitarian function. This is bound to happen whether one is conscious of it or not':

The great majority of industrial town-dwellers are unconscious of it; and it is this that makes their response to experience so unlike that both of the artist and of the ordinary peasant, who can still look at things with more than a specialized, classifying eye.[10]

The analysis offered, or implied, is of course not essentially different from the critique of industrial society that has become, in outline at least, the common possession of many educated minds. Where it differs and where it can still shock us with the force of fresh insight, is in its authenticity. When we read the later Muir, the Muir of *Essays on Literature and Society*, reflecting on the implications of a lapsed cosmogony or on the relationship between personal crisis and social dislocation, we are convinced that he knows, in the deepest way one can know, what he is talking about. Those early years before the departure for Glasgow disclosed a possible, fully human life. They enabled him, almost at the end of his life, to write poetry very much at odds with contemporary movements and, perhaps, the more enduring for it. The apparent naïveté of this is to the point:

It is possible to write a poem about horses for, apart from the work they do for us, they have a life of their own; it is impossible to write a poem about motor cars, except in the false rhetorical vein, for they have no life except what we give them by pushing a starter.[11]

We might be forgiven for suspecting this to be an exaggeration or a revulsion from the symbols of unacceptable advance. But in fact, with the weight of the poetry behind it, it can be seen for Muir to be straightforwardly true. For him the deliberation, the rhetorical effort demanded by poems about cars is an inevitable result of their newness, their lack of continuity with what preceded them. The 'life' to which he refers here is the immemorial life of that 'dread country crystalline' that he celebrated in the early poem *Horses*, a life made palpable through an immediacy of contact with the rituals of country life. Those rituals bear on Muir's poetry throughout his life. His response to them – perhaps we should say his belief in them if by that we imply a deep sense of their fitness in the pattern of things – guarantees an authenticity to poems that in other hands might well have run to attitudinizing or sentimentality. *Petrol Shortage* (discovered in typescript after Muir's death) is a beautiful example of what I mean. He contemplates the scene after the petrol shortage has done its work: no cars run, no planes fly:

All round me is the natural day.
I watch this empty country road
Roll half a century away.

All, one might think, is thus set up for a brief selfconscious idyll. But the feeling and direction of the poem are very much finer, more intelligent than that. A summary of the poem's 'content' would, correctly, describe it as noting the impact of technology and its associated lifestyles, and as expressing a faith in its eventual demise and a return to a proper calm. The achievement of this poem, however, recalls Muir's comments on the 'technique' of poetry. It is, he says, a word 'that always gives me a slightly bewildered feeling; if I can translate it as skill I am more at home with it, for skill is always a quality of the thing that is being said or done, not a general thing at all'. In *Petrol Shortage* the fineness of control seems to express, to be made possible by, the integrity of the feeling. Nothing is forced; the ease and conviction with which the verse is handled seem to belong to that feeling:

> I think, the aeroplanes will pass,
> Power's stupendous equipage,
> And leave with simpler dynasties
> The mute detritus of an age.

> The daring pilot will come down,
> Cold marble wings will mark his place,
> And soft persuasion of the grass
> Restrain the swiftest of his race.

It is a familiar theme of Muir's that technology and the world view that it activates and is activated by have displaced certain human capacities, have made it difficult to realize certain truths that should be axiomatic: human possibilities are narrowed and man's imaginative life impoverished. Muir is unusual (and how strikingly this poem makes clear) in that his conception of such possibilities is at the level of a lived rather than an abstracted experience. So that the peace conceded by the silencing of the engines is for him not just an absence of noise, something for the outward ear to register and the brain to be grateful for. It becomes through contemplation a deeper peace, a peace of which the poet partakes, a road to the recovery of a wholeness that the development of technology has apparently destroyed, irrevocably. The poem is a serene image of such peace, its own active proof of a prophecy 'That only ages can make true'. No amount of 'analysis' would account for the serenity. To read the poem is, for its duration, to live the peace it celebrates and portends.

An Autobiography records something of the ordinary routine of Muir's life in Glasgow: his brief period as an apprentice chauffeur, his work in a beer-bottling factory, his early socialist activities, the friendships he made. But these are surface features. It is the inner life that he is trying to make sense of, that which fascinates him. The 'immense blind dejection' that overtook him as he walked through the Gorbals in Glasgow didn't lead simply to revulsion or indifference. It seemed to heighten his imaginative awareness to the point where chance encounters, scenes glimpsed in the street, might carry an unaccountably disturbing meaning, seemingly framed to embody an otherwise half-articulate knowledge. On one occasion, he had come across a crowd watching 'a muscular, red-haired woman with her arms bare to the shoulder, battering the face of a little shrinking man' and screaming abuse at him as her one-time seducer.

The other memory was of a dull winter Saturday afternoon in Crown Street, another slum. I had been to see some doctor. Again I came on a crowd. Two young men were standing in the centre of it, and one of them, who looked serious and respectable and not particularly angry, raised his fist slowly every now and then, and, as if objectively, hit the other man, who stood in silence and never tried to defend himself. At last an older man said, 'Why dinna you let the chap alane? He hasna hurt you.' But the serious young man replied, 'I ken he hasna hurt me, but I'm gaun tae hurt him!' And with a watchful look round him he raised his fist again. I did not want to see any more; but the scene and particularly the words of the serious young man – the other said nothing at all – took hold of my mind as if they were an answer to some question which, without my knowing it, had been troubling me: perhaps Johnnie's slow and painful death, during which, without being able to return a single blow, he had been battered so pitilessly. In both these memories there was the quality of Scottish Calvinism: the serious young man's reply had the unanswerable, arbitrary logic of predestination; and the encounter of the red-haired woman with her seducer, when both were so greatly changed that their original sin might have been committed in another world, and yet lived on, there in that slum, was a sordid image of fate as Calvin saw it. Somewhere in these two incidents there was a virtue of a dreary kind, behind the flaunted depravity: a recognition of logic and reality (p. 107).

These are real incidents observed by the waking mind. Yet, as Muir tells them, they take on something of the quality of dream. Each picture seems intrinsically intelligible but hard to explain. Muir's words, 'a sordid image of fate', are to the point. The mind would seem to be alert to, to perceive while it creates, images that help it to know itself. Literally it was no doubt the case that the suffering which Muir had experienced and witnessed (we must remember the four deaths in his family) had predisposed him to find in such scenes an 'image of fate'; but until he saw those scenes, those images, his perception of the nature of that suffering had been incomplete. That 'sordid image' had a horrible logic: it fitted the experience of the years in Glasgow. And yet it was, of course, a deeply unsatisfactory view of life's possibilities.

The value of these images may be that they present the nature of the problem with clarity and force, so that the imagination may know the more certainly the direction in which it will have to work. But to understand the problem is not necessarily to know how to deal with it. Muir's acute sensitivity was undoubtedly a handicap in his development as a poet. It can be said of him as it was said of the French poet Gautier that he was a man 'pour qui le monde visible existe'. Here was a youth who had begun to grow towards adulthood in an environment where there was a shared sense that the universe is alive with meaning. In his maturity he would recover and deepen that sense. One or two critics, Michael Hamburger in particular, have said about the best of his poetry that its images are its meaning, that there is an iconic immediacy that demands to be accepted in its own terms, not of analogy, not of parable or allegory, but of an imaginative construct shaped from an insight into the life of things. At this stage of his life, however, his sensitivity led him to a dead-end of anguish and depression which would, as we shall see, delay his beginnings as a poet for many years. His emotional state is again given in a brief picture:

... if I was tired or ill, I often had the feeling, passing through Eglinton Street or Crown Street, that I was dangerously near the ground, deep down in a place from which I might never be able to climb up again, while far above my head, inaccessible, ran a fine, clean highroad (p. 92).

He had indeed lost his bearings and there was no one to give him his proper direction. It comes as a surprise to find him later on referring to the 'countless friends' he had had in Glasgow. But despite the friendships he formed at this time through his work and his involvement with local socialists, he was 'physically and spiritually in a bad way'. He began around this time (1909) to read *The New Age*, a literary periodical which gave him 'an adequate view of contemporary politics and literature'. But his ideas were at war with his temperament. We can, I think, relate his later distrust of mere ideas to this phase in his life. Looking back on it he was able to see clearly enough the lack of connection between the ideas he took up with and the intuitive knowledge he had lost sight of. In so far as he had any faith at all it was a vague faith in a sub-utopian future. This is easy to understand. The present seemed so selfcontained, so discontinuous, so hopeless, that for some time he lost his sense of the value of the past. He says of poetry that he had given it up 'for some time on the excuse that the real song had not yet been sung, and that all the poetry of the past was the prolonged echo of a dead or dying world'. But it was his own world that was dying.

Reading *The New Age* was in some ways a liberation but it led him into further trouble. Stimulated by his reading but 'feeling that my illusive world was beginning to crumble around me', he wrote to the editor, A. R. Orage, asking for his advice. Orage was very kind but the outcome of his advice was disastrous. He advised Muir to take up a great writer, study him in depth until he felt he had an intimate knowledge of 'the workings of a great mind'. Muir chose Nietzsche – 'the choice most likely to maintain me in my suspended brooding over the future and the least likely to lead me to wisdom'. Looking back on it in *An Autobiography* he sees very clearly the nature of Nietzsche's appeal and the absurdity of the choice. Nietzsche offered him a refuge from himself. The fantasy of the Superman enabled him for a time to move on to that 'fine, clean highroad'; but it did so at the cost of his humanity. The chasm between the teaching of this fantasy and the wisdom of his intuitions may be measured if we compare two statements about different periods of his life. 'After a year's association with the Superman', the worried, middle-aged clerks sitting in the tramcar in Glasgow, 'merely filled me with horror'. There is no possible connection between that and this, from a letter written in his maturity: 'Seen deeply enough the life of the most ordinary human creature . . . seems to me portentous, past all theorizing, all relevance to optimism or pessimism' (28 February 1925).

The move to Greenock and the bone factory was a descent into a still lower region. The fourth chapter of the book, 'Fairport' (the name Muir used to disguise the location), is a terrible picture of the aborting spirit. Muir is aware as he writes that he was not likely to have been able to cope with life in such a place. He includes in the chapter a vivid sketch he wrote a few years later which gives an impression of his life in the factory and which, he says, 'shows fairly conclusively that I had sunk into a very bad state'. He had not the resilience and stamina of the 'old, faithful hands in the place who had spent their lives among the bones'. He distinguishes between the factory's effects on him and the objective things that no one could escape: 'Images of stagnation and decay' filled his dreams and 'into my images of the Superman [he was still reading Nietzsche] came the disquieting picture of a gigantic naked race rolling exuberantly among a hill of dead bones, so far beyond good and evil that my mind could not follow them.' But the daily realities were as grotesque or disgusting: 'Respectable families sat at their high teas in a well of stink' and the workers 'carried about with them everywhere the smell of sour fat'. The account of these years indeed produces an image of drastic cultural change: the dignity and pride that men could feel in the Orkneys was impossible; work of this kind could give a man no sense of belonging, could only persuade him of his own insignificance in a meaningless process.

The manner of Muir's appointment at Fairport had followed a typically brutal and impersonal rationalization (as it would now be called) of the firm. His immersion in a shameful situation used up his energies but gave no moral return. He writes of the chronic inefficiency of the organization and the burden he took on himself of defending and explaining away the shortcomings of the place to his distant superiors in Glasgow:

We lived in Fairport in a state of chronic reprobation, always in the wrong, among the filth and the stench, grinding out the profits. The errors were not made by me, but I had to find an excuse for them and drearily lie them away every day, year in, year out. I ended by acquiring a habitual bad conscience, a constant expectation of being accused (p. 133).

There were long-term effects:

This was demoralizing enough, and was the origin, I fancy, of the vague fears which pursued me for years afterwards . . . worst of all was a sort of objective shame that slowly settled within me like a grimy deposit. It was quite unlike the shame a man feels for wrongdoing, being mainly physical (p. 133).

He grew 'dingily absent-minded, morose and solitary'. It is no wonder that he did not properly begin writing poetry until middle life: 'Something in myself was buried . . . the world retreated from me with all its shapes.' In his early life the sensuous visible world had been instinct with meaning. What he describes now is the inner disintegration that follows from the failure of the physical world to be anything other than physical: 'I moved in a crystalline globe or bubble insulated from the life around me, yet filled with the desire to reach it, to be at the very heart of it and lose myself there' (p. 149). It is the language of religious longing, the suffering the more acute because there is no sign of help forthcoming in any of the traditional ways. Still under the influence of Nietzsche, he could not look to the images of Christianity or any other religion to sustain him. He was, truly, cut off from himself, the self that would later come excitedly alive to those images and realize with gratitude that they had all the time been there for his relief and salvation.

The story of his release from that terrible soulless globe is the story of his birth and development as a poet. It began with the two major events of his adult life: his marriage, and a course in psychoanalysis. Since we are concerned here with those happenings in Muir's life that directly impinge on his development as a writer, it is not necessary to do more than note that these took place several years after Fairport. During the war, he had worked in a shipbuilding office and begun contributing epigrams to *The New Age*. These were collected and published in 1918 as *We Moderns* under the pseudonym of Edward Moore. ('A pinchbeck Nietzschean prose peppered with exclamation marks' was how he described his early writing.) He met his future wife in the same year and they married in 1919. Shortly after, they moved to London. What Muir owed to Willa is very simply said in the final sentence of the 'Fairport' chapter: 'If my wife had not encouraged me, it is unlikely that I should have taken the plunge myself; I was still paralysed by my inward conflict. My marriage was the most important event in my life' (p. 154).

After further clerical work, he became assistant to Orage on *The New Age*, began to write drama criticism for *The Scotsman* and to review for *The Athenaeum*. But, though this was auspicious after the dreary years of clerking, London had not cured the old troubles. There was still the anxious failure to make connections, to find himself recognized and affirmed in the life going on around him.

. . . my mingled dread and longing now turned upon itself and reversed its direction, so that as I gazed at an object or a face – it did not matter which, for the choice was not mine – I was no longer trying to establish a connexion with it, but hoping that it – whether animate or inanimate – would establish a connexion with me and prove that I existed (p. 155).

Again, it was Orage who helped him to make the decisive step. For some time *The New Age* had been publishing articles on psychoanalysis. Orage himself was deeply interested in it and, aware of Muir's condition, engineered a meeting between Muir and an analyst. The course of analysis that followed this meeting was to have drastic and very positive results. His 'whole world of ideas invisibly changed'. 'The inventive windings' of his psyche led to all kinds of humiliating disclosures. But eventually they led him into the open air, seemingly freeing his unconscious mind for the passage of the eternal images on which his best poetry is constructed: 'My unconscious mind, having unloaded itself, seemed to have become transparent, so that myths and legends entered it without resistance and passed into my dreams and daydreams' (p. 159). He began through the imagination to relive his life; the dislocation had been so vicious that 'I did not feel so much that I was rediscovering the world of life as that I was discovering it for the first time'. He began 'to learn the visible world all over again'. In Prague, soon after, he spent weeks in 'an orgy of looking'. 'I saw everywhere the visible world straight before my eyes.' The adult poet was being born. The 'image of forever/One and whole' (the phrase comes from the last poem in the collected edition) would have been inconceivable without the re-animation of the visible world and the myths and dreams that henceforth constantly nourished his poetic imagination. Many of these dreams are recorded in the book. He drew on them to do in his own time what he thought the best art did in any age: to provide an 'image of life'; to lay out and clarify the patterns, the eternal crises and recoveries of the spirit that have always marked and will always mark the lives of men.

This phrase, 'an image of life', recurs in Muir's writings and, centrally, acquires a very specific meaning: the image is of a recurring pattern of human experience, uniting the contemporary with the ancient, confirming the agelessness of the imagination and its productions: 'The poetic imagination shows no advance at all and still does what it did in the time of Homer.' What concerns Muir throughout his work is the accessibility of this image to modern man; with the unprecedented rapidity of change – as he was to say in his later essay, 'The poetic imagination', 'the ancestral image grows indistinct and the imagination cannot pierce to it as easily as it once did'.

It is clear that no autobiography can begin with a man's birth, that we extend far beyond any boundary line which we can set for ourselves in the past or the future, and that the life of every man is an endlessly repeated performance of the life of man. It is clear for the same reason that no autobiography can confine itself to conscious life, and that sleep, in which we pass a third of our existence, is a mode of experience, and our dreams a part of reality. In themselves our conscious lives may not be particularly interesting. But what we are not and can never be, our fable, seems to me inconceivably interesting. I should like to write that fable, but I cannot even live it; and all I could do if I related the outward course of my life would be to show how I have deviated from it; though even that is impossible, since I do not know the fable or anybody who knows it. One or two stages in it I can recognize: the age of innocence and the Fall and all the dramatic consequences which issue from the Fall. But these lie behind experience, not on its surface; they are not historical events; they are stages in the fable (pp. 48–9).

Muir seems to conceive of individual men and women as responsive to an unchanging pattern – 'endless change on changeless ground' (*The Window*) – their 'fable', a reality we can never know but that informs all our lives to the extent that without it we cannot conceive of their having any meaning at all. Myth, emblem, dream, metaphor, all are charged with meanings whose source lies with the fable; their value to us is that they make known what we can come at in no other way. Now, more than ever before – and his own story proves it – it is difficult to lay hold on the fable. The press of time, the turmoil of immediate events, mean that we can only with difficulty penetrate to what Muir calls 'the solidest basis of ourselves'.

This conviction was taking shape as he began to make his recovery through psychoanalysis and continued to recover during the 1920s. It informs his first mature critical work (*Transition*, 1926) as it informs his early poetry. Directly, one sees how sharply his reading of contemporary literature is informed by his own experience of such very different worlds as Orkney and Glasgow and why in his poetry he was from the start drawn so readily to write in a mythical mode. In *Transition* he discerns in contemporary literature 'a general distrust of the feelings, a conditional or ironical presentation of them, and sometimes a frank reduction of them to their lowest factors: to those elements which men never distrust even when they distrust everything else'. In this respect, literature faithfully reflects the subversion worked by rapid change: 'In a stable order of society, or in solitude, men may listen to their feelings without much question, for those feelings correspond to the situation; they have a sort of suitability.'[12] Bewilderment, cynicism, confusion follow when circumstances seem to outdate the feelings we bring to them; the feelings atrophy for want of a felt correspondence with the world we inhabit. This perception is even more obviously valid since Muir expressed it in 1926; the 'frank reduction' is everywhere to be seen and to influence new generations.

'Men may listen to their feelings without much question' – it is a fertile phrase. Taken with his phrase about being 'born two hundred years ago', it points to the quality of experience that is behind many of the critical judgements in *Transition*. As we have seen, Muir's childhood and early youth were governed by ancient sanctions and observances alien and incomprehensible on the mainland to which he later travelled. The 'ancestral image' was there tangible and ever present. 'Listening to one's feelings' was possible in ways barely conceivable in the rapidly changing world outside the islands; the feelings, like the circumstances, had a naturalness, an inevitability that the stability of Orcadian life confirmed and reinforced. I imagine Willa Muir must have had something like this in mind when, writing about their first acquaintance and falling in love she said:

We inherited, each of us, a primitive simplicity from our Orkney and Shetland forebears which was likely to be wide open to vibrations from our tribal unconscious. Behind our more or less civilized frontages, Edwin and I had a large area of primitive feeling, a greater proportion of simplicity than is usual in Britain, a simplicity which more sophisticated people call naïveté.[13]

With such a beginning within him, Muir's agonies in the metropolis were inevitable but, given his essential toughness, for the poet and critic the eventual fruits of the collision of values were inestimable. Unlike the mainland poets and writers in whom Muir frequently finds a dismay and rootlessness to match the culture that contains them, he eventually recovered that faith in human capacity and resource, to which the society of the islands bore witness. Cruelly challenged though it was, it was to make possible the final, encompassing vision of wholeness which for most of our contemporaries has become little more than an idea, a nostalgic memory.

To the 'frank reduction of human feeling to those elements which men never distrust even when they distrust everything else', Muir's mature poetry opposes 'images of life' that speak persuasively for a richer vision. Among these, the image of Penelope is perhaps the most significant. 'Alone in her tower' (*The Return of the Greeks*), 'sole at the house's heart' (*The Return of Odysseus*) 'she wove into her fears/Pride and fidelity and love' (*Telemachos Remembers*). Hope, faith, fidelity: the calmness of spirit they belong to is a world that may seem infinitely removed from the distractions and betrayals of the present. Yet Penelope recurs in Muir's poetry as an expression of faith, the very existence of her story a permanent warning to us that we need not be overwhelmed in the turmoil of the times: the pace of change and the vast devastation of war are truly provisional distractions. We must listen to ourselves across the centuries as the voice of humanity speaks in myth and story.

'His poetry, he was sure, came ultimately from The Fable',[14] said Willa Muir. Perhaps the most direct statement about the fable, its relation to the self and its meaning for humanity is to be found in the poem *Twice-Done, Once-Done* from *The Voyage* (1946). Indeed the poem could equally well have been called 'The Story and the Fable'. Succinctly, it acknowledges and clarifies an indebtedness that is the privilege and price of our humanity. Not only is it impossible for us to conceive of an action having meaning unless we are instructed from the past:

> Nothing yet was ever done
> Till it was done again,

Not only is Adam's story, or indeed any story, meaningless unless it prefigures as well as recalls a pattern:

> Had he fallen once for all
> There'd be nothing to tell.

but we can know ourselves only through the gift of our ancestors:

Unless in me my fathers live
I can never show
I am myself

Twice-Done, Once-Done is a forcefully anti-contemporary poem; it restores a mystery to the cant phrase, 'to be myself', a phrase that has surely come to mean almost the reverse of what it means here. Now it tends, whether stridently or smugly, to declare the individual's supposed freedom from tradition rather than his unavoidable dependence on it. Muir's poem locates our sense of ourselves in a dimension that includes all previous experience, all the patterns that enable us to experience anything at all. Passion in the common sense of the word is not a quality of Muir's work; usually any direct personal emotion seems to have been deeply drawn into the poem, the result a level deliberation well suited to his conception of the poet's task. Here, however, there is an unusual, if briefly sustained, air of urgency, particularly in the fourth and last stanzas.

Father Adam and Mother Eve,
Make this pact with me:
Teach me, teach me to believe,
For to believe's to be.

'To believe's to be': a full assent to the poem's own statements is a question not of knowledge but of faith. That faith, like all faiths, can be lost; the truth, or the relevance, of these statements is nowadays especially liable to questioning or dismissal. But Muir's apostrophe here is surely of timeless application: always men's sense of who they are must depend on their capacity for belief. Without a belief in a more encompassing reality than can be provided by immediate circumstances man loses his hold on the fable:

For first and last is every way,
And first and last each soul,
And first and last the passing day,
And first and last the goal.

By the time Muir came to write *Twice-Done, Once-Done* he was near to accepting the truth of Christianity. In the waking visions and trances he experienced during the time he was undergoing analysis in 1920 may be seen the beginnings of that acceptance. They had a profound effect on his sense of humanity. The most detailed and impressive of these visions is described in the 'London' chapter of *An Autobiography*. That description is much too long to quote here; it was a vision that to his analyst amounted to a myth of the creation. To Muir though it was to do with the 'pattern of man's evolution and destiny, not of the creation', and 'our beginning and our end'. At any rate, the conclusions he drew from the experience were far-reaching, liberating him in ways that were to inform his thinking on art, politics and society. That much is made strikingly clear:

My trance gave me an inkling that my personality at least was not and could not be immortal, unless immortality was another name for hell; and when I tried to conceive what was enduring in me beyond the second-rate, ramshackle structure which I had built with time's collaboration, I could not see it in terms of any form or substance for which time had a parallel; in time form and substance are synonyms of separation and bondage, and what the soul strives for and is made for is boundless union and freedom. I realized that immortality is not an idea or a belief, but a state of being in which man keeps alive in himself his perception of that boundless union and freedom, which he can faintly apprehend in time, though its consummation lies beyond time. This realization that human life is not fulfilled in our world, but reaches through all eternity, would have been rejected by me some years before as an act of treachery to man's earthly hopes; but now, in a different way, it was a confirmation of them, for only a race of immortal spirits could create a world fit for immortal spirits to inhabit. This was, of course, an enormous simplification, but it saved me from the more monstrous simplification that 'religion is the opium of the masses,' and that our hope of ultimate union and freedom is a mere mirage leading us away from the concrete possibility of achieving union and freedom in a human society. The theory that the soul is immortal was not invented as a pretext for keeping the rich from being made uncomfortable, or to provide texts to quote against the class-conscious workers in the late nineteenth and early twentieth centuries (p. 170).

Though his London visions brought to mind 'images of the Fall and of the first incarnation, that of Adam' and though they produced the expansion of spirit he recalls, it was no simple 'conversion'. His response at the time was ambivalent; his explanation is quite convincing: 'while there is a sense in which I accept the trance as a revelation of truth, my mind, accustomed to deal with a different kind of experience and apparently fitted only for that, questions each separate detail, finding riddles and discrepancies and reminiscences' (p. 166). Nevertheless, he had by this time begun to get over the worst of his 'infatuation with Nietzsche' and had 'tentatively begun to believe in' immortality again. 'So that the dream did not actually convert me to the belief. But it very much strengthened and at the same time modified it.'

With marriage, psychoanalysis and the Muirs' move to Prague in 1921, a series of chapters in Edwin Muir's life comes to a close. Everything I have quoted and referred to so far has come from that part of *An Autobiography* which was published in 1940 under the title of *The Story and the Fable*. The chapters he added for the 1954 reissue are concerned largely with the Muirs' travels and work in Europe. I do not wish at this point to discuss these chapters in any detail. Though very interesting in themselves, they are not of the first importance in understanding Muir's development as a poet. I shall, however, be referring to them in the course of this study where I think they may help us to read the poetry in a more intelligent way.

The unique merits of *An Autobiography* are not easily brought out in brief quotation. It is only in continuous reading that one realizes one is in the presence of a rare purity of spirit. It is an even-tenored contemplative prose, never calling attention to itself; and yet, within and arising from the personal narrative is a formidable body of perceptions about society, literature and politics. They are the more formidable for being totally free of gesture, having no air of the provisional: they impress us as accretions of experience weighed and ordered through reflection. When, for instance, later in the book Muir speaks against Marxism, it is not just an opinion he is offering us. There is behind his words the immediate personal experience of the Communist putsch in Czechoslovakia; and when he says of this 'calamity' that 'it seemed both irresistible and unnatural, for it is unnatural for human beings to act impersonally towards one another', the common words derive their uncommon force from association with an image of humanity that we have been made to feel is the authentic one. In its quiet way *An Autobiography* continuously affirms the indestructibility of the human spirit. In its scrupulous and modest attention to one man's experience it reminds us that the roots of our thinking are eternally entangled with our feelings; that political philosophies which deny this, deny the nature of man. Man lives by an 'image of life' and for this he naturally looks to the past. The sources of that image are mysterious; in *An Autobiography* we watch it being created through personal recollection and contemplation. In a sense Muir himself was a spectator too. Talking in 1940 of what writing *An Autobiography* had taught him, he said:

There is a law by which the momentary self continuously ousts the permanent self. Consequently to know what we are we must cease for a time to be what we are. Otherwise we live in a perpetual bright oblivion of ourselves, insulated in the moving moment and given a meaning only by the moment.

   This came home to me very sharply after I had finished my autobiography. It is not an original idea; religion has reminded us of it a countless number of times. Yet what matters in an idea is not its originality, but its clarity. And I saw more clearly than I had ever done before that our knowledge of life comes from yesterday, a yesterday which can never change again and is therefore beyond confusion; and that there is the glass into which we must look if we want to see what life is. Our feeling of life comes from the present, our knowledge of life from the past.[15]

'What matters in an idea is not its originality, but its clarity.' In a way, this statement leads us straight to the centre of Muir's work. Most of his life may be seen as a continuous effort to refine and understand that 'idea', to pierce that 'perpetual bright oblivion' (one recalls the 'crystalline globe or bubble' of 'Fairport'), to bring that idea indeed to a state of clarity in which it appears as the right, the natural way of understanding our experience. From that effort comes a body of work – poems, novels, criticism, autobiography – whose essential unity is that they are all in some way concerned with that idea. One of the fascinations of *An Autobiography* is in the repeated insights it gives us into the provenance of the poems as part of that unity. To read the book in conjunction with the poems is to enrich both. To read, for example, the *Ballad of Hector in Hades*, *The Little General*, *The Interrogation*, *The Cloud*, *Horses*, *The Annunciation* and *The Combat* alongside the relevant parts of *An Autobiography* is not to indulge in a pointless tracking down of sources. It is to deepen our understanding of the poetic imagination, the function of poetry, and the relationship between thought and feeling – to understand, in Kathleen Raine's words, that for Muir 'the world of ideas was not a doctrine but an experience'. It is, most specifically, to feel the force of those words of von Hofmannsthal to which Muir refers, both in *An Autobiography* and elsewhere, as a touchstone in our present disorders: 'powerful imaginations are conservative'.

What does this approach yield in practice? One of the most striking things to arise from such a reading is the way in which the poems of Muir's maturity reach back into his early years for their images. Sometimes they are from dreams, sometimes from remembered scenes. Those dreams and scenes had been endowed with their own power all along. Now, in the making of the poem, they are given fresh intensity and meaning. It is impressive to witness this strange continuity of the mind's action across the dislocations of the years. Twenty-five years after leaving Wyre, he began for the first time to dream about it. During the period of his psychoanalysis he had a dream about the family farm, the Bu.

I had a dream later of the Bu itself, though again everything was strangely transfigured and transposed. I was walking up a little winding road; I had been away for a long time, and now, an old man, I had returned. Great trees stood round the house, their foliage darker and thicker than any I had ever seen, the leaves hanging like dark green tongues one over the other in a motionless security which no wind could reach. The walls appeared behind them, thick walls so rounded and softened by time that no jutting angle or corner remained; in the middle was a great wooden gate like the gate of an old castle. Above the house rose a low grey sky, a particular sky arched over it alone: there was nothing but the great walls, the dark trees, and the low, round sky. I stood and looked at the house, filled with quiet expectation, but I did not go in (pp. 64–5).

Twenty-two years later there appeared his poem, *The Return*, clearly based on the dream but with a distinctive pathos and power of suggestion. The dream has been consciously shaped to carry an intelligible meaning. The prose simply presents the picture; in the poem it is understood; the picture is made to speak of the mystery and the pathos of time, of ageing, of memory. We can perhaps best understand the transformation with the help of a comment on 'the poetic imagination' from Muir's essay of that name. Having quoted Coleridge's famous definition of the imagination at its most productive:

a more than usual state of emotion with more than usual order; judgement ever awake and steady self-possession with enthusiasm profound or vehement.

Muir then says:

We must think of the imaginative writer as being both inside and outside the figures and emotions he describes. Wordsworth writes of certain states in which we see into the life of things, and it is the seeing that matters, without that there would be nothing but an intense inarticulate feeling.[16]

'It is the seeing that matters': what Muir means, I think, is that the intense, inarticulate feeling recognizes its embodiment in an 'image of life'. The poet is simultaneously in a state of empathy and detachment: the empathy means he can live within, can experience the life of 'the figures and emotions'; the detachment enables him to present it intelligibly. The passion and the contemplation are simultaneous occurrences. Here is the poem:

The Return

I see myself sometimes, an old old man
Who has walked so long with time as time's true servant,
That he's grown strange to me – who was once myself –
Almost as strange as time, and yet familiar
With old man's staff and legendary cloak,
For see, it is I, it is I. And I return
So altered, so adopted, to the house
Of my own life. There all the doors stand open
Perpetually, and the rooms ring with sweet voices,
And there my long life's seasons sound their changes,
Childhood and youth and manhood all together,
And welcome waits, and not a room but is
My own, beloved and longed for. And the voices,
Sweeter than any sound dreamt of or known,
Call me, recall me. I draw near at last,
An old old man, and scan the ancient walls
Rounded and softened by the compassionate years,
The old and heavy and long-leaved trees that watch
This my inheritance in friendly darkness.
And yet I cannot enter, for all within
Rises before me there, rises against me,
A sweet and terrible labyrinth of longing,
So that I turn aside and take the road
That always, early or late, runs on before.

The seeing is, of course, an act of the imagination. And the power of the imagination is here a mixed blessing. The vision it creates as the mind's eye adopts the view of the old man and looks back at the pattern of his life, is of a transforming sweetness. It transfigures the life being lived now, lived in the ordinariness and familiarity that belongs to the rooms and voices he knows. But this is no commonplace nostalgia, the harsh angles of a lifetime rounded out in recollection. The old man is privileged to see into the life of things past but only at the cost of the terrible longing that arises because the beauty and permanence of what he sees *are* in the past. The truth of what the imagination calls up is as undeniable as that of the woman in Hardy's poem, *The Voice*:

Woman much missed, how you call to me, call to me,
Saying that now you are not as you were
When you had changed from the one who was all to me,
But as at first, when our day was fair.

Muir's wording at times recalls that poem:

> . . . And the voices,
> Sweeter than any sound dreamt of or known,
> Call me, recall me. . . .

With Hardy the woman becomes unbearably real, unbearably absent as time and place summon her into his mind. With Muir the movement of the mind is into the future, so that the true form of the past may be imagined. The feeling that the last lines of the poem express is a complicated one. On the one hand there is satisfaction in the life of the imagination; on the other, there is anguish that the forms it creates cannot be brought into proper relation with life as we know it from moment to moment. All this is in the strange and powerful 'scene' of the last ten lines.

Through the imagination we can grasp that everything will be in its proper place, in its natural relation. The civilized words –'compassionate', 'inheritance' – acquire their proper grace through the imagination which grasps what eludes our ordinary purposeful consciousness because here we are committed to the 'road'. The turning aside to pursue our normal lives is inevitable, natural. But at least we *can* leave the road if only for a short while, and that is natural too. Behind this poem, as behind many others, there is the longing for a state of permanence first known in childhood. In 'Afterthoughts to an Autobiography', Muir describes the feeling he then had of everything being in its proper place:

All these things, which were the work of Time while Time stood still for me, seemed as they should be. I did not know what had moved all these figures into the places where they stood; but I saw the result and was endlessly pleased. Take away the soaring intellect of St. Augustine and the soaring imagination of Blake and how much difference is there between their ultimate vision of life and the first perception of life?[17]

The Return is about the sadness of being unable to attain that ultimate vision for more than a moment, a moment intense enough to make us the more sensitive to our normal failure to see the pattern. For all their quietness, their lack of obvious urgency, many of Muir's poems originate in a permanent tension: a tension between the knowledge that a transcendent vision is natural to man's understanding and the knowledge that it is largely inaccessible. The story of most men's lives is the story of their struggle to realize that vision in one form or another. Muir's poems record that struggle as it was lived in the life of one man. But we read of it as the struggle of Man himself.

In none of his poems is this more startlingly so than in *The Combat* (from *The Labyrinth*, 1949). In the brief chapter, 'Interval', which he wrote to introduce the new chapters for *An Autobiography*, he addressed himself to some profound changes in men's ways of seeing the world that he felt had been accelerated in the thirteen years since he had finished the first part of the book. The major consequence of the era of Hitler and Stalin had been to weaken men's resolve to take responsibility for their own lives, to deny the life of the spirit. So many things had combined to make men feel themselves parts of a gigantic process working itself out without regard for their destinies, a process at once impersonal and inevitable:

I do not believe in the inevitable and the impersonal, these twins which always go together; yet they have come so powerfully into our lives that we have to make a conscious effort now to resist them. This was not so forty or fifty years ago; then there was no pre-occupation with the inevitable or with its corollary the unitary world; this has sprung up since, enfeebling our individual power to live. It has made easier the growth of creeds which deny the significance of life: the creed of pure power which Spengler expressed when he said that 'Man is a *beast of prey*; I shall never tire of saying that': the creed of power directed towards an end in the future, which was formulated by Marx: creeds later to be put in practice by Hitler and Stalin (p. 195).

An Autobiography and the poems, like any imaginative work that tries to see life whole, are affirmations, epiphanies to answer those seemingly irresistible twin forces. Muir speaks with quite unusual authority. Orkney gave him an image of humanity in whose light 'the citizens of that future world [i.e. Glasgow] seemed to me then very precise, docketed, and quaintly dogmatic compared with the Orkney people'; his later direct encounter with the impersonalities of a communist regime meant that he could speak of the threat to humanity with the light of that image behind him. For the origins of the great poem, *The Combat*, we must go back to Wyre. They are partly to be found in a dream recorded in the first chapter of *An Autobiography*. In the dream he saw a bird that seemed to be a heron:

We went towards it, but as we came nearer it spread its tail like a peacock, so that we could see nothing else. As the tail grew I saw that it was not round, but square, an impenetrable grey hedge of feathers; and at once I knew that its body was not a bird's body now, but an animal's, and that behind that gleaming hedge it was walking away from us on four feet padded like a leopard's or a tiger's. Then, confronting it in the field, there appeared an ancient, dirty, earth-coloured animal with a head like that of an old sheep or a mangy dog. Its eyes were soft and brown; it was alone against the splendid-tailed beast; yet it stood its ground and prepared to fight the danger coming towards it, whether that was death or merely humiliation and pain. From their look I could see that the two animals knew each other, that they had fought a countless number of times and after this battle would fight again, that each meeting would be the first meeting, and that the dark, patient animal would always be defeated, and the bright, fierce animal would always win. I did not see the fight, but I knew it would be ruthless and shameful, with a meaning of some kind perhaps, but no comfort (p. 65).

This dream lay half a century or more waiting to be brought into relation with a fuller and more conscious interpretation of life. The eventual upshot, years even after the above description was written, was *The Combat*.

In her book about their life together, Muir's wife Willa tells us that *The Combat* was produced during a period of depression and despair in Czechoslovakia and that soon after the Communist putsch of 1948 'Edwin . . . produced his poem, "The Combat", which steadied us both with its reminder that the armoured Killing Beast could not kill humanity, humble and battered as that might be'. Writing to Douglas Young in 1950 Muir said, 'I think "The Combat" is one of my best poems'. It is surely a great poem; while it is doubtless true that the immediate political crisis provoked it, it is beyond question that the poem transcends that crisis. *The Combat* is at once disturbing and reassuring: the sourness and desperation of some modern political 'philosophies' is there, but so is a redeeming sense of their eventual impotence, their despairing issue. No one could call it an optimistic poem; though

> The killing beast that cannot kill
> Swells and swells in his fury till
> You'd almost think it was despair.

and though humanity will not, finally, yield, the battle is tawdry, squalid. Heroism and the mutual regard of enemies, however bitter, has given way to a grotesque brutality on the one side and a pitiful will to survive on the other. This is not the fields before Troy; it's a 'shabby patch', 'not meant for human eyes'; a world not identical with but much coloured by the heartless real politik that Muir finds reflected in Hemingway's short story, 'The Killers'. To read Muir's essay 'The natural man and the political man' is to see the intellectual basis of that imaginative integration of an ancient dream that *The Combat* represents:

An idea of the change in our attitude to human life may be had by comparing any character in Dickens with any character in the early work of Mr Ernest Hemingway. Dickens was an emotional writer, but he still knew that there was in the individual a struggle between impulse and reason. He was not a religious writer, but his characters still lived on a plane which was partly spiritual and partly natural. Mr Hemingway's early characters live on the natural plane alone. The two gunmen in the short story, 'The Killers', are mechanical murderers, and their victim a mechanical murderee; they are all equally conditioned; and there is nothing to be said about them, except that they evoke the kind of pity and horror one might feel in watching some hunting beast pulling down and killing its prey. The story is astonishingly natural from one point of view, and astonishingly unnatural from another; for after all the characters are not animals but merely men thinking and feeling and acting in an extraordinarily circumscribed way. The murderers have no remorse; the victim has no feeling except animal resignation. The immediate lust to kill, the immediate dread of being killed, are all that remain. There is nothing but sensation.[18]

'The change in our attitude to human life' is undoubtedly at the back of *The Combat*; the affection and admiration that the 'creature', the 'battered bag', inspires, are a measure of Muir's resistance to that change. The resistance is not a question of adopting brave postures; it is an inherent quality of Muir's vision of life. 'The reduction of the image of man' that he finds all around him is challenged by his deepest sense of what man amounts to. *The Combat* is a vision; no one can ever have seen such a terrifying fight, and yet it is all around us. The insignificance to which the latter day image of man condemns us is there in the anonymity of the 'soft round beast as brown as clay',

> Some old used thing to throw away

And yet it will *not* be thrown away, however used up its life may appear to be; 'chivalry and grace' have faded, honour is meaningless – 'the fury had him on his back' – when the struggle has no witness, no audience to lend dignity to the resistance:

> And two small paws like hands flew out
> To right and left as the trees stood by.

One is reminded of Auden's poem, *Musée des Beaux Arts*:

> About suffering they were never wrong,
> The Old Masters: how well they understood
> Its human position; how it takes place
> While someone else is eating or opening a window or just walking dully
> along.

But the comparison gives us the measure of Muir's achievement. One can imagine him protesting that the 'old Masters' understood a very great deal more about the place of suffering in our lives than Auden allows. With Auden, the perception – that suffering is a lonely and disregarded business – is just that: a perception, a curious observation, in its own way provokingly expressed but not, as is Muir's, part of an encompassing interpretation of life. *The Combat* is on 'the shabby patch' but it is also in the universe of *King Lear*:

> And having seen it I accuse
> The crested animal in his pride,
> Arrayed in all the royal hues
> Which hide the claws he well can use
> To tear the heart out of the side.

Body of leopard, eagle's head
And whetted beak, and lion's mane,
And frost-grey hedge of feathers spread
Behind – he seemed of all things bred.
I shall not see his like again.

The 'crested animal' might indeed be Regan or Goneril: splendour divorced from nobility; the appearance of majesty masking the reality of ruthless power.

The emblematic quality of the stanzas quoted is by this time a familiar feature of Muir's poetry. It is unselfconsciously so because natural to his way of conceiving man's moral and spiritual experience. The poem thus has the directness, the undidactic character of a truth grasped and irresistibly recreated. To understand the power of these emblems for Muir and the naturalness with which they enter his poetry we can usefully turn again to *An Autobiography*.

In the first part of that book some of the best, most arresting, writing occurs when Muir describes his early experience of living in a community that had always depended closely on the land and on the animals that had provided its livelihood. The closeness was such that he now realizes the deep, immemorial interpenetration of animal and human life in the imagination of man. Modern living has come between man and animal, making the beast a mere servant, a *service*, the moral and psychological charge that once belonged to such a relationship quite extinguished. That relationship is, says Muir, of a character we can scarcely grasp save through its memorials in art and myth. What they disclose to us is a relation between man and beast based on man's knowledge both of his kinship and of his dependence, a knowledge making for feelings of guilt and the need for atonement. Muir's conviction seems to be that though this knowledge has lost all immediacy, our unconscious memories have not altogether repelled it:

My passion for animals comes partly from being brought up so close to them, in a place where people lived as they had lived for two hundred years; partly from I do not know where (p. 48).

And on the previous page:

I have always been fascinated by a part of us about which we know far less than our remote ancestors did: the part which divined those immediate though concealed relations that made them endow their heroes with the qualities of the animals whose virtues they incarnated, calling a man a bull for strength, a lion for courage, or a fox for cunning. That age is fabulous to us, populated by heraldic men and legendary beasts. . . . The age which felt this connection between men and animals was so much longer than the brief historical period known to us that we cannot conceive it; but our unconscious life goes back into it (p. 47).

'Our dreams and ancestral memories speak a different language' from that of the rational appraisal that sees killing animals as a straightforward necessity. From the mysterious source of this language comes not only an awareness of the 'connection' Muir describes above but also the conviction that we are more than thinking animals; that, in short 'Human beings are understandable only as immortal spirits; they become natural then, as natural as young horses; they are absolutely unnatural if we think of them as a mere part of the natural world' (p. 51).

Both the kinship with animals and all that separates us from them are realized in *The Combat*. The animals referred to in the first three stanzas are, in man's historical imagination, of a noble line: leopard, eagle, lion. But the animal that stands accused is a monstrous amalgam of all three; the litheness, the voracity and the strength divorced from the majesty and nobility they separately represent. Men are of course capable of such singleminded savagery, but it is not men who are in question in the poem: it is Man. The conviction the poem expresses is that however intense the fury, however relentless the determination to extinguish his spirit, Man has resources beyond understanding, resources that reveal the 'natural animal' for the distorted creature of despair it is. Put thus prosaically it is not particularly impressive; experienced as a poem it has the authenticity of deep faith. How rarely one can say such a thing of modern literature. Eliot recalls in the Faber selection of Muir's poems that Muir struck him as one of the few men of absolutely unquestionable integrity he had met in his lifetime. A poem such as *The Combat* tells us something of such integrity. Muir faces the issue; he understands the terrifying ordeal which so many of his contemporaries are compelled to endure at the hands of their fellows; he sees the squalor and the pathos. But he is sustained and his vision authenticated by a faith that evil will not endure. 'The Eternal Man', said Muir, 'has possessed me during most of the time I have been writing my Autobiography and has possessed me too in much of my poetry.' Separately and together, *An Autobiography* and the poems remind us that the springs of intuitive knowledge are mysterious and not to be denied. Muir's own 'thinking' is nourished by intuitions from sources not allowed for in temporal and materialistic philosophies. *The Combat* speaks out of a body of knowledge and experiences variously formulated in his discursive writing but here caught up in a vision that contains and transcends what we would normally call 'thought'. In the words of the closing paragraph of *An Autobiography*: '. . . in the infinite web of things and events chance must be something different from what we think it to be. To comprehend that is not given to us, and to think of it is to recognize a mystery, and to acknowledge the necessity of faith.'

Chapter 2
Beginnings

An assured regular income from Muir's contributions to the American literary periodical, *The Freeman*, enabled him and his wife to leave England for the Continent in 1921. It was there, in Dresden, that 'I seemed at last to recover from the long illness that had seized me when at fourteen I came to Glasgow. I realized that I must live over again the years which I had lived wrongly' (p. 192). The process of reviewing his life that eventually, many years later, was to yield *The Story and the Fable* began there. Writing to a friend in 1936 and encouraging him to write his own autobiography, Muir said: 'I feel there is nothing truer than the saying that one can only realize oneself by losing it; and one way of losing it would be to give it away to whoever likes to have it in the form of an honest and faithful account of it' (19 August 1936). The looking back, stimulated directly by his period of psychoanalysis and waking visions was for him indeed a matter of 'realizing oneself by losing it'. Only in this way could he attempt to discover who he was and thus to contemplate his relations with his fellowmen. The dreams and visions provoked by his analysis had implanted – or, rather, reawakened – a trust in such things as an intimation of immortality, a mode of experience as real as any other. Dreams indeed he describes as part of reality. In living over his life again, as Henry Vaughan says a man must if he is properly to know God,[1] he 'won a new kind of experience'. In 'looking against the direction in which time was hurrying' him, he was able to know 'a moment liberated from time' and to be in some degree 'freed from the order of time'. He looked back and, in recovering 'an image of life more complete than I had known in all the years in between', did indeed discover a phase of his life more like that of a dream than could ever be reached in manhood.

'There is, indeed,' says Yeats, 'a systematic mystic in every poet or painter who, like Rossetti, delights in traditional symbolism, or like Wagner, delights in a personal symbolism, and such men often fall into trances, or have waking dreams . . . and so august a beauty moves before the mind that they forget the things that move before the eyes.'[2] In Muir's case the trances and waking dreams were a prelude rather than an accompaniment to the poetry, a sudden revelation of modes of being that he had until that time ignored. In Dresden (and in nearby Hellerau to which they soon moved) he was, in his wife's words, 'beginning to explore within himself the extraordinary dramas that his London visions had made him aware of. It was not simple nostalgia that took him back to Orkney.'[3] Correctly, Willa Muir speaks of the dramas as having an existence separate from the man who observes them and thus accurately reflects Muir's own sense of their provenance and import: 'It was not I who dreamt it', he says of one of these visions (or dreams, or trances – Muir uses all three words more or less interchangeably), 'but something else which the psychologists call the racial unconscious and for which there are other names.' Muir is not obviously invoking Jung here but what Jung has to say on these matters is directly to the point of Muir's acceptance of his visions. Jung speaks of the psyche awakening 'to spontaneous life' and of the transformation taking place 'at that moment when in dreams or fantasies themes appear whose source in consciousness cannot be shown':

To the patient it is nothing less than a revelation when, from the hidden depths of the psyche, something arises to confront him – something strange that is not the 'I' and is therefore beyond the reach of personal caprice. He has gained access to the sources of psychic life, and this marks the beginning of a cure . . .

That which is so effective is often simply the deep impression made on the patient by the independent way in which his dreams treat of his difficulties . . .

Such experiences reward the sufferer for the pains of the labyrinthine way. From this point forward a light shines through his confusion; he can reconcile himself with the warfare within and so come to bridge the morbid split in his nature upon a high level.[4]

Jung could be describing Muir's progress. The most significant outcome for the man and artist was the transformation of his ideas. The pain and anguish of the years of adolescence and early manhood had disposed him strongly to an acceptance of Nietzsche and the idea of the superman, the being beyond pity and remorse. That, as he came to see, had been a precarious and negative accommodation, successful only in so far as it enabled him to ignore vital parts of his personality. His sufferings during those years had forced him to take refuge in a denial of humanity, in the notion of a company of one from which he could look out and simply observe the meaningless and bestial struggle for life amongst his fellow creatures and sufferers. That notion, though in the short run probably helping him to survive, was really just a notion, an idea deeply at odds with his sensibility, his instinctive respect for and sense of belonging with other men. During the period of his infatuation with Nietzsche he had dismissed immortality as 'an imputation on earthly life and the purity of immediate perception'. And though by the time of his waking visions, Nietzsche's influence on him had begun to wane, it was finally extinguished, criticized and rejected indeed, in a dream about the man himself which, says Muir, was 'a horrible indication of my state at a time when I considered myself beyond good and evil'.

The realization that came to him in Dresden, that he 'must live over again the years in which I had lived wrongly,' is undoubtedly associated with the spontaneous flowering of the psyche that Jung identifies as the signal for recovery. The waking visions had brought proof of a level of being beyond the reach of mere ideas and the productions of time, had produced indeed an exhilarated sense of freedom being possible through the imagination, and of the imagination giving access to elusive truth. The horizons of the spirit had suddenly expanded, bringing a new conviction of meanings to be discerned and contemplated. What Muir came to call his faith cannot of course be accounted for; but it can certainly be related to those many moments in his life – some recorded in the prose writings, others issuing in poetry – when he was aware of a greater reality than 'the I and the not I' (the phrase is from the poem, *The Solitary Place*). We may discern a progression (not without severe setbacks) in which, through a greater and greater awareness of the connection between these unsolicited visitations and the nature of his 'real self', he grew into faith. His poems may be seen as incarnations of the phases in this growth, their increasing fullness of vision enabling him and us to know the shape of that real self – whose reality of course goes beyond the personal self and includes us all – 'the eternal man'.

The Ballad of Hector in Hades was just such an unsolicited revelation. The poem pictures Achilles pursuing Hector around the walls of Troy, killing him and dragging the corpse around the city in triumph. The original myth is, however, changed for Muir's purpose: Hector here returns after death to run the race again in the full knowledge of its outcome. 'Purpose', though, is a doubtful word in this case. Muir's account of how he came to write *Hector in Hades* and his reflections on the result tell us a great deal about his notion of the way the imagination works. The poem which was 'written almost complete at one sitting' and 'came to me quite spontaneously', resolved a problem that had haunted him for thirty years. In *An Autobiography* he describes an incident when he was seven years old in which he had run in fear from a boy who had wanted to fight him. He had been at the time in a phase of hypersensitivity and almost pathological guilt and on that summer afternoon his fears 'took the shape of Freddy Sinclair, and turned him into a terrifying figure of vengeance'. Thirty years on, *Hector in Hades* had exorcised a shame, the very writing of the poem changing the form of the actual incident in his mind and with that his feelings towards it. A particular experience had taken the shape of myth in a familiar folk form, the ballad. Muir's unconscious mind, with trusty logic, had worked out its own resolution, had released him from the bondage of his individual shame and admitted him to the common ground of our terrors: 'I could at last see the incident whole by seeing it as happening, on a grand and tragic scale, to someone else.' But the important thing for us, of course, is that even if we know nothing of the story behind it, the ballad communicates on the ground of our own nightmares, our own fears and apprehensions. (Of the quality of the poem there will be more to say later.)

Muir was convinced that the sudden emergence of a poem, of a picture which would reproduce, accommodate and assuage his fear and shame, was normal. No one can prepare for such moments; they arise unbidden, unaccounted. They are the action of 'the mind within our minds which cannot rest until it has worked out, even against our conscious will, the unresolved questions of our past'. There is nothing of the apocalyptic about such a conviction: no dark Gods lurk behind it, charging the conscious mind with messianic purpose. The moral character of the revelations to be expected from such a source is of an altogether finer quality. In writing of the provenance of *Hector in Hades*, Muir appears as a visionary who waits upon time in order to transcend time. Meaning wells from sources we can never discern but that is no less incontestable for that. 'The mind within our minds brings up those questions when our will is least watchful, in sleep or in moments of intense contemplation':

These solutions of the past projected into the present, deliberately announced as if they were a sibylline declaration that life has a meaning, impress me more deeply than any other kind of experience with the conviction that life does have a meaning quite apart from the thousand meanings which the conscious mind attributes to it: an unexpected yet incontestable meaning which runs in the teeth of ordinary experience, perfectly coherent, yet depending on a different system of connected relations from that by which we consciously live (p. 44).

The important thing to note is that this 'incontestable meaning' has no social, let alone political dimension. The voice that speaks is known only through the language that is given; and that language does not translate itself, cannot be translated into the language of the marketplace where courses of action and men's fates are decided. The poem makes manifest the 'different system of connected relations' and that, in Muir's eyes, would be where the poet differs from the rest of us. Events such as gave rise to *Hector in Hades* 'happen again and again in everyone's life', he says; most of us, though, do not experience them as a transmissible gift, which this poem clearly was. That we can nonetheless make sense of it, and feel grateful for it, is proof that the world from which it comes is our world too. In his understanding of the nature of myth, dream and vision Muir is, again, akin to Jung. The repeated insistence on their value as irreducible 'forms of experience' is common to them both. Each accepts the unconditional quality of dreams and visions; each knows that they are a form of knowledge for which we should seek no discursive equivalent. 'The vision is not something derived or secondary', says Jung, 'and it is not a symptom of something else. It is true symbolic expression – that is, the expression of something existent in its own right, but imperfectly known.'[5] 'What we are to our inward vision, and what man appears to be *sub specie aeternitas* are only expressed by way of myth.'[6]

Those 'solutions of the past projected into the present' were realities, one feels, in which Muir had an instinctive but long suppressed faith.

When in the early days of his poetry writing he came fully to accept the implications of listening to such 'sibylline declarations', he felt the nature of his previous estrangement the more keenly, for moral conclusions follow an acceptance of Muir's persuasion. In his own life, as so many of those who knew him testify, there was a humility and a distrust of posturing and dogma that was the reverse of timidity and indifference. It came, I think, from a feeling that the attitude we should take up towards the theorizings and enterprises of the conscious, deliberating mind is one of vigilant scepticism. Without such a scepticism we are likely to be seduced by false gods, by the appeal of impure solutions to our problems – impure because arrived at in disregard of values that do not urge themselves upon our attention with the same kind of insistence. The lesson is that we are in some ways least capable of right thinking when we are trying hardest to reach a conclusion. To be aware of this is to favour patience and caution; to ignore it is to rest one's faith in the newest, least tried part of the psyche. Muir's best poems will not date because they acknowledge these truths. Our century abounds in experiments – moral, social and political – that have ended in barrenness and destruction. In Muir's perspective, that is only to be expected in an age where rapid change of all kinds makes it more vital than ever to conserve values, to retain an openness to experience that faces backwards as well as forwards.

Such a perspective was beginning to define itself for Muir in Hellerau; it led him to take a highly critical view of his intellectual life up to that time and released in him the energies necessary to his development as a poet. Speaking in *An Autobiography* of the articles he had been producing for *The Freeman*, he says:

I was very little concerned with the truth of what I said; I was simply letting my mind range freely among 'ideas', as if they were a sufficient end in itself. I had started the habit in Glasgow, where ideas were so scarce that any, good or bad, was a treasure to be prized. I had afterwards come under the influence of Orage, the most intelligent merchant of ideas of his time (p. 200).

In Glasgow he had begun taking a weekly paper called *Great Thoughts* from which he acquired 'a passion for thought and thinkers'. He had begun to subscribe to *Chambers's Cyclopaedia of English Literature* which 'brought me back to poetry again'. There was nothing systematic or disciplined in this piecemeal self education – a fact that he came very much to regret. Cut off from his roots in Glasgow, yet hungry for direction, he naturally reached out wherever he could for guidance, without too critical an eye for the intellectual level on which it came. Reading *The New Age* gave him 'an adequate picture of contemporary politics and literature, a thing I badly needed, and with a few vigorous blows shortened a process which would otherwise have taken a long time'. But while intellectually his picture of the world was thus becoming clearer, his emotional condition was such that the development of his taste was against his true nature and conviction. Cynicism, irony, self-advertisement: these are qualities entirely absent from Muir's mature work. Yet at this time he learnt from *The New Age* a 'feeling of superiority' and 'a contempt for sentimentality'; from Heine (from whom he progressed to Nietzsche) he had 'borrowed a quality that did not become me at this stage of life: a habit of speaking about everything ironically'. His socialism (quite incompatible, as he came to see, with his Nietzscheanism) was as much as anything an escape into a totally new future: 'Society was evolving towards [Socialism]; when the evolution reached a certain point revolution would painlessly follow.' For a time, he read 'nothing but books pointing towards the future: Shaw, Ibsen, Whitman, Edward Carpenter'. The callowness of these attachments (as he came to see it) is reflected in the contents of *We Moderns* (1918), Muir's first collection of prose. *We Moderns* brings together epigrams that he had been contributing to *The New Age* since 1916. I do not wish to dwell on it here but it has a place in the story of the remarkable divergence of the later from the earlier work. Muir came fairly soon to see *We Moderns* as in 'the last degree raw, immature, and an expression of a lamentable bad taste, and the product of a prolonged period when 'my life had been a continuous enemy of my inner development'. He is too hard on the book, certainly, for there are good and genuine things in it; but its only lasting significance is as a milestone in the development out of the emotional condition that it on the whole reflects. When in Germany he began to look back on his life for the first time he was 'reliving consciously what I had once lived blindly, hoping in this way to save something of myself'. *We Moderns* was not, he certainly felt, the real Muir, the real self. In its aphoristic cleverness, its declamatory insistence, it belongs to that phase in his life when he was indeed 'between two worlds, one dead, the other powerless to be born'.

Muir's eventual distrust of 'mere ideas' began with the awakening of his imagination in Dresden and Hellerau.

... the perceptions it promised were so much more real than those with which I had been trifling, that these no longer excited me. Some of them vanished altogether and were as if they had never been; others transmuted themselves into imaginative forms, particularly those which touched the ideas of innocence and reconciliation: Eden and the millennial vision of which I had dreamt as a child (pp. 200–1).

This transmutation had not been altogether without precedent. In a couple of memorable pages in *An Autobiography* he describes a quasi-religious conversion to Socialism in which 'everything, including myself, was transfigured'. It is worth quoting at length because it very clearly shows that despite the element of falseness – 'it was false in being earthly and nothing more; indeed that alone was what made it false' – the experience was of a kind essentially the same as those which he came to value so much in the dreams and visions of his maturity:

There are times in every man's life when he seems to become for a little while a part of the fable, and to be recapitulating some legendary drama which, as it has recurred a countless number of times in time, is ageless. The realization of the Fall is one of those events, and the purifications which happen in one's life belong to them too. The realization of the Fall is a realization of a universal event; and the two purifications which I have described, the one in Kirkwall and the one in Glasgow, brought with them images of universal purification. After that night in Kirkwall I felt that not only myself but every one was saved, or would some time be saved; and my conversion to Socialism had a similar effect. It was as if I had stepped into a fable which was always there, invisibly waiting for anyone who wished to enter it. Before, ugliness, disease, vice, and disfigurement had repelled me; but now, as if all mankind were made of some incorruptible substance, I felt no repugnance, no disgust, but a spontaneous attraction to every human being. I felt this most intensely during the first May Day demonstration I attended. That day is still enveloped in a golden mist, and I have no distinct memory of it, except that it was warm and sunny. I can remember the banners floating heavily in the windless air, their folds sometimes touching like a caress the heads and faces of the people marching behind them. I can remember a tall, dark, handsome man wearing a brown velvet jacket and carrying a yellow-haired little girl on his shoulder, and a pot-bellied, unhealthy man who walked beside me, and some middle-aged working-class women with shapeless bodies which seemed to have been broken into several pieces and clumsily stuck together again, and a crowd of well-to-do and slum children all mixed together. But what I am most conscious of is the feeling that all distinction had fallen away like a burden carried in some other place, and that all substance had been transmuted.

I do not know what value such experiences have; I feel that they should 'go into' life; yet there seems to be no technique by which one can accomplish the work of their inclusion. They stick out from my workaday existence, which I cannot lead without making distinctions, without recognizing that some people are wise and some foolish, some good and some bad, some clean and some dirty, and that, for instance, if I associate with dirty people I may catch a contagious disease and transmit it to my family or my friends. I admit the validity of psychological explanations of these states; my squalid years and my sudden escape from them in adolescence clearly contributed something to my condition. Yet that condition was so palpable and self-evident that these explanations, though I acknowledge their weight, have no genuine effect upon it, and in the end I must regard it simply as a form of experience. It is a form of experience which I have had oftener in dreams than in waking life, for dreams go without a hitch into the fable, and waking life does not (pp. 114–15).

It is strange to find him using a word like 'technique': one would expect him to reject the very idea of a transfiguration being a matter of manipulation. He would have to wait until Rome to see that such experiences do not 'go into life' but are *in* life, surround us, inhabit us, are part of our essential selves, awaiting realization and recognition.

The full story of this stage in his life is in *An Autobiography* but it is useful, I think, to have the picture briefly before us so as to get an immediate sense of how sharply the best of *First Poems* break with that period in which Muir's life had been 'a continuous enemy' of his inner development.

In recalling his early years in *An Autobiography* Muir attempts to recover a quality of perception when *everything* had the character of an unsolicited revelation, indeed of dream. In the passage following the statement that no autobiography can begin with a man's birth he speaks of sleep as 'a mode of experience and our dreams a part of reality'. In dreams time is of no significance, and so it was in his childhood. What is called up in *An Autobiography* and in some of the best of *First Poems* is 'the vast boundless calm while time still sat on the wrist of the day with its wings folded'. Every aspect of life on the island seemed timelessly related; the ordinary and the fabulous were one, the animal world was immemorial; the mind ever open and responsive to pictures of agelessness. Certainly Muir's first experience of family and surroundings took hold of his imagination with an immediacy and intensity denied to those who live in more complex environments. When trying to recall this immediacy he seems naturally to use the imagery of the islands and the sea: his mother and father were 'fixed allegorical figures in a timeless landscape', his father 'rising out of changelessness made them more, not less solid, as if they were condensed into something more real than humanity . . . and now I can see them only as a stationary pattern, changing yet always the same' (p. 25). In these quotations we sense the forming presence in so much of Muir's poetry and, indeed, the grounds of his belief in immortality: 'We think and feel and believe immortalty in our first few years, simply because time does not exist for us.' It is as though the landscape of his boyhood ratified these immediate impressions, making them fundamentally proof against the trials of time and adult experience. Muir could begin to write poetry only when he had made those impressions live for himself again. But it would be a mistake to think of his beginnings as simply a matter of deliberate, intense recollection. His critical work in the early 1920s is of a piece with it. *First Poems* contains six ballads (though only three were retained in *Collected Poems*). The best thing in his second collection of prose, *Latitudes* (1924), is undoubtedly 'A Note on the Scottish Ballads'. Muir's lifelong admiration for and fascination with the Scottish ballads is deeply significant to his development as an artist. In reading that essay we come almost as close to understanding the character of his beginnings as a poet as we do through *An Autobiography*.

Muir was later embarrassed to have written *Latitudes* – 'so much mere nonsense combined with overweening confidence' (22 May 1958). And it is true that there is a merely conventional 'brilliance' about much of the prose. It runs frequently to aphorism, has the knowing air of a deliberately provocative writer; it fairly consistently promises more than it delivers, drawing the reader on in the expectation of sharp insight but in the event lapsing into vague suggestiveness or plain obscurity. 'A Note on the Scottish Ballads', however, is wholly without these faults, surely one of the 'choice forlorn fragments' that did not cause Muir to feel embarrassed. It is indeed criticism of the first order. Muir writes from within his subject; a passionate admiration joins with a lucid, unsentimental intelligence to elaborate a view of the ballads (and, incidentally, of art in general) which compels the reader's engagement.

Muir demonstrates in this essay those qualities that he later claimed were lacking in much modern literary criticism. A good critic 'apprehends by a native affinity the virtues of a work of imagination and rejoices in them'. In the essay on the ballads, Muir has that native affinity and it illuminates his subject at every turn. Eliot said of Arnold that only a great critic could quote with the sureness and persuasiveness that is his. Time and again, here, Muir quotes briefly from Scottish and English ballads to clinch his case for the former's superiority. He does not so much develop an argument, we feel, as demonstrate the obvious; though behind the obviousness lies the skill and sensitivity of the demonstrator. He speaks of 'that simplicity of stark, fundamental human things which the ballads more perfectly than any other poetry express':[7]

The unquenchability of desire, the inexorability of separation, the lapse of time, and all these seen against something eternal and as if, expressed in a few lines, they were what human beings have felt from the beginning of time and must feel until time ends: these things, uttered with entire simplicity, are what at its best Scottish poetry can give us, and it can give them with the intensity and inevitability of great poetry.[8]

The 'Note on the Scottish Ballads' still stands as a fine piece of independent literary criticism, with that impersonality proper to writing that 'sees the object as in itself it really is'. In addition, however, for the chronicler of Muir's life and the student of his poetry, it stands in a vital relation to the act of 'looking against the direction in which time was hurrying me' that Muir was undertaking at the time of writing the essay (1923). The critical writing is of a piece with his 'rediscovering the world of life'. What he discovered in recollecting the Orkney boyhood was, above all, simplicity. Throughout his writing he refers to the 'bareness and simplicity' of the landscape and, in *An Autobiography* is quite clear about its importance in the life of the imagination:

The little island was not too big for a child to see in it an image of life; land and sea and sky, good and evil, happiness and grief, life and death discovered themselves to me there; and the landscape was so simple that it made these things simple too (p. 206).

The bareness and simplicity of that landscape is something he loved and evoked and one feels this attachment must be related to his instinctive avoidance, in both poetry and prose, of rhetoric and luxuriance. The ballads might indeed be described in much the same terms as he uses for the landscape and the imaginative life it shaped. He repeatedly stresses 'this simple vision of life as a thing of sin and pleasure, passing, but passing with an intense vividness as of a flame, before something eternal'[9] as a possession both of the Scottish peasantry and of the ballads themselves. He frequently uses the word 'unconditional' in this essay to describe this vision and the word occurs often in his writings to indicate an absence of the provisional, a purity of vision or feeling. The ballads clearly figured for him as an example of the kind of impersonality to which all art should aspire. They came out of a simple but profound faith about the value of human life and a similar trust in the power of words and music to express it. And in the ballads he found a view of life that seemed analogous to, or rather to express, the essence of life as he knew it on Wyre. In his childhood, as he remembered it, there was enough left of the culture of which the ballads once formed a part for him to feel the continuity of their vision and his own earthly life. It is therefore highly significant that he speaks of the best ballads displaying 'a vision of unconditional clearness like that of a child' and, having quoted from the ballad, *Jamie Douglas*, says that there 'the qualities of the velvet, the crimson, the gold and silver are seen as they are seen in childhood, for the first time, and with something solid in the vision of them';[10] significant, too, that he sees the absence of imagery in the ballads as making 'the real form and colour of things stand out with a distinctness which is that, not of things seen by daylight, but of those more absolute, more incapable of being questioned, which we see in dreams'.[11]

The 'something solid in the vision of the colours' in *Jamie Douglas* was thus part of the world as he first knew it and indeed may speak too for the quality of its evocation in *An Autobiography*. He says there that 'the sense of deep and solid peace' associated with his earliest memories 'has come back to me since only in dreams' and, in describing a scarlet suit he wore at his baptism, that 'it must have been the first time that I saw the colour of gold and scarlet, for it is this suit that makes me remember that day, and it still burns in my memory more brightly than anything I have ever seen since' (p. 18). Temperamentally, then, by virtue of his early days on Wyre, he was drawn to the ballad form whose nobility was that of a fundamental vision and a common possession. The fact that the 'old songs, rooted for so long in the life of the people', were still there in his childhood must have helped to sustain him, a true vision that he could hold to through the doubts and confusions of his personal life. The joint preoccupation with the ballads and with the rediscovery of his childhood in the early 1920s is thus logical, the one recalling the essential vision of the other and providing a standard for his own art. In the light of this it is not surprising that his first collection of poems (1925) should contain six ballads. John Holms, a friend of Muir who influenced him very much, talked of them as 'having more of the ballad spirit than any imitations I have read – in his case the form is entirely natural – he writes in ballad form more quickly and easily than in any other. A pure question of race.'[12] This last sentence is to the point. We may now feel Holms's assessment of the ballads to be too high, but he rightly recognized the relative ease with which Muir handled the form as arising from a native affinity. In recalling his early years and in studying the ballads he was reanimating a vital and long-suppressed part of his imaginative life. It was that rather than the pressure of contemporary poetic example that counted in his early poetic development. For his beginnings were very unusual indeed. As he saw it, he began writing poetry ten or fifteen years after he should have done and then:

I had no training; I was too old to submit myself to contemporary influences; and I had acquired in Scotland a deference to ideas which had made my entrance into poetry difficult. Though my imagination had begun to work I had no technique by which I could give expression to it. There were the rhythms of English poetry on the one hand, the images in my mind on the other. All I could do at the start was to force the one, creaking and complaining, into the mould of the other (p. 205).

He was an instinctive poet in a straightforward sense: 'I began to write poetry simply because what I wanted to say could not have gone properly into prose. I wanted so much to say it that I had no thought left to study the form in which alone it could be said' (p. 206). The most startling illustration of this urgency and, also, the most finished and satisfying poem in this volume is *The Ballad of Hector in Hades*. Unlike *The Ballad of the Soul* which does not sufficiently improve upon the incoherence of the waking vision from which it derives, *Hector in Hades* has a finality, an impersonal authority that frees it from the circumstances that lie behind it.

Some of Muir's best poems are based on scenes or characters from the Trojan war and this is the first. In its absence of imagery, its sustained concentration on the immediate physical facts as they come into Hector's vision, the poem recalls indeed Muir's characterization of the Scottish ballads. The essay was published the year before the poem: 'the real form and colour of things' stand out 'with a distinctness which is that not of things seen by daylight, but of those more absolute, more incapable of being questioned which we see in dreams':

The grasses puff a little dust
    Where my footsteps fall.
I cast a shadow as I pass
    The little wayside wall.

The strip of grass on either hand
    Sparkles in the light;
I only see that little space
    To the left and to the right,

And in that space our shadows run,
    His shadow there and mine,
The little flowers, the tiny mounds,
    The grasses frail and fine.

The landscape of the poem is not just the scene of the action that Hector relives. It *is* that, and it comes urgently to mind as we read the poem – the ballad moves in time with the onset of terror. But we don't see the landscape as a scenario, a background. Hector's nightmare is an image of terror for any time, an unchanging story. Nothing is in its proper place, nothing moves at its proper speed. The world is both in the shape of the fear within, yet alien in a new and final way:

I run. If I turned back again
   The earth must turn with me,
The mountains planted on the plain,
   The sky clamped to the sea.

Speaking of his early poetry, Muir gives the impression that it was only later on that he fully understood what he had been trying to do. In *An Autobiography* he says that as the memories of childhood returned to him in Dresden and Hellerau, 'I went on writing a poetry of symbols drawn from memory without realizing that I was doing so. I continued to do this for ten years before I became aware of it, and then only when it was pointed out' (p. 206). In beginning to write poetry and in thus recovering the 'image of life' he had known on Wyre, Muir does for himself and the reader what he later said von Hofmannsthal does in his poems and plays: he 'preserves a lost world and gives it back to us as part of our experience'. Orkney had taught him 'something inherent in every good order' and in unconsciously 'writing a poetry of symbols drawn from memory' he was reaching back through time to rediscover that lost world and the childish power of divining concealed tragedy that eventually yielded *Hector in Hades*. The poems, though, that most directly summon that world are the first two in the *Collected Poems*: *Childhood* and *Horses*.

Muir may have spoken of forcing the images of his mind 'creaking and complaining' into the given rhythms of English poetry. But that would hardly be a fair comment on *Childhood*. The discovery of the life of the imagination was so intense an experience that questions of technique did not preoccupy him at this or any other stage of his poetic development. There is, one feels, an implicit trust in that intensity of vision which, as T. S. Eliot remarked, 'unconsciously produced the right, the inevitable way of saying what he wanted to say'. Here are the first and last stanzas.

Long time he lay upon the sunny hill,
   To his father's house below securely bound.
Far off the silent, changing sound was still,
   With the black islands lying thick around.
         *   *   *
Grey tiny rocks slept round him where he lay,
   Moveless as they, more still as evening came,
The grasses threw straight shadows far away,
   And from the house his mother called his name.

The poem recreates the calm and security of the island childhood. Though, obviously, it is the adult looking back on that scene, the adult's special perspective is excluded. It is a direct entrée into a state of feeling whose reality the power of the expression vouches for. The second and last lines of *Childhood* establish the boundaries within which such a feeling was possible, though such is the power of Muir's imagining that the last line comes as a reminder of the foundations on which that claim is based. The physical presence of the sound and the islands is there, but arrested in the poem as they were in the days being recalled. The world is at once physical and symbolic, at once the world of ordinary perception and that of dream: the control of the verse is such that we view the scene as possessing the mind, the outward form of a deep peace that can be made known through the beauties of sound and rhythm:

> Over the sound a ship so slow would pass
>   That in the black hill's gloom it seemed to lie.
> The evening sound was smooth like sunken glass,
>   And time seemed finished ere the ship passed by.

In his poem *The Retreat*, Henry Vaughan speaks of how, his soul 'gazing on some gilded cloud, or flower', he would 'in those weaker glories spy/Some shadows of eternity'. There is the shadow of something eternal in *Childhood*. One recalls Muir's identifying the essential qualities of the Scots ballads as their absence of reflection, of thought, their 'vision of unconditional clearness like that of a child'; and there is nothing that could be called reflection here. Instead it is a picture, a picture of everything in its place, of the dignity and aptness of the human and the non-human world. As such it is very much the experience of the state of childhood as Muir recalls and explores it in *An Autobiography* and, more explicitly, in the postscript to the book that he produced in 1940 under the title of *Yesterday's Mirror*. There he links the vision of the child with that of the greatest mystics and poets in that in both cases there is a perception of 'a fundamental rightness in human life, in spite of its evil'. Of the vast differences between the child and, for instance, St Augustine or Blake, there is the fact that they 'knew evil and had passed through experience to another innocence, while there is no choice for our first innocence but to lose itself in experience'.[13] Time stands still in this poem and we experience something of the child's way of seeing while we read it. For it is a picture of innocence, of before the Fall, and unless we have such pictures we cannot know what we have fallen from.

The odd archaism and the distinctly uncontemporary flavour of *Childhood* are not in the least distracting. *Horses*, on the other hand, is clearer evidence of the difficulties Muir said he had in beginning to write poetry. There is no point in making much of them; they are clearly the growing pains of a writer with something powerful to express. The adult eye is fixed upon early experience more deliberately than in *Childhood*, remembering and evoking the terrible mute potency of the farm horses, and here and there the borrowed robes are obvious. The final stanza is Wordsworthian, in its regret for the fading vision and in its closing cadences recalling that 'dread country crystalline'

> Where the blank field and the still-standing tree
> Were bright and fearful presences to me.

Only intermittently does the poem take fire, before subsiding into ordinariness, into the kind of generality represented by 'warm and glowing with mysterious fire' and 'gleamed with a cruel, apocalyptic light'. At its best, though, it strikes a Blake-like image out of the recollection that nonetheless belongs to Muir himself:

> Their manes the leaping ire of the wind
> Lifted with rage invisible and blind.

Blake, Wordsworth, the Old Testament, these are voices in the song; but the vision, though imperfectly realized, is still palpably authentic. The prose passage about the farm horses quoted in chapter 1 clearly describes the same scene and would convince us of that. But we don't need that extraneous evidence. These horses, like the rocks, the islands and the sea of *Childhood*, are farm horses; but they are simultaneously covered with a glory from some impenetrable region of which at its best the poem gives us some intimation. But 'that dread country crystalline' that, in the words of *An Autobiography*, 'I loved and dreaded . . . as an explorer loves and dreads a strange country which he has not yet entered', is only intermittently present. We know that Muir felt inadequate to the expression of such things in poetry. The awakening that came upon him in Dresden and Hellerau in 1922 was the beginning of salvation, a rediscovery of life through the imagination. But the beginning was, as he said, 'sluggish'. (The corresponding passage is understandably more accomplished, more complete. Fifteen or so years on he had lived through the period of 're-discovering the world of life', and had a surer hold on it. There we have a picture of unqualified power and precision which, occurring in the midst of a narrative dealing with both the visionary and the ordinary, conveys an authentic feeling of the one being present in the other.)

There are no 'ideas' in the best of *First Poems*. It is the physical world and the life of the spirit as it inhabits or finds an echo there that they express. There is wonder in *When the trees grow bare on the high hills*, the poem following the parallel movement of the leaves falling and the heart growing light. There is the succession of loosely strung pictures of the uncomprehending earth in *Autumn in Prague*: summer is gone, the time of growth, of plenty, of fertility. Now, in autumn, we feel the immemorial unity, the still concord that summer disguises. The stubble, the trees, the girl, the gossamers, the sea, all related, all in their proper place. Muir's childhood memory connects, it seems, with Prague now, and finds there qualities of the dream wherein all is perfect and unchanging:

> The stubble shines in the dry field,
> Gilded by the pale sun.
> The trees, unburdened, with light limbs,
> Shiver in the cold light.
> In the meadow the goat-herd,

A young girl,
Sits with bent head,
Blind, covered head,
Bowed to the earth,
Like a tree
Dreaming a long-held dream.

But the outstanding poem of this kind is *October at Hellbrunn*, surely an example of the poet 'seeing into the life of things'. (I quote from the final version of the poem. As with other 'first poems' included in the collected edition Muir made some amendments, changing a word here, deleting an archaism there.)

The near-drawn stone-smooth sky, closed in and grey,
    Broods on the garden, and the turf is still.
The dim lake shines, oppressed the fountains play,
    And shadowless weight lies on the wooded hill.

The patient trees rise separate, as if deep
    They listened dreaming through the hollow ground,
Each in a single and divided sleep,
    While few sad leaves fall heedless with no sound.

The physical scene is made present. We are looking at familiar objects in familiar surroundings. And yet there is a palpable sense of something within and behind the scene whose location is everywhere and nowhere. We may point to the obviously animistic 'oppressed the fountains play' and 'the patient trees rise separate', but they are not figures of speech, interpretative guidemarks. Rather, they bring into momentary focus a pervading emotion of which we can probably give no more precise an account than to recall Yeats' 'continuous indefinable symbolism which is the substance of style'. Marble cherubs there may be in 'the wavering lake', but this garden is haunted by spirits older than time; the poem conjures these spirits out of 'the stone-smooth sky', the 'wooded hill', the 'hidden fountain', and they speak for themselves in a beautifully sustained evocation:

The marble cherubs in the wavering lake
    Stand up more still, as if they kept all there,
The trees, the plots, in thrall. Their shadows make
    The water clear and hollow as the air.

The silent afternoon draws in, and dark
    The trees rise now, grown heavier is the ground,
And breaking through the silence of the park
    Farther a hidden fountain flings its sound.

There is no doubt that by this time – '*October at Hellbrunn*' was published in 1924 – Muir's poetic gift was unmistakeably declaring itself and, through it, those imaginative sympathies so long dammed up.

None of the poems in this first collection, though, deals directly with the moral and spiritual dilemmas that preoccupy him in most of his poetry (though *Betrayal* – see chapter 3 – points the way). What they mainly seem to be doing is establishing a foundation for that poetry, assisting Muir in his 'rediscovery' of life. *Childhood, Horses, When the trees grow bare, Autumn in Prague, October at Hellbrunn*: all in their different ways recall or evoke moments 'liberated from the order of time' and that will eventually be seen to be the only hope of grace. All of them, too, celebrate the visual, sensible world. One remembers that in Prague Muir had begun to 'indulge in an orgy of looking'.

Chapter 3

The Enchanted Knight

Time wakens a longing more poignant than all the longings caused by the division of lovers in space, for there is no road back into its country. Our bodies were not made for that journey; only the imagination can venture upon it; and the setting out, the road, and the arrival: all is imagination (p. 224).

It would be quite wrong to see Muir as a sentimentalist endlessly nostalgic for a precious harmony known in childhood only to be destroyed by the merciless circumstance of adult life. Division entered his world early; some of the best writing in the early parts of *An Autobiography* describes that phase of his childhood. The circumstances in which 'contradiction' came into his life were particular to him; but he is quite clear that the phase itself is natural and universal – 'a phase of emotional and mental strain [which] brings with it a sense of guilt'. In his case the end of innocence was signalled by 'a passion of fear and guilt'. He describes the absurd but paralysing terror that overtook him after being warned by his father not to interfere with some poisonous sheepdip on the farm; his irrational and terrible failure to persuade himself that he had not indeed touched it and his efforts physically to scrub away the contamination. The period in his life with which this was associated was one in which he became conscious of death and 'the sense of an unseen tragedy being played out around me'; the result was a sense of estrangement that in fact and in the way he expresses it prefigures that more ominous and terrifying estrangement he was to experience in Glasgow. He had 'actually gone away into a world where every object was touched with fear, yet a world of the same size as the ordinary world and corresponding to it in every detail: a sort of parallel world divided by an endless, unbreakable sheet of glass from the actual world'. Obviously Muir was a child of exceptionally keen sensibility, but he is no doubt right in holding that the condition he describes is essentially a phase in the growth of every human being. He of course recovered from this early disturbance, but from that point 'the world my eyes saw was a different world from my first childish one, which never returned again'.

His way of describing what has been lost is important to an understanding of the trials of his youth and early manhood: 'a perfectly solid world, for the days did not undermine it but merely rounded it, or rather repeated it, as if there were only one day endlessly rising and setting'. That world could not of course survive but the effect of the break-up of his family and particularly the deaths of his brothers was to obliterate his knowledge that it had ever existed. All that happened to the family in Glasgow was experienced by Muir as the pitiless triumph of time, a triumph for which the hostility of the new environment provided a viciously apt setting and for which the sufferings of his brothers seemed to give irresistible proof. To put it this way may seem to colour things too much. But it does not. Time was Muir's 'obsession' – as we have seen, his own word. Nothing was more painful for him to write about than the apparently meaningless deaths of his brothers. In *An Autobiography*, he 'hurried over these years because they are still painful and still blurred in my mind'. The impersonality of the city to which the family had migrated must have been felt the more intensely in the helpless observation of this suffering. (One brother died from consumption, the other of a brain tumour.) It was as if the spirit of that impersonality had actively entered the family and was bent on its destruction. Of his brother Johnnie's agonizing death (to be dealt with more fully in the novel, *Poor Tom*) he wrote:

the attacks strengthened methodically, as if a power beyond our knowledge or reach were performing some dreadful operation on him which could neither be hurried nor retarded; it was like the infallible consummation of an objective process . . . that impersonal, systematic torture (pp. 102–3).

What point could there possibly be in such torture? He could find 'no answer to that question, except that life was ruled by an iron law'. Time was the insidious agent of that iron law. Muir's development as a poet begins, as we have seen, with a revival of the imagination, an effort to recover an image of wholeness that would place his own agonies, his estrangement from himself, as the provisional things they were. 'It is in our nature to ignore time', he says, and 'we pay no attention to him until he tugs us by the sleeve or claps his policeman's hand on our shoulder.' Most of the work in *First Poems* may be seen as an attempt to reaffirm the reality of that natural inattentiveness. It is evoked in such poems as *Childhood* and *Horses*. What they do not do, though, is to bring the experience of timelessness recalled and affirmed into relation with an adult awareness of time's effects. That will be the burden of much of Muir's work; but there is no sign of it in *First Poems* – except in the extraordinary *Betrayal*:

Sometimes I see, caught in a snare,
  One with a foolish lovely face,
Who stands with scattered moon-struck air
  Alone, in a wild woody place.

She was entrapped there long ago.
  Yet fowler none has come to see
His prize; though all the tree-trunks show
  A front of silent treachery.

'She' is Beauty and 'He who entrapped her long ago,/And kills her, is unpitying Time'. According to Butter[1], *Betrayal* was one of the early poems against which, in manuscript lists and in his own copy, he eventually wrote 'bad' or some stronger expression of disapproval. One wonders whether his dislike would be to do with the power of the vision here being associated with so bleak, so negative a view of life. There had been much in Muir's personal life to invite such a view. In *An Autobiography* he speaks of his brother Willie's approaching death in words that directly suggest the poem: 'I scarcely dared to speak as we walked along the little paths, seeing nothing round us, both of us thinking of that invisible, deadly, and yet peaceable enemy quietly working beyond our reach.' Absorbed into the impersonality of the ballad form, the blackness of the vision is less supportable than, say, in the novel, *Poor Tom*. The prose descriptions there may be harrowing but they are provisional in the sense that they arise from and all the time refer to particulars. Here, in the poem, is a betrayal of all life; the images of pathos, foolishness, treachery, sadism, follow one another in an indictment of all creation. So that when we read that 'nothing now of Beauty stays,/Save her divine and witless smile', 'divine' is an empty counter, a convention without substance, a mockery. In *Betrayal* there is a disturbing challenge in the very sureness of movement and diction. The universe is poisoned, its fairest shows an unregarding part of a destructive pattern. Muir's imagination is the familiar of the chill workings of the enemy within. How much so is clear from the just and perfectly placed word 'inly', here:

> He slays her with invisible hands,
>   And inly wastes her flesh away,

This pitiless vision, then, belongs essentially to a period of Muir's life which, looking back on it, he felt to be 'a heap of dismal rubbish . . . I climbed out of those years like a man struggling out of a quagmire, but that rubbish still encumbered me for a long time with post-mortem persistence'. *Variations on a Time Theme*, published in 1934, is a measure of that post-mortem persistence. It is a collection of ten separate but thematically related poems whose interest now is on the whole limited to its value as evidence of Muir's difficulty in finding a form for the expression of the philosophical problems that beset him. His first attempts to make use of biblical myth and the language of heraldry are, with hindsight, interesting experiments in modes within which he was later to work with real success. But as a whole the poetry hardly deserves the detailed attention its frequent obscurity demands. In a letter to an anthologist who was including the second poem of the seven in a collection of contemporary verse, he confessed that 'it was written in a mood of unusual dejection. The painful emotion in the poem comes from a simultaneous feeling of immortality and mortality'.[2] The anthologist presumably asked for some explanation of the symbolism and certainly it needs it.

> At the dead centre of the boundless plain
> Does our way end? Our horses pace and pace
> Like steeds for ever labouring on a shield,
> Keeping their solitary heraldic courses.

The horses and their riders clearly are symbolic but they do not possess that intimacy, that instant familiarity that belongs to the very unphilosophic symbolism of the best of *First Poems*. There is here no intensity; the symbols have no charge, the verse is generally flaccid, the whole obscure. It has the air of notes for a poem and certainly later works deal far more successfully with 'the feeling that we, as immortal spirits, are imprisoned in a very small and from all appearances fortuitously selected length of time'.[3] The dejection has mastered the expression. In some writers the result would be rhetoric or sentimentality. In Muir it is lifelessness.

> Time has such curious stretches, we are told,
> And generation after generation
> May travel them, sad stationary journey,
> Of what device, what meaning?   (section 2)

When the poetry in *Variations on a Time Theme* has life it is a borrowed life.

> After the fever this long convalescence,
> Chapped blood and growing pains, waiting for life,
> Turning away from hope, too dull for speculation.
> How did we come here to this broken wood?   (section 1)

The obvious source is Eliot's *The Wasteland*. Muir is hardly ever derivative and even here, when most obviously so, the result is not without its own stern authority. The equivocations with which the mind is teased –

> Or did we choose, and if we chose
> Did we choose idly, following the fawning way,
> Or after years of obstinate dubitation,
> Night sweats, rehearsed refusals, choose at last
> For only the choice was left?   (section 1)

– are not whimsical or factitious, but the chief interest of the poem (and this is a small interest) is really as a collection of pointers, of motifs for the work of his maturity. One is not convinced that Muir's large questions (this section consists almost entirely of questions) arise out of the fullest acquaintance with his feelings. They would not, surely, have permitted the wholly uncharacteristic echo of that 'obstinate dubitation'. When one brings to mind the clearly developing grasp on the significance of his own and humanity's past in *First Poems* the closing question here, which asks whether

we 'between the impotent dead/And the unborn', can 'till these
nameless fields', seems somewhat false (The echo here is Arnold:
'Wandering between two worlds, one dead,/The other powerless
to be born'⁴). Muir wears borrowed robes, speaking more for a
common sensibility than subjecting that sensibility to his own deepest
convictions. I think he probably shared this feeling that the poems
in this series were untrue to what he came to call his 'solidest
foundation'. Certainly he was far from satisfied with them. In a letter
to a lady who had admired his earlier poems, he doubted whether
she would like these as much: 'I myself did not get nearly so much
pleasure in the writing of them – indeed, a good deal of bitterness
in some cases – whereas my earlier ones were the fruit of very fortunate
moments for me. And we must write, and feel as we can.'⁵

For a poet whose aim was simplicity, (a 'singleness of spirit' such as
around this time he deplored the lack of in Joyce,) *Variations on a Time
Theme* could not have been satisfactory. Here and there odd lines and
images are struck that seem to come nearer to a genuine imaginative
realization of the 'problems' that beset him. But in general the writing is
strained.

In the introductory chapter to his book of critical essays on modern
literature, *Transition* (1926), Muir draws an important distinction
between ordinary writers and those of the first rank.

The mark of the former [he says] is that they accept the spirit of the age both
consciously and unconsciously; their conscious is accordingly a mere passive
reflection of a general unconscious, and is incapable of being turned back into
that unconscious to discover and objectify what is there. They are mere
expressions of the thing of which they should be the contemplators.⁶

The difference between the verse most typical of *Variations on a Time
Theme* and the best of his next collection, *Journeys and Places* (1937) is
broadly suggested in this quotation. There is in the later volume an
impressive growth of imaginative range and power. The problem of time
still presses but does not constrain the poet in the way of *Variations*.
Instead we do indeed have the first instance of Muir as 'contemplator' in
the sense used above. The pilgrimage, the long journey in search of a
resting place for the spirit properly begins in this volume; and though the
best poems record the anguish of defeat and impossibility of arrival,
they do not for the most part express emotion in a personally direct way.
For the first time there is a degree of objectivity that gives us the poems
not as the expression of personal crisis but as the image of a common
condition. The titles of the best poems suggest the direction in which
Muir's art will develop: *Tristram's Journey, Hölderlin's Journey, The
Fall, Troy, A Trojan Slave, Merlin, The Enchanted Knight.* These are
some of the means by which Muir seeks to 'objectify what is there' in 'the
general unconscious': myth, legend, folk-tale. For him, their significance in his own life is such that he is deeply convinced of their potency
in interpreting and clarifying the present age. The timeless stuff of myth,

the notation of the unconscious, becomes an instrument in the poet's struggle to make meaning out of the contemporary scene – a scene he describes in *Transition* as being for the artist one of bewilderment and pervading uncertainty. From *Journeys and Places* onwards Muir is revealed ever more clearly as a writer who, unlike most of his contemporaries, is able to accept the significance of these things at a level deep enough for him to bring them into revealing relation with the 'wasteland' that, like his contemporaries, he so keenly felt.

The act of contemplation results in the creation of an image that calls up and holds the energies and tensions recognizably present within our own culture. Such images can be more disturbing than more direct comment and engagement because they seem both to contain and transcend their origins. I stress the *public* nature of these poems for even when their roots are demonstrably personal, the full-grown work is not. There is no finer illustration of this in the work of Muir's poetic output than *The Enchanted Knight*.

Lulled by La Belle Dame Sans Merci he lies
  In the bare wood below the blackening hill.
The plough drives nearer now, the shadow flies
  Past him across the plain, but he lies still.

Long since the rust its gardens here has planned,
  Flowering his armour like an autumn field.
From his sharp breast-plate to his iron hand
  A spider's web is stretched, a phantom shield.

When footsteps pound the turf beside his ear
  Armies pass through his dream in endless line,
And one by one his ancient friends appear;
  They pass all day, but he can make no sign.

When a bird cries within the silent grove
  The long-lost voice goes by, he makes to rise
And follow, but his cold limbs never move,
  And on the turf unstirred his shadow lies.

But if a withered leaf should drift
  Across his face and rest, the dread drops start
Chill on his forehead. Now he tries to lift
  The insulting weight that stays and breaks his heart.

When the Muirs returned to Cambridge after the Czech Communist putsch of 1948, Willa Muir was reminded of *The Enchanted Knight* lying stricken in a field. She suspected that her husband 'might be in a state of despair about the whole human race and was refusing to belong to it'.[7] That suggests the enduring power of the poem. *The Enchanted Knight* gives expression to a desolating phase in the life of the spirit that we may know not just once but unpredictably and at any time. It had been known to Muir as a boy emerging from childhood when he had for a time lived in 'a sort of parallel world divided by an endless, unbreakable sheet of glass from the actual world': it had been known in the early days after he moved to London when he would 'gaze at an object or a face – it did not matter which for the choice was not mine – I was no longer trying to establish a connexion with it, but hoping that it – whether animate or inanimate – would establish a connection with me and prove that I existed'; it was experienced, severely, at the time of which Willa Muir speaks, as a falling 'plumb into a dead pocket of life'. But of course it was in the years of his working in 'Fairport' that the experience of being 'far away from myself' had been most desperate. Despite the friendships he eventually formed at this time he was 'physically and spiritually in a bad way'. He went through 'a second Heine phrase' drawn by the 'sickly graveyard' strain in Heine's poetry:

I identified myself with the dead man who knew so well that he was dead. Something in myself was buried, and I was only half there as I worked in the office and wandered about the roads. I felt that I had gone far away from myself (p. 145).

'The world retreated from me with all its shapes.' He describes how he would find himself 'gazing at things – hillsides, woods, ships, houses, trifling objects in shop-windows, with a dry yearning'. When the world of shapes retreated, the self retreated. The word 'shapes' is important. Muir was now moving in a world whose fundamental difference from that of his childhood was that physical objects were no longer instinct with meaning. In his early years his sense of himself had been deeply, indissociably bound up with the physical scene around him, a scene that, as for Wordsworth, carried with it 'a sense of something far more deeply interfused'. What he records is a yearning for that something more and his powerlessness to bring it about.

I have said that *An Autobiography* is the record of the growth of a poet's mind. To have read about these various experiences of self-estrangement is, when one comes to *The Enchanted Knight*, to realize more fully the kind of triumph of art that that poem represents. When in the twenties Muir was taking his first hesitant steps as a poet, he was also developing a theory of art from which in essence he never departed and that sheds a good deal of light on the nature of that triumph. With an assertiveness that he later regretted, but with an undeniable vigour of intelligence, he rejected personal agony as a source of art and with that a considerable body of contemporary literature. In his essay 'Against profundity' (1922) he argued that 'the intellectual and artistic character of the present age . . . is a tremendous and tortured desire, among all writers . . . to descend into their own depths', to explore what has hitherto been 'beneath the threshold of artistic expression and to establish there a kingdom of art, an interesting, sad and intense kingdom of the blind'.[8] The essay contains a vigorous statement of what he sees as the true function of art and artists. He recognizes that he describes the ideal, but what is it that the great artists have, those 'who have the power of refreshing us'?

To throw oneself out, for ever and always; to strive upwards into sharper light and air. . . . Life is comprehended only in the throwing of it outward, clearly and completely; what introspection shows us is only what introspection itself has tortured and thwarted, the suffering, passive body of our vivisected selves.[9]

The passion in such affirmations – and they occur frequently in *Latitudes* – is that of a man who recognizes in art a truer reflection of life than he is at present able to arrive at through his own efforts of will and imagination. ('Life would be impossible for us without Shakespeare, Mozart, Homer, Goethe, who have opened the second book of revelation to us'). It is, too, that of a critic who, in articulating a definition of the kind of art that has 'the power of refreshing us', more clearly understands the nature of the poetry he must try to write. In his essay on George Douglas (1923) he says of 'classical art' that 'it is so securely objective that whatever circumstances of grief, of turpitude or of horror it may describe, it raises no echo in our ordinary subjective emotions and is entirely incapable of corrupting us'.[10]

It is in a sense given by these quotations that we may see the best art as revealing to us that 'real self' of which Muir says it is so difficult for us to gain a glimpse. (In Germany in the twenties he had been 'trying to form an intelligible picture' of his life and thus 'save something of myself'.) The best art gives us back that real self, compels upon us a kind of knowledge quite beyond our daily, transitory selves since they are preoccupied in time, with all that time brings in distorting pressure and distraction. Paradoxically such art can have more to say to us than the art which reflects contemporary suffering in detail because it gives us a perspective, an eternal perspective on the present.

The Enchanted Knight raises 'no echo in our ordinary subjective emotions'. It is the triumph of Muir's art to have converted intense personal suffering into a form that, incidentally, perfectly illustrates his idea of the classical. Keats and Heine are no more felt as essential presences in the poem than are the personal emotions at its root. The imagination seems to have produced a poem of unconditional purity; a spiritual state of subtle complexion has been evoked, we feel, in the only language in which it could be grasped – more, the only language in which it exists. So that for Muir as for his reader, the gap between intuition and created poem has vanished:

The poetic state, the state in which poetry is produced, is a state balanced more or less exactly between the conscious and the unconscious, between inspiration and formulation; something is happening to the poet, and at the same time he is shaping it towards an end in his mind (5 April 1936).

The lulling of the Knight by la Belle Dame Sans Merci is into a state of death in life, a state in which the sensuous world and its meanings can receive no acknowledgement, awaken no response. The armies that 'pass through his dream' and 'the bird that cries within the silent grove/The long-lost voice', are agonizing reminders of the lost and potentially real world. *The Enchanted Knight* is a figure of humanity's losses. He seems to stand for that level of our being or phase of our spirit in which we know that we suffer from a paralysis of the feelings; in which, sporadically and unavailingly, we will try to come alive in some now unorthodox but once simple and regular way. Our limbs are 'cold'; but every so often we know what we have lost. Some visitation from the past, some imperfect memory, 'a withered leaf', catches at us with its intimation of what that might be; only to find us impotent to acknowledge its force through our own living. Blackmur suggests the mystery and the power of this poem in his comment on the way our minds receive it: 'As we think in an earlier form of ourselves, so we use a different alphabet of feelings; and in that form and that alphabet we believe preciously in what in its present form we greet only with the attraction of horror . . .'[11]

In his paralysis the Knight can make no contact with what life has to offer in beauty, in friendship, in whatever makes it more than an 'insulting' burden (how right and how original that word is!) Amongst the things the Knight seems to speak for is a failure of imagination and faith that is a recurrent theme in *Journeys and Places*. It is most arrestingly dealt with in *The Hill*, a poem that would seem to possess the distinctive imaginative self-sufficiency of Muir's best poems and that clearly 'derives' from an experience recorded in *Scottish Journey* (1935). Coming from the moorlands to the west coast of Scotland he

could not make out what the tiny louse-like forms could be that were crawling over the broad, soiled, mud-coloured sands, until I realized that they must be bathers. From that height and distance, where these shapes were only by inference human, they presented a strangely sad and ignominious spectacle, and the simultaneous knowledge that I was looking at human flesh, yards and yards of human flesh assembled there as by some meaningless feat of mass production, was such a shock that I hastily started the car again so as to reach the shore and see for myself that these were human beings. They were, I found to my relief. But the sand looked as dirty near at hand as it had looked from the distance.[12]

The traveller in the poem, the 'he' of so many of Muir's poems of spiritual searching, approaches the hill first from the north and then from the south and, looking upon the 'same' scene, sees visions as incompatible as good and evil themselves. The first stanza presents a scene recognizably that of the prose description but it has become generalized, a realized intuition of the sadness of humanity in the mass:

> And turning north around the hill,
> The flat sea like an adder curled,
> And a flat rock amid the sea
> That gazes towards the ugly town,
> And on the sands, flat and brown,
> A thousand naked bodies hurled
> Like an army overthrown.

The biblical simile, the repetition of 'flat', the likening of the bathers to an overthrown army, the predominantly monosyllabic diction and jaded rhythms, produce an image of humanity anonymous and debased.

The second stanza on the other hand is a picture of pure imagination, a vision of purity, freedom and loveliness spelt out with the elation of sudden discovery:

> And turning south around the hill,
> Fields flowering in the curling waves,
> And shooting from the white sea-walls
> Like a thousand waterfalls,
> Rapturous divers never still.
> Motion and gladness. O this hill
> Was made to show these cliffs and caves.

These are incompatible visions. Which is true? The poem takes no stand, places its faith in neither. The 'he' of the poem has 'never stood again upon that hill', never presumably again seen things in either simple light. The third and final stanza with its picture of him living far away, knowing nothing of how to reach the hill and not knowing which side he would come out on were he to find it, is an arresting image of the becalmed spirit, or of a mind powerfully persuaded of the truth of certain illuminations but for the most part living in a place where such illuminations are unknown. The power of the poem is to persuade *us* of the possibility of both visions but to leave us, with the poet, unable to connect them. There is, indeed, no suggestion that they could be connected. He does not know whether he will be

> With the bright divers never still,
> Or on the sad dishonoured sands.

The countless pathways that separate him from the hill must, it seems, lead to one or the other; the sadness is in not knowing which is the true end of the journey: beauty or squalor.

The Hill we see to be based on an actual, physical journey Muir made; but as a metaphor of spiritual questing, the idea of a journey occupied a central position in his poetry from this point on. Muir of course did not invent the metaphor; it is, indeed, one of the most familiar of all religious symbolisms, and in making use of it in his distinctive way he implicitly invites comparison with those poets for whom the symbolism is both the expression and the sustenance of their belief. For Henry Vaughan the way was not easy to discover, nor the place of arrival easy to discern:

> Man hath still either toys or care;
> He hath no root, nor to one place is tied,
> But ever restless and irregular
>   About this earth doth run and ride.
> He knows he hath a home, but scarce knows where;
>   He says it is so far,
> That he hath quite forgot how to go there.
> (Henry Vaughan: *Man*)

According to Vaughan,

> Man is the shuttle, to whose winding quest
> And passage through these looms
> God ordered motion, but ordained no rest.

But 'busy, restless, thing' though man may be (*The Pursuit*) belief confers on the believer a power of accepting this as a blessed part of his estate. Vaughan in his poems shares that acceptance, so that when he speaks of the anguish and bewilderment of the search these things are made tolerable, indeed good, through that acceptance. Through his poems he celebrates a condition that cannot be explained or understood but only accepted; the celebration is the acceptance, an imaginative and spiritual triumph over the uncertainties with which it deals.

Muir, on the other hand, while he shares the yearning, the desire to accept, can at this stage believe neither in God nor in the power of the imagination to create a refuge from the ceaseless going foward of time. The most pained and obsessive of *Variations on a Time Theme* had posed the problem at its most explicit. The seventh variation is an anguished and angry cri de coeur, a seemingly despairing acknowledgement of the potency of time's weapons, recalling in its very phrasing the enslavement of Macbeth – 'cabin'd, cribb'd, confin'd' – to his self-created hell:

> Ransomed from darkness and released in Time,
> Caught, pinioned, blinded, sealed and cased in Time;
> Summoned, elected, armed and crowned by Time,
> Tried and condemned, stripped and disowned by Time;   (section 7)

If there could be no escape from Time, then 'we're the mock of Time,/While lost and empty lies Eternity'.

With *The Stationary Journey* (the first poem in *Journeys and Places*) the awareness of time's potency has not diminished but the form and imaginings of the poem suggest the direction Muir's art will take, even though Muir himself at this stage sees the imagination as doing little more than enable man to realize his helplessness the more painfully. The enslavement to Time is, as in the seventh 'variation', expressed through a physical figure:

> Here at my earthly station set,
>   The revolutions of the year
> Bear me bound and only let
>   This astronomic world appear.

What follows is an experiment in the mind's capacity to transcend that bondage, to attain freedom through its power to 'reverse my course/Through ever-deepening yesterday'. The attempt yields images of strange intensity:

I would see eld's frosted hair
  Burn black again and passion rage
On to its source and die away
  At last in childhood's tranquil age.

The imagination takes the poet and, potentially, every man through 'the dark backward and abysm of time' until he is brought up against 'transmutation's blank'. The journey is possible through the imagination but comes to a dead end, unfulfilled, at its limits:

Eternity's the fatal flaw
  Through which run out world, life and soul.
And there in transmutation's blank
  No mortal mind has ever read,
Or told what soul and shape are, there,
  Blue wave, red rose, and Plato's head.

'World, life and soul' run out, can never be fully entered in their true form because time binds and propels its subjects who, for that very reason, can never penetrate to the forms and essences that lie within those experiences. 'Transmutation's blank' remains an unattainable ideal.

For the reader what is achieved through the imagination in *The Stationary Journey* seems in some ways to contradict its conclusion – that what the imagination has called up is nothing but 'a dream' (here, unusually, used in its everyday sense). The experience of reading the result is of touching that faculty in man from which, if consolation is to come at all, consolation will come. For Muir, however, though it is man's gift to be able to track backwards in time, revisiting the major stopping places in the ceaseless journey forward, he can never lose his consciousness that the imagination can only exercise itself *in* time. That is why 'Imagination's one long day' has only the quality of a dream. For the reader there is a tension between what the imagination palpably does accomplish here and Muir's own feeling about it. The poem seems very adequately to give form to his intuitions, to make impressively real the nature of the inadequacy that he finds in human nature. The astonishing ninth and tenth stanzas (number 9 is quoted above) –

For there Immortal Being in
  Solidity more pure than stone
Sleeps through the circle, pillar, arch,
  Spiral, cone, and pentagon.

– express very precisely a metaphysical perception about the nature of being. We should be grateful, one would think, that the imagination permits us an entrée in such a region. So why the lament, why the anguished conclusion that it is all a dream? What, it seems to me, traps Muir at this stage is the obsession with looking back; the poem experiments with the idea that he may arrive at a vision of the whole if he can discern and connect every step that has led up to the present moment. Charlemagne, Jesus, Venus, Hannibal, David, Homer – legend, myth, religion – all attest to a meaning running through time but all are irrecoverably finished, complete; their meaning could only be known if we could relive their lives, their own development in time. What Muir cannot accept is that within 'imagination's one long day' there may be what he seeks, that what Blake called 'symbolic imagination' is 'a representation of what actually exists really and unchangeably'. It follows from what Blake says that the unchangeable is there for the artist, if he has faith and wisdom enough, to summon forth. Muir here lacks the faith but it is a deeper wisdom that produces the poem. What is brought before our eyes in *The Stationary Journey* is the 'shaping spirit' itself as it tries to assert its hold on the unchangeable. The urge to alight in that elusive region is in human nature itself and the poem gives it form while at the same time denying it can do anything of the sort. The reason for that denial is suggested perhaps by Muir's later reflections on the completion of his autobiography:

To write a book describing one human being is strictly an impossibility; for what we require for real self-knowledge is the power to stop the sun and make it revolve in the opposite direction, taking us back stage by stage through manhood to youth and through youth to childhood, missing nothing, until it conducts us to the mystery from which we started. But at the most we can take only a few chance leaps backwards while Time hurries us on; and those fortuitous leaps we afterwards call our life.[13]

Later on in the same essay he talks of art as

the sum of the moments in which men have glanced into that yesterday which can never change; and when we read, or look at a picture, or listen to music, we are released from the moment to contemplate that mirror in which all the forms of life lie outspread. There is accordingly something divine in art, since it moulds a living world out of our dead yesterdays, reliving life, and since in dealing with what can never change again it lets itself be purified by the unchangeable.

Whether deliberately or not, this description of art recalls Blake's claim that with poetry, painting and music we have 'the three powers in man of conversing with Paradise which the flood of time and space did not sweep away'. In *The Stationary Journey*, however, there is no hint of Paradise nor of the possibility of ever knowing it. The outer world of the present time does not exist; all the heroic or significant action is in the past, the only life is through memory. In that outer world, whether through people, landscape or building or through their contemplation in art, Muir would eventually discern the 'forms of life outspread'. Here, however, he is denied the insight that was later to be his. There is a curiously negative, cut-off feeling about *The Stationary Journey*. There is a passion, a yearning to establish some spiritual resting place but a sense that he is looking in the wrong direction. The passion can find no object outside itself. There is the will to believe, but nothing to believe in.

It was the transfiguring imagination that created the 'rapturous divers' of *The Hill*. But the traveller glimpsed them only once, before returning to that state of bemused longing that in one form or another finds expression throughout *Journeys and Places*. The picture presented in *The Mountains* (like *The Stationary Journey*, a personal statement) is of a man 'rooted' in the present, 'held by the mystery of the rock', bewildered where to turn, divided between simple longing for the past and a longing to be beyond time's bound altogether, but at the same time

> Dreaming of a peak whose height
>   Will show me every hill,
> A single mountain on whose side
>   Life blooms for ever and is still.

The use of the word 'dreaming' suggests (as 'dream' did in *The Stationary Journey*) that the vision of stillness within action, of the timeless within time, is a hopeless one.

Muir is not as a poet much given to direct personal statement of this sort, and indeed the most powerful expressions of bemusement and spiritual longing are to be found in the least personal poems in this volume. Both *Tristram's Journey* and *Hölderlin's Journey* are securely objective, raising 'no echo in our ordinary subjective emotions', inhabiting a landscape that belongs not to Muir alone but to us all in those states of feeling to which they give body. Both Tristram and Hölderlin are pilgrims 'in search of that which sought them'. That phrase is from *The Mythical Journey*, a not particularly successful attempt in blank verse to map the journey from the non-humanity of the dark primeval time through to a settled and civilized age in which the 'little hills' and 'the winding valleys' form a pattern that is their meaning. The 'he' of that poem wanders through time in a constant search for 'that which sought him', his only security being the knowledge that there must exist some purpose in the journey. He knows this in his heart, though it's an 'impotent heart'; he seeks

> One whose form and features,
> Race and speech he did not know, shapeless, tongueless,

One is reminded of Muir's eventual discovery of Christ and indeed the wanderings here are a foretaste of those of the much later poem, *The Labyrinth*, where the nightmare is redeemed by a serene conviction of some deeper purpose. Though in *The Mythical Journey*,

> The gods reclined and conversed with each other
> From summit to summit

as they will do in the vision that includes *The Labyrinth*, it is recognized here as a desperate hope, a dream rather than a vision. He calls it a 'living dream sprung from a dying vision' because at least it sustains him:

> Beneath its branches
> He builds in faith and doubt his shaking house.

Both Tristram and Hölderlin seek 'one whose form and features' they do know and know with an intimacy that makes the agony of separation the more acute. Each journeys through a landscape that reflects and is indifferent to his loneliness and derangement. Convinced of Iseult's infidelity, Tristram rides out from Tintagel, loses his mind, and having lived in mental torment and violent action, is captured and returned to King Mark's castle. Muir always adapts myth to his own purposes and here the end of the episode is different from the Malory version on which it is based. Tristram's identity is revealed when Iseult's hound leaps up and licks his face; the result is not just recognition but Tristram's return to sanity and wholeness, to the inward peace destroyed by Iseult's apparent unfaithfulness. As in *Hector in Hades*, there is a solidness and an immediacy in the detail of the physical scene in *Tristram's Journey* that again calls to mind the words with which Muir characterized the best Scots ballads; there is again that 'distinctness . . . not of things seen by daylight, but of those more absolute, more incapable of being questioned which we see in dreams':

> He rode out from Tintagel gate,
>   He heard his charger slowly pace,
> And ever hung a cloud of gnats
>   Three feet before his face.

> At a wood's border he turned round
>   And saw the distant castle side,
> Iseult looking towards the wood,
>   Mark's window gaping wide.

> He turned again and slowly rode
>   Into the forest's flickering shade,
> And now as sunk in waters green
>   Were armour, helm, and blade.

The power of this makes the resolution – 'he was in his place' – unsatisfactory. The assurance is borrowed, I think, from the legend itself; the legend has not been fully made over into the shape of the dominating emotions of the poem. The alienation is real enough, but the homecoming is wish rather than fact.

Hölderlin's Journey is based on the true story of the German poet. The Diotima of Muir's poem is the Diotima of Hölderlin's own. In Frankfurt, Hölderlin had been dismissed by his employer, the husband of 'Diotima', had found employment in Switzerland and Bordeaux and later returned home both mentally and physically ill. It is the return that Muir's poem deals with. The detail of both *Tristram* and *Hölderlin* is imagined with the directness of Hector's nightmare flight in *Hector in Hades*. The ring of hills within which Tristram awoke arises here too, and with the same chilling effect. The land through which Hölderlin wanders is inhuman; man is outside nature; it surrounds him – opaque, indifferent, unreadable – 'a shallow candour was their all'. The horror deepens after the 'hills of lies' have been left behind. The sudden appearance of a living deer 'with its rock crystal eyes' and the stone deer's head on the gate's pillar, is an irresistible image not of life in death but of the reverse; Hölderlin tells his own story:

'On either pillar of the gate
    A deer's head watched within the stone.
The living deer with quiet look
    Seemed to be gazing on

Its pictured death – and suddenly
    I knew, Diotima was dead,
As if a single thought had sprung
    From the cold and the living head.

From that point the landscape deepens in indifference. Iron enters the soul of the world:

'Upon the swarming towns of iron
    The bells hailed down their iron peals,
Above the iron bells the swallows
    Glided on iron wheels.

And the insight contained in the deer's head is not just that Diotima is dead but that the search was fruitless, the outcome determined before it was ever begun:

'Before I left the starting place;
    Empty the course, the garland gone,
And all that race as motionless
    As these two heads of stone.'

There is bitterness surely in the final picture of Hölderlin,

Dragging in pain a broken mind
And giving thanks to God and men.

What has Hölderlin to give thanks to God and men *for*? It is of *Hölderlin's Journey* that Muir spoke in a letter to Stephen Spender, who had asked him for a poem for *The Left Review*: 'It is a purely imaginary and I am afraid personal description of Hölderlin's real journey which has haunted me ever since I first read about it; why, I don't know enough about myself to say.' (undated letter, 1936) What most 'haunts' Muir produces in many of the poems in *Journeys and Places* memorably harsh and implacable images, pictures of a spiritual stasis within which the poems arise to make their unconscious protest. Here, most strikingly, it is the image of an iron universe. In *Tristram's Journey* it is of the failure to remember:

> But now he searched the towers, the sward,
>   And struggled something to recall,
> A stone, a shadow. Blank the lake,
>   And empty every wall.

In *The Road* there are several images of an irredeemably determined world, encapsulated in the brief, brutal 'And there within the womb/The cell of doom'. In *The Stationary Journey* – a title that could stand for the general tenor of these poems – there is the already quoted image of the 'Immortal Being in/Solidity more pure than Stone'. The alternatives are all a dream. The tension in these poems is between a vivid conviction that 'the lawless roads ran wrong through all the land' (*Hölderlin's Journey*), that man cannot connect with a transcendent or immanent reality, and the painful reaching after the assurance that he can. *The Hill* gave us alternative visions, but overwhelmingly it is the negative one that prevails so far. It is that which carries imaginative conviction. The horror is palpable; the glory is only a dream.

We may nevertheless see in Muir's developing power of projecting his personal crises in the form of story and picture a promise of eventual release. The sheer power of the negative images that he so consistently produces at the climactic or crucial points in the poems so far discussed would seem to promise redemption through imagination. At this stage he cannot know whether he will be

> With the bright divers never still
> Or on the sad dishonoured sands

But though he cannot see it in this way, the poems themselves are strong in affirming the possibility of a more positive vision than present circumstances will allow. It is in this sense that we may speak of the poems making an unconscious protest against the vision they express: none more so than *Merlin*:

> O Merlin in your crystal cave
> Deep in the diamond of the day,
> Will there ever be a singer
> Whose music will smooth away
> The furrow drawn by Adam's finger
> Across the meadow and the wave?

Merlin seems to come from a deeper level of the mind than the repetitious insistences of the seventh *Variation on a Time Theme*. It seems to be more than half a rebuttal of *The Stationary Journey's* gloomy resignation to 'Time led in chains from post to post/Of the all-conquering Zodiac ring'. It is as though, even in the creation of images of despair, the imagination will unaccountably produce 'an unsolicited act of help where no help was known to be'. That this is how we might see the matter is indeed suggested by a comment that Muir made on the poem in a radio broadcast of 1952: 'Merlin I can scarcely say how I came to write; it more or less wrote itself.'[14] The assurance and beauty of this poem make the questioning in the lines quoted seem almost formal. *Merlin*, with its haunting description of the singer/artist's art seems to be answering the question in the only possible way. Literally, of course, the answer to the question is 'no'. On the other hand, the fact that the imagination is able to crystallize the ideal so finely surely promises liberation from the despair and pessimism of the earlier poems. *Merlin* expresses the constant aspiration of Muir's poetry and at the same time acknowledges that it can never be realized. But in asking the question Muir implicitly accepts the transforming power of the imagination that, however imperfectly, reveals for our contemplation the forms of our experiences. The latter section of the poem with its calm succession of traditional images drawn from myth and fairy tale, breathes faith in these archetypes, uses them in the assurance of their continuing meaning for all humanity. Having such meaning, they in themselves bear witness to Merlin's power:

> Or a runner who'll outrun
> Man's long shadow driving on,
> Break through the gate of memory
> And hang the apple on the tree?
> Will your magic ever show
> The sleeping bride shut in her bower,
> The day wreathed in its mound of snow
> And Time locked in his tower?

The growth of poetic power was not accompanied by a growth in public interest in Muir's work. He would have sat very uncomfortably in any representative anthology of verse of the 1930s. His letters of the mid-1930s show him quite without illusion on this score. Grateful for Spender's praise of *Journeys and Places*, he says that he never expects his poems to be liked and in a letter to Alec Aitken that they have 'never taken on . . . and that is naturally discouraging, but would never make me give up the writing of it when the impulse comes' (23 July 1938). I want to look more closely at his own view of the 1930s and of the responsibilities of the artist in the next chapter. *Journeys and Places* provides its own kind of evidence. It is part of Muir's strength and clarity that he on the whole resists the most direct and contemporary engagement; his deepest convictions tell him that the most lasting and valuable response is that which assimilates but is not controlled by the emergencies of the age. The compelling political pressures and conflicts of the day press on his imagination. Frequently the issue is a poem in which the pressures making for a dehumanized, fractured, brave new world are objectified and brought into critical relation with the wholeness they deny.

When he does produce an obviously contemporary poem it is distinctively his, owing nothing to fashion or the persuasion of the day. The general atmosphere of depression and foreboding in the 1930s seems to suffuse *The Town Betrayed* but the betrayal is seen in mythic terms:

> Fierce Agamemnon's form I see,
> Watching as if his tents were time
> And Troy eternity.

and the threat to the town is seen as part of a recurring event such as attaches to the names of Achilles, Siegfried, Lancelot. But the nature of the betrayal, the manner of the assault is given in a modern idiom that reminds one of Auden. The inexorable mechanics of modern warfare update an old ritual:

> Far inland now the glittering swords
> In order rise, in order fall,
> In order on the dubious field
> The dubious trumpets call.

'Dubious' is the contemporary note as is the sinister reference in the next stanza to the powers of life and death vested in 'men obsessed and neat'. The strength of the ballad-like verse here is that it facilitates a bringing together of ancient and modern, of traditional imagery and association with the all too contemporary. It is startling that we are able to pass immediately and without incongruity from the three stanzas that accuse the 'men obsessed and neat' to this:

> Our cattle wander at their will.
> To-day a horse pranced proudly by.
> The dogs run wild. Vultures and kites
> Wait in the towers for us to die.

That belongs to a world which, in discursive terms, has no relation to the one in which men decree doom to distant peoples. But such is the ease with which Muir is able to suggest continuity within discontinuity, the recurrence of old events in new guises, that we accept the idea of a Shakespearean universe without demur. What we are given is a picture in which, as in *Troy*, wars and betrayals, past and future, coalesce, but with no loss of distinction between ancient and modern practice.

In *Troy*, a crazed old man fights on alone after the departure of the Greeks, oblivious that the war is over, a prey eventually to 'some chance robber seeking treasure/under Troy's riven roots'. Here, undeniably, is a work of unconditional strength and maturity. *Tristram's Journey* and *Hölderlin's Journey* were decisive moves in the direction of an objective 'image of life', an image in which personal emotion was subordinate to a more comprehensive reading of human life. Here the subordination is fully achieved: we don't reflect on any personal anguish that may lie behind its composition. It springs, we feel, authentically from life as men may know it at any time, in any place. The myth of Troy, source of inspiration and renewal for countless writers, here inspires the kind of objectivity that we feel belongs to myth unadulterated. The pathos and tenderness of the poem are inseparable from the images that evoke them. There is one curt summary of their significance – 'Proud history has such sackends'. Yet even these sackends take their colouring from the surrounding descriptions of nightmare squalor:

> The rat-hordes,
> Moving, were grey dust shifting in grey dust.

The opening of the poem comes upon us with the suddenness of a landscape seen whole in a moment:

> He all that time among the sewers of Troy
> Scouring for scraps.

Everything that follows has a monumental inevitability about it: the insane and noble bravery of the old man; the subterranean nightmare of the scene of action; the casual evil of the robbers; the equal perfunctoriness of the old man's death. All are rendered with an admirable imaginative sureness of word and image to give, for instance, the exact and disturbingly pathetic strength of this:

> His arms grew meagre as a boy's,
> And all that flourished in that hollow famine
> Was his long, white, round beard.

where the studied carefulness of the last line's description seems to acknowledge the dignity the old man's beard represents and the pathos of its appearance in this scene. The scene, as in *Tristram* and *Hölderlin*, is not merely that of the physical action. In the intensity of his solitary campaign that scene is the landscape of the old man's mind; but it is also a picture of a time desolately out of joint, mad with discord, bereft of grace.

> Oh, sturdily
> He swung his staff and sent the bold rats skipping
> Across the scurfy hills and worm-wet valleys,
> Crying: 'Achilles, Ajax, turn and fight!
> Stop cowards!'

In his essay on Henryson's *Testament of Cresseid*, Muir praises 'the finest effects of style in the poem' as the outcome 'of a simple and yet surprising humanity'. That style is seen in 'the fewest possible words, words which seem just adequate and no more, and in that appear to achieve a more secure finality: all that might have been said being made superfluous by the few simple words that are said'.[15] Muir's mastery in *Troy*, it seems to me, may be accounted for along the same lines; it is a mastery of story, of proportion, of correct emphasis, of detail; we do not feel we are present at a local incident peculiar to that war alone. The old man is archetypal – 'He might have been Priam's self' – a form of our aspirations, our 'best selves' and, as Muir presents him, a token of hope in extremity:

> Yet he withstood them, a brave, mad old man,
> And fought the rats for Troy.

The echo of Lear cannot be accidental, and it seems to me that for all the cruelty and inhumanity of the picture, it is suffused with a love built on faith – a faith like that which sustains the 'old battered thing' in *The Combat*. The old man dies his agonized and inconsequential death but his final days display an indefeasible spirit. The last few lines of the poem are a picture of the recurring desolations of war. They have a monumental character that seems to affirm the indestructibility of the human spirit, grossly affronted as it is – the old man's killers are, after all, not Greeks but Trojans, fellow-countrymen, not state enemies.

> Proud history has such sackends. He was taken
> At last by some chance robber seeking treasure
> Under Troy's riven roots. Dragged to the surface.
> And there he saw Troy like a burial ground
> With tumbled walls for tombs, the smooth sward wrinkled
> As Time's last wave had long since passed that way,
> The sky, the sea, Mount Ida and the islands,
> No sail from edge to edge, the Greeks clean gone.
> They stretched him on a rock and wrenched his limbs,
> Asking: 'Where is the treasure?' till he died.

This is an 'image of life' in Muir's use of that phrase: a picture of humanity of a kind free from the contingencies of the present, valid for all time. It is, certainly, a poem for our own age (it was written in 1937): the nobility of the old man is under hideous pressure, the atmosphere of the poem is dark. Yet it is unconditional in the sense that it cannot date until the cruelties and braveries it records are extinguished in human societies. I sense that here Muir had reached that 'solidest foundation' of himself that he said he was only rarely on. The poem has the technical assurance that comes from complete imaginative conviction.

Chapter 4

The Narrow Place

The bounded is loathed by its possessor. The same dull round, even of a universe, would soon become a mill with complicated wheels.
William Blake[1]

Nearly all the poems in *Journeys and Places* were written during the 1930s. So were some of those brought together in the 1943 collection, *The Narrow Place*. But we cannot think of any of them as 1930s poems. And yet neither do they in any sense stand aside from that decade. As *Troy* suggests, they take its pressure more deeply and in quite different ways from the poetry of the main stream. Muir kept his own counsel in the most unsympathetic of times. The solitariness of his position and the quality of his achievement can, I think, be better appreciated if we see what made the 1930s so little productive of enduring verse. It is equally important to see how securely opposed to the conventional wisdom was Muir's view of the artist's responsibility 'in a time of mortal shocks'. The coherence and strength of that view enabled him to produce work that, while distinctively his own, now seems to speak more directly of the general condition than much of the selfconsciously contemporary verse of the 1930s.

I have said that Muir's beginnings as a poet in the early 1920s were unusually instinctive. He began writing poetry with a strong if not very articulate sense of what he wanted to say and a kind of purity of intention that kept him free of any school or fashion. So that in reviewing his work from the mid-1920s on one does not think of it as a progression, a succession of discrete phases. Rather, there is the sense of the poetry more confidently and clearly realizing the intuitive ideals with which he had set out. With experience, his intuitive sense of the nature of art and of his own poetic gift grew more sure: as his life became more ordered, so also did his art. There was a reciprocal relationship and he was aware of it:

Your statement [he wrote to a friend] that you have been literally growing up with your work, that this presents difficulties as well as rewards – that is, I feel, the mark of all true creative living, and I think anyone who endures it is happy, is privileged, when he can give it the second-life, the victory of art. I have often said to you that I value my poetry more than my criticism (though I think that the latter approximates far more closely to excellence of form); and it is for this reason, that I feel art is for me the only way of growing, of becoming myself more purely, and I value it for myself, I know it is my *good*, the only real good for me (17 March 1925).

That was written in 1925 but it clearly held good for Muir throughout his life. There is the closest relationship between the looking back over his own life, his thinking about the nature of poetry and the quality of his own poetic expression. This consistency was the result of a rare kind of emotional and intellectual honesty that compelled him to be true to his experience in the face of all kinds of distractions that threatened to distort it. It yielded poetry and criticism of rare purity. The purity is tough, the sign of a determination to be true to his best insights and to measure the day against them. It is in no way remote or abstract. As briefly remarked in the previous chapter, Muir was totally at odds with the major trends in the poetry of the 1930s; and this is the more impressive when we realize how intelligently thought out his position was. In a decade when *ideas* about what a poet should be and do often seemed more exciting and important than poetry itself, Muir's own ideas remained faithfully in touch with his experience. This indeed is the truth of Kathleen Raine's statement about the world of ideas being for him 'not a doctrine but an experience': he had to be an outsider in an age when, as he later said, such clarity as the representative poets of the 1930s achieved was 'an ideological and not an imaginative clarity'.[2]

In his book *A Hope for Poetry* (1934), C. Day Lewis tackled the difficult question of poetry and political ideas. He did so with considerable awareness of where the difficulty lay. But some of his formulations suggest the kind of narrowing of the idea of poetry to which Muir would have been instinctively antipathetic – and they point incidentally, to the character of Muir's own writing. In answering 'the orthodox criticism that the poet should never associate himself with any system, political or economic, except to the extent that it provides stimulus and material for his poetry', Day Lewis says:

A man, by developing the poetic faculty in himself, does not automatically secede from his common humanity. It is true that some artists have cultivated the former successfully to the almost complete exclusion of the latter, and some but by no means all great poets have been – in Keats' phrase – men that 'have not any individuality, any determined character'. But this kind of passive, plastic nature, where the whole man is metamorphosed into an impersonal poetic instrument, is, I believe, rare.[3]

The 'poetic faculty' or, as it is elsewhere called, 'the poetic self', has here become detached from the whole personality. Day Lewis seems to assume that it is inherently out of touch with 'common humanity'. But it is clear that 'common humanity' is an ideological concept with its roots in the politics and social conditions of the day. The possibility that in attending to the development of his 'poetic faculty', a man might the more surely express and call out to a common humanity is ignored. There is something philistine about the idea that the rest of the man needs to get together with 'the poetic self' in order to put it on a useful basis. At root, it reflects a lack of confidence in the power of poetry to connect with politics and economics in its own way. It expresses the anxiety of the 1930s poets to find a role for themselves that they could believe in; and it shows the intellectual distortions produced by expecting the power of the arts to declare itself in immediate, material ways – by changing attitudes and altering the course of events. Day Lewis's passage is, in these ways, representative. It isn't possible to tell what use he would have in 1934, for the kind of nature where 'the whole man is metamorphosed into an impersonal poetic instrument'. Not much, probably. For what, usefully, could he be the instrument of? In fact the impersonality of the best art is not an obstacle to the expression of 'common humanity' – in what we might call the traditional understanding of that phrase; it is the means to that expression. By natural gift and background Muir was instinctively aware of this; this fact is the key to his lack of sympathy with the 'poetic' of the times. By the 1930s that awareness was fully conscious and he knew he was unlikely to have wide appeal. Already, in the mid-1920s the direction which his art would follow was becoming clear. He speaks in a letter in 1924 of wishing to 'get a certain pathos of distance in contemplating human life' (he is referring there to *Chorus of the Newly Dead*) and of wishing to include as 'little mere thought as possible; no mention of God, but an assumption of infinite and incalculable powers behind the visible drama' (7 May 1924). In another letter he expresses his objection to 'felicities' in poetry. He does it in what is for him a remarkably vehement way:

Neat poetry is a kind of poetry in which a disagreeable kind of personal superiority is asserted, and as poetry is concerned in my mind with great themes and is the response of the individual mind to those at the few moments when it is raised above itself, that assertion of superiority is false psychologically, repellent and foolish.

Personal assertiveness is, for Muir, at odds with the proper function and stance of the poet. And in this he is in a tradition that, as he later pointed out in 'The Poetic Imagination', we can find articulated in Plato's 'Ion, or of The Iliad'. The poet's stance is appropriately one of humility, of a patient readiness to profit from those 'few moments'. He should indeed see himself, in C. Day Lewis's phrase, as an impersonal poetic instrument.

In *Transition* Muir had identified the secondrate artists of any period as those who are 'mere expressions of the thing of which as artists they should be the contemplators'. There too he had said that 'in the modern world the power most solidly obnoxious to the artists is not the public but the intelligentsia'. The intelligentsia, like the secondrate writers, are expressive of the 'spirit of the age' whereas their proper function is to 'interrogate it'. In the 1930s it is hardly an exaggeration to say that the distinction between artists – the representative poets, at least – and the intelligentsia, is lost in the claim of the first group to be identical with the second. I shall have more to say in this chapter about the pressure of events on Muir's writing of poetry, but we can perhaps better understand his response to them by looking a little more closely at his conception of the artist's way of working. To get a clear idea of how he saw his own responsibility as a poet is to put oneself in a better position to appreciate what he achieved during the late thirties. It was a time when, as probably never before, there were plenty of people (writers and writers about writers) to tell a poet what his responsibility was, clamorously, and often dogmatically.

What is remarkable about Muir's conception is its consistency. In the 1950s it is, fundamentally, what it was in the 1920s. It bears on the literary criticism of his early maturity. The crispness and acuity there belong to a mind in possession of ideas about the nature of art and the modern artist's responsibility that are already axiomatic. Here is what he had to say about Huxley and Joyce. I shall not want to quote at length again from the early critical work. This will, I hope, make the point not only about the sureness of touch, the determined independence, but that the quality of the criticism has not really had its due:

The difference in quality between Mr Joyce's work and Mr Huxley's is very suggestive. Superficial resemblances there are many; both writers are irreligious, both are disillusioned, both are ironical; and the temper of the age is all three. Yet the difference between Mr Joyce's *quality* and Mr Huxley's is infinite. It may be indicated broadly by saying that while Mr Huxley's disillusionment is a thing which, with trifling variations, may be found among half the writers in London and Paris, Mr Joyce's may not. In reading Mr Huxley we may, if we choose, assume his disillusionment, take it for granted as comfortably as we take any habitual assumption. But when disillusionment is objectified as it is in *Ulysses*, we can no longer do this; we are compelled to reckon with it. We are not at liberty to adopt it as it stands; for this disillusionment is no longer an attitude, but rather all that an attitude by its nature hides and keeps us from seeing. To accept it is not thus to accept another disguise or defence; it is rather to accept in some measure ourselves. For its effect Mr Huxley's work depends on the fact that we do tend to make the assumptions he makes; but once his mood is not accepted as self-evident, his irony becomes empty; we are left with a mere attitude, seductively presented, which has no grounds for existing save that it is the attitude of a great number of people who question it as little as Mr Huxley does. This is to say that Mr Huxley's novels, in spite of admirable qualities, a graceful style, wit, remarkable tact in avoiding the *bête*, belong to the literature of fashion. A change of mood would take half their appositeness from them. *Ulysses*, on the other hand, depends very little for its comprehension on the mood which its readers take to it; for their floating disillusionment, halfconscious and vague, is there so profoundly grasped and completely objectified, that the general mood fades, evaporates, becomes unreal, beside it. We feel that this attitude has been radically modified, that henceforth it must become more real, or, if it persists, more unreal.[4]

These perceptions help us to understand Muir's view of himself as an artist. In the letter quoted earlier he says that his own poetry has no 'felicities, and I dislike felicities from the bottom of my heart – they give me a faint sickly feeling'. This dislike is part of the objection to the artist displaying what in the extract above he calls an 'attitude'. Fundamentally, an attitude is the ego asserting itself, confronting experience, putting its imprint on it and presenting itself to the world. For Muir the artist's ego is of no importance; worse, it is an obstacle crowding out his proper function, which is to become a conduit, a medium for impersonal truths that link him with 'common humanity' in an understanding that transcends the local origins of the poem.

In any case, the origin is often mysterious: not only the direct welling up of dream but the untraceable and spontaneous forming of phrase and line are the start of many a poem. He frequently spoke of lines coming to him 'spontaneously' and of poems 'coming from I know not where'. His wife confirms it:

He always waited for his poems, never saying to himself: I am going to write a poem about such and such. Sometimes a line 'came up', as he said, that proved in time to belong to the very middle of a poem rather than the beginning, and he simply waited until he knew what the poem was going to be. Once it was composed and written down he would revise it, again and again.[5]

Muir was aware of the mystery and humble before it. His most complete answer to those who might accuse him of remoteness from actual social and political circumstances is to be found in the late poem, *The Poet*. It is not in fact a finished work; it was written a couple of years before his death and he referred to it himself as only a note for a poem. It was never revised, but it repays examination. There is a life's work behind it; its strength is that of a considered challenge to conventional conceptions of understanding and an acknowledgement of how little we really know.

> And in bewilderment
> My tongue shall tell
> What mind had never meant
> Nor memory stored.
> In such bewilderment
> Love's parable
> Into the world was sent
> To stammer its word.

In the word 'bewilderment' is acknowledged the necessary humility before the secret source. Though the 'word', the poem, is the eventual point at which the source makes itself known, its mystery is beyond all knowing. Neither conscious intention nor formulation – 'what mind had never meant' – nor the remembered experience, are at the root of things. If memory is involved here it is not of a personal nature; the Christian allusion in 'parable' suggests instead that what the word gives us in its imperfect, 'stammering' way, is an intimation of immortality, a shadow of the source, exalting and humbling.

> What I shall never know
> I must make known.

> Where traveller never went
> Is my domain.
> Dear disembodiment
> Through which is shown
> The shapes that come and go
> And turn again.

I think the full understanding of the first two lines here hinges on the divergent meanings of 'know' and 'known'. 'Known' surely associates itself with the realm of meaning acknowledged in Shakespeare's 'bodies forth the forms of things unknown'. 'Know' refers us to the commonplace meaning: the conscious cognition, the appropriation of something external to us. 'Known' implies a making, a creative act in which there is no distinction between knower and known. The puzzling part of this stanza is the word 'disembodiment'. Presumably it relates to the incompleteness of the creative act: we are given through the poem nothing indeed but an intimation of the mystery, an image of 'the shapes that come and go/And turn again'. These shapes, the ground figures of our existence, are not to be apprehended in any other way. Were they to be apprehended, embodied to us, we would not be as we are. Our existence would not be human; it would not be the mystery that it is, and we would not need the faith that the last stanza enjoins and celebrates:

> Heaven-sent perplexity –
> If thought should thieve
> One word of the mystery
> All would be wrong.
> Most faithful fantasy
> That can believe
> Its immortality
> And make a song.

The perplexity is welcome, indeed a condition of our humanity; and while the poem acknowledges the 'bewilderment' of the poet, mediator of 'love's parable', the final stanza surely speaks too about the obstacles that man can himself put before it. What is required is faith, acceptance, openness – 'negative capability' in short – so that the truth may well up in 'song'. 'Thought' belongs here with the 'know' of the first stanza: the rational, discursive, explicatory powers of the mind whose bent is always towards devaluing 'fantasy', though that 'fantasy' can indeed give them a foundation from which they may be more responsibly and truthfully exercised.

If we can see the relationship between the 'thought' and the 'fantasy' in this way we may more readily see in what way Muir's poems carry social and political significance. Only by consulting the wisdom of past generations, whether it be laid up in books or carried in our bones, can we know whether our 'thinking' is leading us into the light or into the darkness. It was only in the darkest years of his life that Muir was not persuaded of the necessity of this. Explicitly, when defending and explaining the position he outlined in his broadcast talk, 'The decline of the imagination', he said in a letter to Alec Aitken: 'For we have so much knowledge of things, and so little knowledge of ourselves. I am trying to gratify my plea for imagination, and my conviction that our development for the last three or four centuries has been a lop-sided one' (28 June 1951).

He speaks in the same letter of his 'experience of life' coming to him not 'through science but through the often blind gropings of an imperfect imagination'. In his essay on 'Contemporary poetry' in *Transition* he had talked of the impact of 'science, enlightenment, scepticism' on the 'supremely creative, the poetic power' and said that these things 'make us look coldly, and involuntarily, automatically so, upon the things which the poet must contemplate with passion. The theorist's impersonality of intellect becomes insensibly an impersonality of feeling.'[6] The 'passion' is to see things whole, to resist the invasion of one mode of seeing into the whole of human experience. Where the spirit of enlightenment seeks to explain or explain away, to hold off the world the better to manipulate it, the poet endeavours to make it whole, to represent and express its meaning through an 'image of life'.

The passion then is the passion of contemplation, not of action; the allegiance is to a view of life, not to an attitude. The calmness and contemplativeness of Muir's own poetry is a powerful corrective to a misplaced faith in the likelihood of totally new remedies for our disorders. Writing to Stephen Spender in 1935, he expresses his distrust of fashion and of the 'spirit of emulation' which makes us feel when

something new appears . . . almost in conscience bound to produce something that is new, whereas if we wrote from the solidest basis within ourselves we should produce something that is new. I know that in my own experience I have generally to burst through to that solid foundation (at least it always feels like that) and only rarely touch it: for to me it is the most difficult thing in the world to reach. I am very rarely in it, most of my life is somewhere else (4 May 1935).

From this vantage point the poet cannot regard himself as a saviour or as the originator of a new mode of sensibility. His position and power are necessarily conservative in that it is from the 'solidest basis within' himself that the possibility of coherence and meaning arises. He brings the new into relation with the old, a vital task in an age characterized by apparently grotesque discontinuities. But he can do this in no deliberate way; he must await the opportunity to burst through to that 'solid foundation'. And though Muir, according to his wife, never lost his conviction that 'his poetry came ultimately from the Fable', he was aware that for him as for others the illumination or the communion might be only too easily thwarted. In the exquisite little poem, *The Visitor*, the poet/speaker begs his family, 'Brother and sister, wife and son', to leave him that he may allow his 'ghost' to enter. This is not, he assures them, because he does not love them, but

Lest while I speak he is already flown,
Offended by the din
Of this half-uttered scarcely whispered plea
(So delicate is he).

Only with care, scruple and good fortune is he likely to make his communion. The tone is one of tender impatience, of anxiety that the 'din' has made it impossible. It is as though the speaker, in saying 'I would be alone', knows how difficult it is for those he loves to know his meaning; but the love for his family and the necessity of being alone are not exclusive of one another. This 'visitor' – his muse, his genius, his 'true self' – can gain access only when a special hospitality is offered. It is significant that we have in the lines quoted a homely image to enfold an ineffable meaning: it does not matter that Muir goes no further in defining the nature of his visitor. It is of its nature that it cannot be understood in the way that the 'great tidings' of his family can. It might be objected that he has failed to make articulate what can mean nothing to us until it is. But no; what *The Visitor* does is to present an image of the 'hidden source' in ordinary life; or rather of its being perceived and felt and demanding an answering movement in the consciousness of its host. And its host is aware that the hospitality he so desperately wishes to offer can be ruined by the last people from whom he would expect active opposition. Hence the solicitude on the one hand and the anxious impatience on the other.

The notion of the 'solid foundation' is central to what Muir thinks of himself as doing through the exercise of the imagination in his poetry: there is implied in this notion something very like a Jungian conception of the unconscious, a permanent psychical content to which we are only fitfully granted access. Such access cannot be engineered for a purpose; the purpose of our gaining access is mysterious. But the result is what matters for the poet and his readers: an 'image of life', a guarantee of continuity and relation at the deepest level. Muir's language when talking of these matters is quasi-religious: 'I think that probably before every poet there hangs an idea of a freer style than he can ever reach, or that he only reaches in moments of supreme inspiration, or in isolated lines given by grace' (4 May 1935). The allusion to Jung is perhaps in general terms obvious enough. What is much more striking is that the personal stories of these two men resemble each other in so many essential ways. The collective, or racial, unconscious – as an abstraction the phrase has passed into our general vocabulary: but for these men it was not an abstraction; it was an experience. Anyone who reads Jung's autobiographical *Memories, Dreams, Reflections* (1963) alongside Muir's *An Autobiography* must be startled by the similarity of the conclusions they draw from their experiences. Not only has each man travelled the same road, albeit from very different starting points, but their very words seem often to echo one another as if in unconscious affirmation of the other's vision. Just as Muir speaks of that 'solid foundation' underlying the shifts of the conscious world of attitude and appearance, so Jung says that 'in spite of all uncertainties, I feel a solidity underlying all existence and a continuity in my mode of being'.[7] I make the comparison here not simply because the two men's reports on their experience have so many arresting verbal similarities but because a reading of each enhances our understanding of the other. With Jung the 'evidence' for the truth of his intuitions and images is, like Muir's, a matter of convincingly recollected detail, of the gradual revelation of pattern. The lesson to be learnt from the pattern is with him supported by a wealth of clinical observation – though 'clinical' is an unfortunate word, with its suggestion of detachment and precision, since it tends to obscure the central role of intuition in Jung's psychology. For the truth of Muir's intuitions we may of course go to the poetry. Each man's record displays a religious sensibility that in an earlier age would have expressed itself in an inherited language of religious belief and observance. As it is they must forge their own. Time and again one finds oneself noticing statements that might have come from either man. Each frequently has the strongest sense of being acted on rather than being the agent. Jung, speaking of a sense of destiny: 'this gave me an inner security, and, though I could never prove it to myself, it proved itself to me. I did not have this certainty, *it* had me.'[8] Muir, of one of his London waking dreams: 'It was not *I* who dreamt it but something else, which the psychologists call the racial unconscious, and for which there are other names' (p. 164). Of dream, Jung: 'To me dreams are a part of nature, which harbours no intention to deceive, but expresses something as best it can. These *forms of life* [my italics], too, have no wish to deceive our eyes, but we may deceive ourselves because our eyes are short-sighted.'[9] Muir on the 'transfiguration' of the Mayday demonstration in Glasgow: 'in the end I must simply regard it as a *form of experience* [my italics]. It is a form of experience I have had oftener in dreams than in waking life' (p. 115). Jung: 'What we are to our inward vision, and what man appears to be '*sub specie aeternitas*', can only be experienced by way of myth.'[10] Muir, of the dream that led to *The Combat*: 'I set it down to show how early impressions may grow and take on the form of myth' (p. 65). I shall want here and there to point up the parallels between Muir and Jung, particularly in so far as their interpretations of experience lead to similar conclusions in the area of political morality. One could without difficulty select from Jung's writing to make a running commentary on Muir's poetry, each seeming to provided a ratification of the other's work. Their general compatibility can, however, be most graphically illustrated in the following juxtaposition of passages from their respective autobiographies. Muir's amounts to a definitive statement about the purpose of writing the book. Jung's passage first:

Critical rationalism has apparently eliminated, along with so many other mythic conceptions, the idea of life after death. This could only have happened because nowadays most people identify themselves almost exclusively with their consciousness, and imagine that they are only what they know about themselves. . . . In view of all this, I lend an attentive ear to the strange myths of the psyche, and take a careful look at the varied events that come my way, regardless of whether or not they fit in with my theoretical postulates.

Unfortunately, the mythic side of man is given short shrift, nowadays. He can no longer create fables. As a result a great deal escapes him; for it is important and salutary to speak also of incomprehensible things. Such talk is like the telling of a good ghost story, as we sit by the fireside and smoke a pipe.[11]

And Muir's:

My belief in immortality, so far as I can divine its origin, and that is not far, seems to be connected with the same impulse which urges me to know myself. I can never know myself; but the closer I come to knowledge of myself the more certain I must feel that I am immortal, and, conversely, the more certain I am of my immortality the more intimately I must come to know myself. For I shall attend and listen to a class of experiences which the disbeliever in immortality ignores or dismisses as irrelevant to temporal life. The experiences I mean are of little practical use and have no particular economic or political interest. They come when I am least aware of myself as a personality moulded by my will and time: in moments of contemplation when I am unconscious of my body, or indeed that I have a body with separate members; in moments of grief or prostration; in happy hours with friends; and, because self-forgetfulness is most complete then, in dreams and daydreams and in that floating, half-discarnate state which precedes and follows sleep. In these hours there seems to me to be knowledge of my real self and simultaneously knowledge of immortality. Sleep tells us things both about ourselves and the world which we could not discover otherwise. Our dreams are part of experience; earlier ages acknowledged this. If I describe a great number of dreams in this book I do so intentionally, for I should like to save from the miscellaneous dross of experience a few glints of immortality (p. 54).

Like Jung, Muir is interested in relating only those moments when 'the imperishable world irrupts into this transitory one'. The experiences that command his attention as a writer come from what he elsewhere calls the 'universal unchanging underground' on which 'our most precious experience takes place'. It was not the kind of attention for which the poets of the 1930s on the whole wanted to be noticed.

Much of the verse of the 1930s now seems to stand apart from any major tradition of English poetry, quaintly provisional, selfconscious, dominated by the social and political crises of the day. For all the poetic factions and dissensions that the historians of the period record, for all the genuine differences that can be observed between those writing in the early years of the decade and the 'new generation' that Day Lewis announced in the postscript (1936) to *A Hope for Poetry*, it is perhaps the decade of all decades which asks to be thought of as having its own identity. The explicitness and selfconsciousness with which, through poetry and statements about poetry, the decade expressed itself, ensure that we shall think of it so. It is easy enough now to see how deadly to the life of the imagination would be so anxious an effort to write and to justify poetry that would be politically relevant and influence events. T. S. Eliot, himself then very much out of fashion with the younger poets, said that the verse of the period 'suffered by being more and more restricted to its own resources, as well as by the obsession with politics'.[12] The verse itself is the clearest and, with its less talented practitioners, the most embarrassing proof of the sterility that the obsession led to. Rex Warner sounded the exhilaration of the moment in tones that conjure the kindred spirits of public school camaraderie, jolly adolescent adventure and callow enthusiasm for the cause:

> Come then companions. This is the spring of blood,
> heart's hey-day, movement of masses, beginning of good.[13]

It is of course very easy to put down verse of this kind. But it is not part of my purpose to give a balanced account of the decade that produced so much of this kind of thing. The more extreme examples can, though, directly suggest the obstacles to public recognition and to confidence in one's own gifts that so peculiar a phase might present. The first number of *The Left Review* (for which, later Spender asked Muir for a socialist poem) were quite clear on the function of the writer: 'A writer's usefulness depends on his influence: that is to say, on the size and enthusiasm of his public: or, in the case of writers' writers, on his ability to set scores of other pens working.'[14] The broadening of the objectives of poetry to take account of the major political and social crises, both at home and abroad, was clearly an exciting departure, a rescuing of poetry from the charge of effeteness and irrelevance. But the broadening was in imaginative terms a narrowing, a dispersal of imaginative energies that, had they been concentrated on ends more natural to the talents of individual writers, might have yielded better and, indeed, more 'relevant' verse. In his essay on *King Lear* Muir remarked that 'a man may have political sense, and political sense of a high kind, without falling into any of these categories (i.e. the conventional political classifications by party); for his mind, while working politically, may not think in terms of any of them'.[15] It is difficult to imagine intelligent men in any age disagreeing with that. But for most writers in the 1930s, the emergencies of the day had to be met with something more direct. Political sense must not only inform the poetry, it must scream out of it in protest or exhortation. As Julian Symons points out in his book about the period, there were men of sensibility and talent editing *The Left Review*; but the overwhelming compulsion of the day was to view the function of the paper and its contributors in a narrowly political way. 'It is the strongest argument for a Writers' International', said its first editor, 'that it can bring writers into touch with life. "Life" in this context equals the class struggle.'[16] It was a time when a literary periodical (*Contemporary Poetry and Prose*, 1936) could give over its back cover to the sign: 'Support the Spanish People Against Fascism'.

The flirtation with Communism and the largely uncritical acceptance of the Soviet Union as the vision of a humane future are by now well documented. It is in this respect particularly that the anxiety to bind the writing of poetry to the world of action is now seen to have been so misguided. Certainly Englishmen, poets among them, died in Spain. But there were many more whose espousal of Communism was a more or less mental thing, uninformed by fact and observation. The besetting danger of that mentality – to be unanswerably proved by events still to be disclosed or to happen in the Soviet Union – was the danger of abstraction, of an inclination to explain and excuse barbarism in the light of an overreaching grand design. 'Will the use of violence in the particular, concrete situation benefit the majority of persons concerned?'[17] was the criterion by which, Day Lewis suggested, one should measure inhumanity. 'What we saw during the 1930s', says Julian Symons, writing in personal recollection, 'was an attempt to deny utterly the validity of individual knowledge and observation.'[18] This generalization is itself an abstraction to be distrusted and tested in the way of all abstractions. But as a broad characterization of the myopia which afflicted a very great number of intellectuals, long on enthusiasm but short on information, it suggests well enough how hostile the 1930s could be to the life of the imagination.

By temperament and background Muir was, as will now be clear, unlikely to be attracted by the prevailing literary ethos of the 1930s. He was also comparatively old. He was not amongst those who 'were in the nursery in 1914'. To Edmund Blunden, reviewing an Oxford volume of undergraduate verse in 1931, those who had been had 'grown up amid unnerving conditions and such as destroy vision'.[19] The 1930s are a young man's decade, the decade of youthful energies and idealisms burning for a cause to follow. Muir's understanding of where the present insistence on politicizing poetry is leading is set out in an essay he contributed to *The London Mercury* of November 1934 (the very same month as the second number of *The Left Review* already quoted). The title is 'The present language of poetry'. It starts with a brief historical analysis of the reasons why there is now 'no general and accepted language for poetry' and why there is a demand for an individual idiom, acknowledges the work of Auden and Spender (even though it 'often betrays the idiom of a class or set') and then considers 'the whole school of engineering poetry, which, though of far less excellence enjoys considerable influence as a literary fashion':

The sudden boom in engineering imagery in poetry cannot be understood without taking into account the increasing influence of Communism. The tendency of poetry as well as thought, when an old and semi-religious belief has fallen, is to turn to a purely earthly one. That happened at the beginning of the romantic movement, when many of the English poets looked towards the French Revolution. The popularity of engineering imagery at present is due to a belief in the inevitable approaching salvation of society through the use of machinery, and this makes it more than a curious literary fashion. But the periods when poetry has held a purely earthly – that is, political and historical – belief have always been short; and whether Communism prevails politically or not, the mode of Communist poetry is bound to be fleeting; for though some poetry may influence our political beliefs the permanent aim of poetry is not political. It may be, indeed, that the present political preoccupation of poetry is one of the obstacles to the creation of a general poetic convention. For such conventions spring from a deeper level of life than political forms or ideals; and except for some of Mr Eliot's and Mr Auden's poems there is hardly any contemporary poetry which comes from that deeper level. A general poetic convention includes it as part of itself. But in a time like our own it can be reached only by a sort of water-divining or digging, and what the poet draws up from it is almost a private secret, or a secret at most which will be understood by a few intimate friends.

One imagines that the ideal cure for the present malady of poetry would be a perfect simplicity; but perfect simplicity is the most difficult thing to achieve in a world without general beliefs. The one fact that seems clear – and it is not very comforting – is that until a general convention of poetic diction is discovered or created poetry will exist in a state of suppression, as it does now. How such conventions are created we do not know. It may be that society will have to be fairly radically changed before that can happen. If so, poets should be speaking at the street-corners instead of writing Communist poetry. The fact that they are not there may argue either their political ineptitude, or the fact that poetry is not finally political, and will continue to be written in every age, and against the most crushing disabilities, by those who feel the impulse to do so.[20]

Muir was not always so forthright. The discomfort and difficulty that he occasionally felt around this time comes out strongly in a letter to Spender in 1936. He sends him *Hölderlin's Journey* with a nervous reservation that 'I don't know if it has much relevance to the present world'. The letter ends with an anxious reference to the fascists in Spain and their sympathisers in Italy, Germany and Portugal, and Muir appears uneasy at what he sees, only half-apologetically, as his incapacity to produce verse of a conscious political character:

I find that while consciously I am a socialist, and would like to write poetry that would in some way express that fact, when I actually start to write, something else comes up which seems to have nothing to do with socialism, or is connected with it in some way too obscure for me to detect (July–November 1936).

In another letter written around the same time, he contrasts himself with Spender in his 'inability to care more for public things than for personal things'. He understands that 'public things should rouse in you an emotion as spontaneous as a personal emotion. I can see that. But I can't bring about the necessary transformation in myself, perhaps because I was born in a different age, and on top of that in a different world' (19 November 1936). This of course is exactly to the point. Spender had asked for a poem for *The Left Review*. The 'necessary transformation' is not, one imagines, something he could have brought himself to try to bring about.

The views on the relations between poetry and politics that Muir held in the 1930s are consistent with those he expressed much later in such essays as 'The politics of King Lear' and 'The natural man and the political man'. The consistency is the key to his toughness and the capacity to go on writing his own distinctive, utterly unfashionable poetry in a period so inimical to it. It was perhaps too kind to say, as he later did, that the poets of the 1930s had ideological but not imaginative clarity, because clearly there was a good deal of ideological naïveté too. But his own imaginative clarity was linked to an insight into the deeper implications of current politics and social change that made him aware of threats to the independence of the artist that we now appreciate easily enough. Writing to Spender in 1937, he recognizes the humanity, the essential decency of the impulse of 'Left Literature' but it 'seems to me in danger of being dehumanized, formalised, throttled by an automatic ideology, which denies humanity except in great bulk; so huge that it has no relation to our lives' (6 October 1937). Muir was aware, unconventionally at this time, that Nazism and Communism were not polar opposites, that of the essence of each was a denial of the soul and a dynamic that worked itself out in disregard for the life of the individual. His friendship with the Austrian writer, Broch, whose work the Muirs had translated, brought him into contact with the evils of the Nazi régime (Broch had been imprisoned after Hitler invaded Austria). But his resistance to the ideas of Communism – after the war to be for him so resoundingly justified by the Russians' behaviour in Prague – was, I think, a natural outcome of 'spontaneous piety', an inherited sense of humanity which, when united with a sober and acute intelligence, enabled him to analyse and reject the delusions to which so many less well grounded sensibilities were giving in. Eliot speaks of the 'possibilities of refreshment' for the language that come 'from its several centres: apart from the vocabulary, poems by Englishmen, Welshmen, Scots and Irishmen, all written in English, continue to show differences in their music'.[21] The difference between the typical poetry of the day and what Muir was writing is due to the major difference of origin. With his classical and deeply held view of the poet as seer, he had both a protection against the trends of the time and a base from which to criticize them. 'Propagandist poetry', he wrote in a review in 1940, 'is essentially rhetoric, and rhetoric is an instrument of the will, not of the imagination.'[22] The injunctions, exhortations and accusations that writers were prone to issue and to submit to in the 1930s were in these terms the expressions of the will and thus likely to prove abortive. I think he would have agreed with Yeats that 'we make out of the quarrel with others rhetoric, but of the quarrel with ourselves, poetry'.

As we have seen, Muir's imagination compelled him to view men and affairs in ways that could not easily be reconciled with the prevailing rhetoric. But it was not this that prevented him from producing as much poetry as he would like to have done in the years just before and just after the beginning of the war. The Muirs were in financial difficulties. They had had ten years as translators (their translations of Kafka being of course the most notable). Muir had done regular reviewing for *The*

Listener. But the demand for German translations had dried up at the beginning of the war and (how grotesque this now seems) Muir found himself once more a clerk; this time in the Government food office in Dundee. (He had hoped to get a job as a teacher but found it impossible for lack of paper qualifications: 'In the eyes of the Scottish educational authorities', said Willa Muir, 'he was practically illiterate and could not be allowed to teach anywhere'.[23]) When he was not working at the office, most of Muir's energies went into caring for his wife who had been dangerously ill in 1939 and was in precarious health for the next few years. By 1942 Muir himself went down with heart strain (aggravated by heavy work as a member of the Home Guard) and was ordered to rest completely for six weeks.

His letters during these years make it clear that though the impulse to write was there – 'numerous lines in poetry keep occurring to me' – the opportunity to make something of them on the whole was not – 'I have not the time or energy to follow them into the poems that should follow them; and this is what I regret most' (15 November 1940). In any case, though he was immune to the hectoring injunctions to adopt political stances, he could like anyone else be depressed and discouraged by the times. His view of the artist's and intellectual's responsibility in a time of such terrifying crisis is that of a contemplative withdrawing to a position from which he can continue to do work of a kind that will keep the alternative before men's eyes: 'It seems to me that this is a time when anyone who serves the intellect and the imagination must stick to his work as hard as he can' (4 January 1940). From his letters it is clear that for him it is in some ways necessary to ignore the immediate world the better to engage with it. He felt that immediacy of suffering was no guarantee of good art. In fact for him he felt the opposite was likely to be the case. At a time when, he says, 'my mind is being teased by fragmentary intimations of poems more than it has been for some time', he sends Spender a poem he distrusts because, unlike another to which he alludes – which 'came out of contemplation and not out of distress' – it 'came simply out of distress of mind which I tried to deal with and is probably far too monitory' (2 August 1940). (The poem is *In a Time of Mortal Shocks*, omitted from the collected edition.) Previously, in a letter to George Barker, he had spoken of his desire to write 'a recitation, a chorus on the subject of refugees'. He feels it is 'a wonderful theme' but himself feels 'far from wonderful' – 'a lot of my energy is wasted in trying to ignore this mad comic-opera world' (21 May 1939). Only about a third of *The Refugees* (the original poem was published in 1939) appeared, amended, in *The Narrow Place* and it isn't difficult to see why he should have been dissatisfied with it. 'It was inspired by quite sincere feeling, but never *rose* to the right height, the pity and indignation never transmitting themselves, except in one or two lines in the last part!' (4 January 1940). The opening of the section that is retained is rather fine, evocative of a creeping, deceptively unspectacular menace and complacent inertness that belong to the special atmosphere of the months before the outbreak of war but that can stand for any such event and the response we make to it:

> A crack ran through our hearthstone long ago,
> And from the fissure we watched gently grow
> The tame domesticated danger,
> Yet lived in comfort in our haunted rooms.

But the poise of these lines, though equalled by others here and there in the poem, is more usually in contrast with lines like these:

> This is our punishment. We came
> Here without blame, yet with blame,
> Dark blame of others, but our blame also.
> This stroke was bound to fall,
> Though not to fall so.

As a whole the poem is too discursive: an unresolved and deeply disturbing problem is *discussed*, the result an uncharacteristic prosiness that recalls some of the less successful of the 'place' poems in *Journeys and Places*. There too one feels that Muir was too close to his own feelings, unable to assimilate them to a more impersonal 'image of life'. The result is lifelessness.

The Refugees and such poems as *Scotland 1941* and *The River* have an unusual contemporariness for Muir and I think that in the works of his maturity they represent his least happy mode. They are all, one would have thought, in some ways good poems; but at the same time one can see why he might have been dissatisfied with them. His language in these poems loses something of its deliberate remoteness from the poetic idiom of the time. He speaks in *The River* of 'trained terrors, the well-practised partings' – words well suited indeed to what they describe, but in their very pointedness, their directness, more than normally limited to the historical time to which they belong. In the same poem there is an unusual *playing* with words, in this case to evoke the soldier off to the front:

> He,
> A bundle of clouts creased as with tribulations,
> Bristling with spikes and spits and bolts of steel,
> Bound in with belts,

It is in such a context that Muir can run to bathos, to banality: 'The disciplined soldiers come to conquer nothing.' The minatory tone that he deplores is there in *The Refugees*, in the last line at its most obvious: 'We must shape here a new philosophy.' It is there in *Scotland 1941*: 'How could we read our souls and learn to be?' So is the banality:

> And spiritual defeat wrapped warm in riches,
> No Pride but pride of pelf.

These poems have much to be said for them. There is for instance something fine in the anger that produced *Scotland 1941* and it does give us a clear idea of why, for Muir, Scotland was often a source of such disappointment – a 'narrow place' indeed where Knox and Melville had stripped 'the peopled hill and altar bare'. But they lack the disturbing power of his best: they advertise their origins in actual events too obviously; and, in the case of *Scotland 1941* and *The Refugees*, they bring the 'I' to the fore in a manner that limits their force. They are about Muir's problems rather than about those of men everywhere and at all times.

Muir would certainly have agreed with Jung that 'what is essential in a work of art is that it should rise far above the realm of personal life and speak from the spirit and heart of the poet to the spirit and heart of mankind'.[24] The best, the most disturbing poems of these years, are indeed those in which he rises above that realm by reaching most deeply into it. The hectic political gesturing and exhortation of the thirties produced no response in him. What he did respond to was the world of which they were a part and of which he in some ways saw them as a symptom. The poet who could write

> Yes, why do we all seeing a communist feel small. That small
> Catspaw ruffles our calm
>
> Mark him workers, and all who wish the world aright –
> He is what your sons will, the road these times must take[25]

or engage in the anticapitalist histrionics of this:

> It is now or never, the hour of the knife,
> The break with the past, the major operation[26]

could be written off as merely fashionably self-indulgent. But the fashion was a portent. And what is portended is embodied in such nightmare poems of Muir's as *The City* and *Then*. It was a sign of that growing disregard for the life of the spirit which to Muir was the central objection to Communism. His views were very clear and, as usual, the outcome of the most serious examination of his experience and his intuitions. Frequently in his letters and sometimes explicitly in his poems (*The Solitary Place*), he expresses his detestation of a 'purely historical view' of humanity, which he takes Marxism to be: 'I can't get away from the thought that the Marxist conception of life is a conception where there is no God, no divine spirit, either immanent or transcendent . . . any interpretation of history which leaves it out must be mutilated, a monstrosity' (3 February 1940). We have seen that his acceptance of the child's vision acted as an insurance against any such mutilation in his own view of the world. But present times were proving the power and seductiveness of such an interpretation. In another letter written around this time he notes the resistance of orthodox Marxists to the evidence of the inhumanities that are being committed in the name of their creed: 'Russia's latest exploits in Finland must have shaken some even of the Marxians, though I haven't yet met one who admits it. But they seem to have lost all capacity for thought, so far as thought means judgement' (26 January 1940). I have already noted this phenomenon, the attachment to an orthodox doctrine that can deal with concrete evidence of cruelty either by ignoring it or accommodating it within an abstract scheme. It is the latter feature, the ease of accommodation, that particularly horrifies Muir. In the letter from which this last quotation comes, he outlines for Herbert Read a possible essay on Calvinism and Communism. It is their similarities that engage him. Each, as he sees it, has wrath as a main feature in its creed. The Calvinist sees a divine principle in wrath; the Communist the only liberating human principle. 'I think both theories are extraordinarily alike here, alike, that is, in elevating the form of most human activity (which I suppose is struggle and anger) into the principle of human activity, and beyond that, into the principle of good, at least of advancement.' Although his comments on the 1930s writers are mild, the implication is clear. In espousing a creed that denies the soul, a poet goes against his calling and in so doing assists, where he should resist, the reduction in the idea of human nature that such a denial implies. Hence the need for those 'who serve the imagination' to stick to their proper work. Muir's truest, most profound response to a world that seemed to be following the 'road these times must take' is not the poems of contemporary allusion and detail. It is in such poems as *The City* and *Then*. In the first, which appeared in September 1938, humanity misses its spiritual mark in a misconceived quest for the millenial home, for a delusive perfection beyond human reach, dissolving in wrath as the delusion persists. It is a poem of great pathos and pity, and cheerless with the conviction that this *is* humanity. Muir here knows the temptation, understands the impulse to reach beyond 'an order natural and wise', but offers no consolation. The 'dead land' pitted with 'blind whirling places' is now, Europe 1938, and the 'we' of the poem are responsible[27] for the now unstoppable drift of events. But it is not a poem against Nazism, against Communism or against Calvinism. Rather, it is in touch with whatever there is of evil in any creed men follow that blinds them to their natures. And, as we have seen, it is fundamental to Muir's critique of the age that it distorts man's image of himself and surrounds him with false aims:

The City

Day after day we kept the dusty road,
  And nearer came small-towered Jerusalem,
Nearer and nearer. Lightened of the goad,
  Our beasts went on as if the air wafted them.

We saw the other troops with music move
  Between the mountain meadows, far and clear,
Onwards towards the city, and above
  The ridge the fresh young firmament looked near.

All stood so silent in the silent air,
  The little houses set on every hill,
A tree before each house. The people were
  Tranquil, not sad nor glad. How they could till

Their simple fields, here, almost at the end,
  Perplexed us. We were filled with dumb surprise
At wells and mills, and could not understand
  This was an order natural and wise.

We looked away. Yet some of us declared:
  'Let us stay here. We ask no more than this,'
Though we were now so close, we who had dared
  Half the world's spite to hit the mark of bliss.

So we went on to the end. But there we found
  A dead land pitted with blind whirling places,
And crowds of angry men who held their ground
  With blank blue eyes and raging rubicund faces.

We drew our swords and in our minds we saw
  The streets of the holy city running with blood,
And centuries of fear and power and awe,
  And all our children in the deadly wood.

Though the mixture of historical and mythical reference keeps the poem's narrative in touch with the landmarks of our own minds, it somehow goes beyond them. It reaches into a region whose distinguishing features are those of allegory and prophecy. The journey to Jerusalem, the ambition to 'hit the mark of bliss', not only evokes the Biblical stories but stands as a type of all such aspirations. The simple scene – 'an order natural and wise' – that the travellers reject, would seem to be a type of that quiet fulfilment that knows nothing of agonies and ecstasies, 'not sad nor glad', but exists in a limited but sane tranquillity. The price of high aspiration, high hope indeed, can be a terrible revelation of man's self-ignorance. The travellers reach a heart of darkness, a hell where 'ignorant armies clash by night' and the doom of unborn generations is read in the images of present terror.

When one accounts for a poem like this it is with an inevitable sense of reducing its strangeness to a manageable and thus misrepresented shape. For within *The City* we do not have a precise map of historical actuality, nor a precise prophecy of future horrors. Instead it gives a form to the quality of our aspirations, of our dreams of fulfilment, of our bewilderment, our overreaching folly – and despair. The picture of the last two stanzas is comfortless, inhuman; and the inhumanity we recognize as that of our time and indeed any time in which men have put aside brotherhood, 'put aside the sorrowful years' (*The Ring*), and join arms without mercy. There is no change of pace in the final stanza. Indeed the easy quatrains of *The City* are, deliberately, undramatic, unvaried in pace. It is, we feel, a finished story, so much so that the drawing of swords is merely a sad, expected action to which there was no alternative. There is something in this poem of the very inevitability, the deadly certitude of recurrence that at one time possessed Muir as a reality. The 'blank blue eyes' and 'raging rubicund faces', – anonymous, automatic – are a figure for that 'hiatus in the soul' that is the root of evil; they are, too, in their recurrence, from the same archaic ground as the terrifying disembodied forces awaiting embodiment in *Then*.

If wrath is the principle of human advancement, of the good, it might look for a text in *Then*. If ever one of Muir's poems shaped the agonies of the present after the archetypes of an intuitive imagination, this is it. It is easy to understand the difficulty a reader in 1940 might have in coming to grips with it. Its idiom is strange, oblique. And yet, now, the date seems the reasonable one, and more so in the light of Muir's analysis of Calvinism and Communism as grounded in wrath:

Then
There were no men and women then at all,
But the flesh lying alone,
And angry shadows fighting on a wall
That now and then sent out a groan
Buried in lime and stone,
And sweated now and then like tortured wood
Big drops that looked yet did not look like blood.

And yet as each drop came a shadow faded
And left the wall.
There was a lull
Until another in its shadow arrayed it,
Came, fought and left a blood-mark on the wall;
And that was all; the blood was all.

If there had been women there they might have wept
For the poor blood, unowned, unwanted,
Blank as forgotten script.
The wall was haunted
By mute maternal presences whose sighing
Fluttered the fighting shadows and shook the wall
As if that fury of death itself were dying.

Without ceremony, we are in a region of archaic simplicity. The flesh is envisaged as awaiting habitation by a life force; the fighting shadows and their bloody outcome are a vision of original sin; the pathos of the last section is that then, as now, sorrow was ineffectual. It is an image of original and changeless suffering. While the stimulus was surely the darkness of the present, the result amounts to a bleak interpretation of man in history – a story of inherent aggressiveness, cruelty and relentless blood-letting, redeemed only by the ineffectual sorrowing of the womanly part of mankind. Not women, note. The sighing in the poem is that of 'mute maternal presences'. Muir seems in this poem to be in touch with the very grounds of our being, to be sharing a knowledge of its changeless features that is very much akin to the kind of knowledge possessed by primitive communities. In his essay, 'Archaic man', Jung describes the 'mana conception' of life as 'one which has it that there exists something like a widely distributed force in the external world that produces all those effects which are out of the common' and, speculating on its implications, he asks: 'Were the dissociated psychic contents – to use our modern terms – ever parts of the psyches of individuals, or were they rather from the very beginning psychic entities existing in themselves according to the primitive view as ghosts, ancestral spirits and the like.'[28] The poem seems to make contact with a more archaic knowledge of life prior to the stage in man's development when such a concept would have been understood. Some words of Willa Muir that I have already referred to are to the point: '. . . for we inherited, each of us, a primitive simplicity from our Orkney and Shetland forebears which was likely to be wide open to our tribal unconscious.' 'Vibrations from the tribal unconscious' – the phrase rings true as a description of what in this poem is given a shape through which we can relate it to our own world: a world in which the recurrence of bloody wars, whether territorial or ideological, seems at times inexorably determined by forces more inscrutable than any we can discern and affect. I say *seems*. This was certainly not Muir's considered view of the origins of events, but we have in *Then* a vision that relates an archaic sense of man's relations to the universe to the deterministic, purely historical view of the world that Muir detested so much.

Then is not, of course, a vision that a Marxist or a Calvinist would recognize. The poem admits the possibility of wrath as the originating principle of creation; it is a part of human nature. But undeniably, too, pity exists – mute, unregarded, impotent, but nonetheless beyond destruction. In that poor fact lies the hope that the final section registers: that the powers of evil will eventually at least be constrained through the persuasion of an equal impulse of humanity. In rejecting wrath as a principle of good, Muir said that he felt

pretty certain . . . that the spring of advancement, the thing that has always had to be fought for, did not come out of opposition or anger at all, though when it enters the world of action it rouses anger, until, when the anger has burned itself out, it emerges in a somewhat defaced but still positive and workable form (26 January 1940).

That hope, it seems to me, is built into *Then*.

It is created anew in Muir's first working of the myth of Penelope's faithful waiting for Odysseus – *The Return of Odysseus*. The poem began as one of those 'fragmentary intimations of poems' that seem to have arisen in protest at the times and the threat they posed to the life of the spirit. In 1939, with the horrors of Fascism, the persecution of the Jews and the inevitability of war crowding in on everyone's senses, Muir, I think, began to see what was happening as a realization of that merely temporal-historical view of life that he instinctively detested. 'The break with the past, the major operation' that Day Lewis had invoked and welcomed was being engineered in ways unimagined in those words.

Germany and Italy were denying the witness of their own best culture which, if only it had been listened to, would have been heard eloquently proclaiming the barbarism of the 'merely historical view'.

The capacity to recognize immaterial realities is almost dead, it seems to me; is quite dead in the sphere of action at any rate, the sphere in which Hitler, Mussolini and Chamberlain move. And in the last resort we live by immaterial realities; that is our real life; the rest is more or less machinery. We are moved about, caught, wedged, clamped in this machinery; and that is what is called history (16 January 1939).

And that is what is called Time, we might add. 'Moved about, caught, wedged, clamped' – the feeling echoes the remorseless cataloguing of Time's action in *Variations on a Time Theme* – 'caught, pinioned, blinded, sealed and cased in Time'. And it *is* an echo, not a fortuitous parallel of phrasing. Muir's earlier nightmare has become the disease of the world. What could be done? Those who serve the intellect and the imagination must, as we have seen, 'Stick to their work as hard as they can'. At least the work would bear witness that words like 'intellect' and 'imagination' had meaning. It is perfectly reasonable that the rulers of Fascist or Marxist societies should regard language as a tool for their manipulation since the historical-progressive view of the world implicitly regards the moral content of language as expendable: it demeans the witness of the past as no more than a phase in a continuously improving process; the perspective is always that of the present moment or of the envisioned Utopia. It would be whistling in the dark to tell Hitler, Mussolini or Stalin that 'Mozart, Shakespeare and Homer are the second book of revelation'! Muir though, by now freed from that dreadful sense of time's oppression, can see what is happening, knows what is at risk and knows his own resources. The darkening modern world is fully present in *The Return of Odysseus* and so is a sense of its provisionality, of its unnaturalness. Muir's characteristic unselfconsciousness with language, his ability to work in the vocabulary of traditional moral certainties is of a piece with a sensibility that cannot conceive of an existence without 'immaterial realities'. The story of Penelope conserves our sense of human worth as surely as she conserves Odysseus' house.

The poem is in two pictures: first, Odysseus' house, scene of dilapidation, desecration and neglect. Insecure where it should be solid and safe – 'the lolling latches gave to every hand'; public where it should be close and private – 'the walls mere walls to lean on as you talked'; a common place of assembly for degenerates of all sorts – 'traitor, babbler, tout and bargainer': Odysseus' house is a corrupt little world in which 'you could be yourself'. While in *Twice-Done, Once-Done* to 'be yourself' was impossible unless you acknowledged your dependence on past selves, the phrase here, though critically placed by the poem as a whole, is used with its everyday meaning. 'You could be yourself' only in conditions the very reverse of those that the other poem says are necessary. This 'self' is very much a modern notion, recognizing its own indulgence as its only duty, blind to the consequences for its own habitat. The second picture is of Penelope. She chooses her task – 'endless undoing of endless doing' – as a duty; her action is entirely different in quality and direction; it is an act of faith in the value of behaviour that has nothing to recommend it to those who merely wish to be themselves:

> Odysseus, this is duty,
> To do and undo, to keep a vacant gate
> Where order and right and hope and peace can enter.

The 'lolling latches' of the outer doors invite the common intruder, invite licence and abuse; the 'vacant gate' bears witness to a quite different quality of openness: a patient, suffering determination to keep alive a sense of human possibilities that the common intruder would spit upon. 'Order and right and hope and peace' must be positively chosen and worked for. Penelope's endless weaving becomes a sign of that determination, the more moving for her not knowing that, despite her weariness and fear that it will be all in vain,

> even then Odysseus on the long
> And winding road of the world was on his way.

Chapter 5

The Solid Foundation

Man is never helped in his suffering by what he thinks for himself but only by revelations of a wisdom greater than his own. It is this which lifts him out of his distress.

(C. G. Jung)

The City, Then and *The Return of Odysseus* are brought together in the 1943 volume, *The Narrow Place*. It is a mature collection of verse in the sense that almost without exception, the poems seem to have arisen from that 'solid foundation' and in so doing to be marked by a new assurance, imaginative and technical. This is not to say that the conflicts and uncertainties of the earlier writing have been resolved. Indeed, as Muir grew older (all these poems were written in his fifties) he saw more clearly the *necessity* of conflict, the naturalness of its place in human life. But by this time he was winning through to a view of good and evil that rescued him from the spiritual stagnation that often seemed to threaten in *Journeys and Places*. The late 1930s and the 1940s were for him a time of reckoning in many respects; and the writing of his autobiography seems to have clarified his thinking in a number of ways. 'All these thoughts' – that is about his philosophy (or rather, his lack of one), his ideas about time and the problem of evil – 'have been roused (and clarified in my mind) by writing my life: there is very little in the book itself about them' (4 January 1940).

When *The Narrow Place* first appeared, it was divided into two sections, the second being under the heading of 'Postscript'. The division was made, one imagines, to mark a turning point, a gladness and a promise newly revealed. For 'Postscript' consists of a dozen poems that in one way or another signify an arrival, an emergence from the darkness of 'the narrow place'. Muir has grown towards the affirmations of such beautiful poems as *The Annunciation*, *The Confirmation, The Commemoration* and, indeed, *The Return of Odysseus*, poems of calm and moving splendour. These might have been planned to answer the anxious questionings and melancholy doubts of *The Human Fold*, *The Narrow Place* and *The Recurrence* of the first section. One should read this volume as a whole and, indeed, in the order in which the poems appear. To do so is to follow a growth into a kind of faith (I say 'kind of' to reflect the tentativeness with which Muir himself used the word), a conviction that will finally have put paid to the destructive uncertainties associated with his obsession with time at its most intense. The metaphor of growth is the correct one for it draws attention to the fundamental fact that faith cannot be inherited. Its enduring qualities are *created*; the alternatives have been contemplated – faced and rejected. And this, too, is surely one true test of the work of art that continues to have something to say to us: that its affirmations arise from conflict. Much art is simply dipped in the mainstream of conventional feeling and gives us no sense that its affirmations and denials have been fought for; the artist has allowed the current to do his work for him to provide the body of feeling without which we do not feel we are in the presence of a work of art at all. As we have seen, the cruel trials of Muir's early life for a time disposed him strongly towards an acceptance of Nietzsche. Eventually he grew beyond the doctrine of the Eternal Recurrence. That growth is recorded in a number of poems; in *The Recurrence* the doctrine is spelt out in its appalling implications with an intensity and a sureness that can only come from its having been previously assimilated and accepted. In other words, its repudiation is not just an intellectual matter, an attitude towards a possible way of viewing the world. It arises from those implications having been contemplated as they have affected his life; the poetic result in *The Recurrence* is a succession of generalizations that bear the unmistakable imprint of their founding experiences:

> All has been that can ever be,
> And this sole eternity
> Cannot cancel, cannot add
> One to your delights or tears,
> Or a million million years
> Tear the nightmare from the mad.

The most hideous implication is that which forms the conclusion of the poem, though by then the affirming voice is strong to deny its plausibility:

> What is not will surely be
> In the changed unchanging reign,
> Else the Actor on the Tree
> Would loll at ease, miming pain,
> And counterfeit mortality.

Christ's suffering and sacrifice would be without meaning, the self-indulgent cruelty of a mocking God, were all predetermined. The hideous image of the lolling actor expresses the revulsion that such an action provokes. The meaning of the crucifixion lies in its having been freely chosen when it might have been avoided. In the paradox of the 'changed, unchanging reign' is the possibility of salvation: life has its recurrences, the basic rhythms and assurances; but within that predictability lies a broad field of possibility. Together these two aspects of life make for a significance that in the world of the eternal recurrence would be unthinkable: the significance that man creates anew for himself within the dignifying and reassuring 'reign'.

The Recurrence rejects the painful challenge of Nietzsche's ancient wheel. The 'heart' cannot, will not, accept its despairing doctrine even though the 'eye' can see no other explanation of human life:

> But the heart makes reply:
> This is only what the eye
> From its tower on the turning field
> Sees and sees and cannot tell why,
> Quarterings on the turning shield,
> The great non-stop heraldic show.
> And the heart and the mind know,
> What has been can never return,

It is a statement of faith, a convincing one, a gesture of the free spirit. On the occasions when he is not capable of the gesture but burdened with the problem, when he attempts to wrestle intellectually with the question of free will and determinism, the result is unsatisfactory, prosy. This – the opening of *The Wheel* – may represent the kind of stillbirth I mean:

> How can I turn this wheel that turns my life,
> Create another hand to move this hand
> Not moved by me, who am not the mover,
> Nor, though I love and hate, the lover,
> The hater?

Not at all typical of the 1943 volume, this kind of writing was much more evident in *Journeys and Places*. The last nine 'place' poems of that collection are, after *Variations on a Time Theme*, perhaps the least satisfactory and rewarding that Muir wrote. All those poems in their various ways express the frustration of knowing one's confinement in time but being powerless to affect it. But Muir seems imaginatively trapped in his dilemma, unable to strike out into the objective forms that will contain but not be bound by his obsession with time. There is such a world of difference between the realizations, the projections of *Hölderlin's Journey* or *Troy* or *The Town Betrayed* and the groping philosophizing of such a poem as *The Solitary Place*, where one's sense is of the mind imprisoned within an overwhelming dilemma, of the imagination stifled. Similarly in *The Private Place* there is an effort of the will, a conscious determination to overcome the problem of time and the limitations of the self. But the willed quality deadens the verse and wearies the reader.

There is distress in *The Human Fold* but it is under control in a way that the anguish of some of the 'place' poems is not. *The Human Fold* is a wasteland that is very much more than the projection of a private nightmare. It has the objectivity of a familiar picture – of spiritual desolation, of directions lost and values cheapened; but it is a picture with the freshness and clarity that comes from its having passed through the individual imagination and been found true. The self-interrogation and philosophizing of *The Wheel* are absent; in their place a contemplativeness that seems the more assured because of the criticism to which the vision of desolation is submitted. And the source of this criticism is of the essence. In Jung's words, help comes through 'revelations of a greater wisdom than his own'. As so often in Muir's poetry, it isn't easy to separate technical competence from imaginative conviction – he would not have accepted the distinction himself. Yeats speaks of those 'intuitions of coming technical power which every creator feels and learns to rely upon'.[2] This linking of intuition and technical power puts the emphasis where it belongs and recognizes the deep interrelations between imaginative insight, moral growth and the exercise of technique: 'coming technical power' is coming imaginative power. This volume as a whole shows a range and a flexibility in the use of verse forms that is new to Muir's poetry. But his own modest disclaimer suggests we will do more justice to his achievement by stressing the what rather than the how:

I am not good at discussing the technical points of verse; the word 'technique' always gives me a slightly bewildered feeling; if I can translate it as skill, I am more at home with it, for skill is always a quality of the thing that is being said or done, not a general thing at all. A thing asks to be said and the only test is whether it is said well (2 July 1952).

By this time Muir's control of the short line is increasingly sure and suited to his purpose. The strong stresses of the first fourteen lines of *The Human Fold* emphasize the bitterness and the weariness of a familiar and still resented scene – 'the stationary farce'.

> Here penned within the human fold
> No longer now we shake the bars,
> Although the ever-moving stars
> Night after night in order rolled
> Rebuke this stationary farce.

All overdone and all heard before, we might think. The burden lifts slightly as the poet admits the occasional glimpse of an order within which some sort of meaning is possible. It comes in the familiar heraldic guise – 'the dragon with his tears of gold'. But it cannot destroy the present sense of imprisonment and futility. Men have a made-to-measure glance; everything shrinks, in other words, to the scale of the meanest, most ordinary transaction.

Suddenly, startlingly, there come the four lines that close the first section of the poem as they close the second.

Yet looking at each countenance
I read this burden in them all:
'I lean my cheek from eternity
For time to slap, for time to slap.
I gather my bones from the bottomless clay
To lay my head in the light's lap.'

By what long way, by what dark way,
From what unpredetermined place,
Did we creep severally to this hole
And bring no memory and no grace
To furnish evidence of the soul,
Though come of an ancient race?
All gone, where now we cannot say,
Altar and shrine and boundary stone,
And of the legends of our day
This one remains alone:
'They loved and might have loved for ever,
But public trouble and private care
Faith and hope and love can sever
And strip the bed and the altar bare.'
Forward our towering shadows fall
Upon the naked nicheless wall,
And all we see is that shadow-dance.
Yet looking at each countenance
I read this burden in them all:
'I lean my cheek from eternity
For time to slap, for time to slap.
I gather my bones from the bottomless clay
To lay my head in the light's lap'.

Those last four lines of each section are beautiful, unearthly, as befits a wholly unlooked for dispensation. As in *Variations on a Time Theme*, Muir rehearses the agonies of alienation, of vanished mystery and observance – 'no memory and no grace/To furnish evidence of the soul'. But those disturbing and unaccountably moving lines come upon us as they came upon Muir. For they arose in a dream which he describes in his diary:

A dream, or rather a voice, which came to me in halfsleep this morning, after being knocked up. The voice spoke from behind and a little above me, and said, 'I lean my cheek from Eternity for Time to slap.' At the same time I had a faint image of someone in white – a dim impression of a shroud – pushing his or her cheek against some transparent thin substance, slightly crinkling it; a feeling of an insubstantial displacement. I am certain I could never have framed that sentence except in sleep, though it seems so wonderful to me now, awake.[3]

From sleep, from a region of which the conscious mind has so little understanding, comes a beauty that challenges and accuses the insistent pessimism that the poem records. There is no doubting the genuineness of that bleak vision of life without 'genuine liberty'. All the more wonderful then that it is forced to admit the challenge of this unsolicited image of tenderness and beauty. (Muir clearly felt it to be in some way elemental, a gift of grace: it recurs in the much later poem, *The Usurpers*.) But to admit the challenge is not to have the total view transformed. The illumination does not at this point 'go into life'.

In *The Narrow Place* (the title poem of the 1943 volume) the mystery is summoned with an intensity new to Muir's poetry. The short lines, the staccato rhythms, create again that landscape of despair, the 'hole' of *The Human Fold*; the tightness and aridity are felt in the movement of the verse and called up in the thinned blood and dehumanized faces that

> have lost all look of hate or love
> And keep but what they have.

It is a 'parsimonious ground', pitiful in the little that it will let live. And yet – and this is the miracle to which the voice that spoke through *The Human Fold* bears witness – under the 'little wild half-leafless tree' that the ground does support

> we sometimes feel such ease
> As if it were ten thousand trees
> And for its foliage had
> Robbed half the world of shade.
> All the woods in grief
> Bowed down by leaf and bird and leaf
> From all their branches could not weep
> A sleep such as that sleep.

The final section begins with a command to spiritual effort, to a broadening of awareness that is within man's power if only he opens himself to what is within him and can interpret it aright:

> Sleep underneath the tree.
> It is your murdering eyes that make
> The sterile hill, the standing lake,
> And the leaf-breaking wind.
> Then shut your eyes and see,
> Sleep on and do not wake
> Till there is movement in the lake,
> And the club-headed water-serpents break
> In emerald lightnings through the slime,
> Making a mark on Time.

The command to sleep is a command to see. Sleep becomes a figure for a vision killed by mere sight, the faculty that produces the first part of the poem and, indeed, that part of his own life from which the poet is endeavouring to escape. The final three lines are mysterious and suggestive beyond explication; they speak of orders of experience denied by 'murdering eyes'. Beyond reach of the rational, analytical, 'murdering eyes' the club-headed water-serpents await their moment. Arising from the unknowable depths of the psyche they await the moment when they will emerge, burst through the previously 'standing lake' and in making their mark on time, redeem its cruelties. They *are* the timeless in time, the final answer to the deceits of 'the stationary farce'.

In this poem the two orders of experience – the temporal and the eternal – are again juxtaposed, but with a vital difference. The magical lines that came from 'looking at each countenance' in *The Human Fold* were there totally beyond solicitation, a gift. Here, on the other hand, the gift, though deeply mysterious, is within us, awaiting our recognition, carrying its promise of a new order. The working out of Edwin Muir's salvation is one way of describing these poems, but how inadequate that would be; for it is their achievement and lasting value to possess that impersonality that enables every man to find the image of his own being within them. The transformations that await the 'we' and the 'you' of this poem, await us all, for we are all creatures of a time whose image is that of a 'narrow place'. Muir maps that place with an objectivity that gives form to a general spiritual condition. The desolation from which he seeks release is, no doubt, a recurring state, one of the transformations of the spirit that will never be altogether transcended because a permanent aspect of our humanity. That desolation, though, is more acute in an age that has stripped 'the bed and the altar bare'; the outer world seems so often only to echo and confirm it.

Something of the power of *The Narrow Place* then is its being in no particular place. The roads, the mountain walls, the much-trodden mound are not in the least naturalistic, any more than are the ten thousand trees, the leaf and the branches. But though not naturalistic, they are natural. They have the rooted power of familiar symbols; we do not as we read find ourselves wanting to decode them. This is the essence of Muir at his best: that he had a native sense of the world as a 'dictionary of types and symbols' (Yeats) and the power to give them poetic life. I fancy that the kind of unselfconscious trust in the use of symbolism in the lines such as those quoted may be an obstacle to some modern readers. The unselfconsciousness is not common in modern poetry. One has to live with poetry like this, has to become familiar with its imaginative mode. My own experience is that it grows into one's mind rather slowly but then attaches itself with a sureness that belongs to the truth of the vision. Muir's 'spontaneous piety' means that he is deeply at home with that dictionary of types and symbols. Behind the unselfconsciousness is an intimacy of understanding that the first part of *An Autobiography* displays and that is made explicit in this extract from his diary for 1938: '. . . had the sudden realization that my dreaming pleasure in nature, in grass, weeds, flowers, trees, *paths* [his italics] . . . comes from familiarity, a trustful feeling to all these things, as if they were old friends! all memory, like friendship.'[4]

That 'trustful feeling', however, does not lead to a poetry of sensuous imagery. Its effect can best be suggested by Muir's characterization of

Hölderlin, the poet to whom he was so attached and from whom he undoubtedly learnt much: 'His poetry had always been symbolical in a very definite way; when he wrote a poem on the oak, for instance, he did not mean any oak that could be seen by the eye, but an ideal. The palpable world was impalpable to him, and ideas palpable.'[5] When Muir's own work is 'difficult' it is, I think, not because of recondite allusion (it is never 'clever') topical content or the 'wrestle with meaning'. It is, rather, because he works in a mode suggested by those words on Hölderlin. In those words, it is the 'idea' of the palpable world that he deals with in *The Ring*. In some ways this is the essence of Muir.

The Ring

Long since we were a family, a people,
The legends say; an old kind-hearted king
Was our foster father, and our life a fable.

Nature in wrath broke through the grassy ring
Where all our gathered treasures lay in sleep –
Many a rich and many a childish thing.

She filled with hoofs and horns the quiet keep.
Her herds beat down the turf and nosed the shrine
In bestial wonder, bull and adder and ape,

Lion and fox, all dressed by fancy fine
In human flesh and armed with arrows and spears;
But on the brow of each a secret sign

That haughtily put aside the sorrowful years
Or struck them down in stationary rage;
Yet they had tears that were not like our tears,

And new, all new, for Nature knows no age.
Fatherless, sonless, homeless haunters, they
Had never known the vow and the pilgrimage,

Poured from one fount into the faithless day.
We are their sons, but long ago we heard
Our fathers or our fathers' fathers say

Out of their dream the long-forgotten word
That rounded again the ring where sleeping lay
Our treasures, still unrusted and unmarred.

Into this poem comes his knowledge of the deep interpenetration of the human and the animal world in the symbolism by which we come to know our natures; in it too is the conviction that through dreams and sleep – sources of archetypal wisdom – we can recover those 'treasures' that 'the narrow place' had threatened to squeeze out of our lives. It is a picture, a reading of the human condition that is the fullest to date in Muir's work. The myth of the Fall informs the poem and takes on an imaginative reality in the linking of the legends of the first stanza with the dreams of the last. These legends tell of a time when there was no time, when 'our life was a fable'. In reading this poem we understand

Nature not as an abstraction, nor as the sum of the creatures in whose form the destruction comes. The creatures have the 'true legendary quality'; they compose both the strength and the weakness, the innocence and the evil in the world, and, as such, are more than merely animal. As in *The Combat*, they are touched with pride and greed, the productions of 'fancy fine'. Most hurtfully, they know only the moment – 'for Nature knows no age', the 'vow and the pilgrimage' are empty words, dependent for their meaning on a sense both of past and present that they have never had. And the outcome is us – 'we are their sons'. But there is hope in the 'long-forgotten word'. That the word came out of a dream, that gift which connects us with all that we have forgotten – it is that which closes the ring and makes us whole. It is as if to say that despite all those who have never known the vow and the pilgrimage, the possibility of grace is within us, a distant voice that is yet our own since we are unavoidably of the same family as once knew perfection. That perfection is not of course to be located historically; it is, rather, a permanency, a potentiality in human nature. It can be ignored but it cannot in the end be denied. We have immortal longings that survive the vanishing of 'grace' and 'evidence of the soul'. The 'long-forgotten word' is the badge and symbol of grace.

Muir is one of those writers whom we know better for knowing his 'world'. His essay on *King Lear*, written some five years after *The Ring*, relates – incidentally – the mythical picture in the poem to the mythical elements in Shakespeare's play. He advances a view of *King Lear* as the 'mythical drama of the transmutation of civilization'. It is, as he sees it, a play that gives body to two totally incompatible views of human nature: the one grounded in respect for memory, continuity, tradition, the other acknowledging only 'a continuous present divested of all associations, denuded of memory and the depth memory brings to life'. The collision between these two views is a conflict of nature and society – 'for nature is always new and has no background; it is society that is old'. What particularly engages Muir is the way in which, though 'the old world still echoed in [Shakespeare's] ears, he was aware of the new as we are aware of the future, that is as an inchoate prophetic dream'. The final paragraph of the essay casts a strong light on *The Ring*. It establishes the provenance of the images in the poem: they belong within the traditions that make *King Lear* a living work and that both in *An Autobiography* and in this poem prove to have a continuing vitality, to be a well-spring of the imagination:

Lear is very old, almost Saturnian in his legendary age, the kingdom in him exists as a memory and no longer as a fact; the old order lies in ruin, and the new is not an order. The communal tradition, filled with memory, has been smashed by an individualism that exists in its perpetual shallow present. The judgment on the new generation is passed by a member of it who does not belong spiritually to it: Edgar. It is remarkable that in the scenes where Lear, the Fool and Edgar are together, it is Edgar, the only sane man, who conjures up the deepest images of horror. For he is of the new generation, and knows it as Lear cannot. When Lear asks him who he is, he replies by giving a portrait of his brother Edmund:

A servingman, proud in heart and mind; that curled my hair, wore gloves in my cap, served the lust of my mistress' heart, and did the act of darkness with her; swore as many oaths as I spake words, and broke them in the sweet face of heaven; one that slept in the contriving of lust, and waked to do it. Wine loved I deeply, dice dearly, and in woman out-paramoured the Turk: false of heart, light of ear, bloody of hand; hog in sloth, fox in stealth, wolf in greediness, dog in madness, lion in prey.

That is a picture of an animal with human faculties, made corrupt and legendary by the proudly curled hair. It is a picture, too, of the man of policy in the latest style, who regards the sacred order of society as his prey, and recognises only two realities, interest and force, the gods of the new age.[6]

In *Collected Poems, The Ring* is followed by *The Return of Odysseus*. The sequence is surely deliberate. The traitor, tout and babbler who infest Odysseus' house *are* the herds that 'nosed the shrine'. Penelope and Odysseus are partners to the vow and the pilgrimage; her fidelity and endurance protect, indeed are part of the 'treasures, still unrusted and unmarred'. The fidelity is chosen, the endurance made possible, by 'the word that rounded again the ring'. It is a gravely beautiful poem and it is easy to see why it originally appeared in the 'Postscript' section of *The Narrow Place*. If one compares it with almost anything from *Journeys and Places* and with the poems of the first section in *The Narrow Place*, one sees very directly a marked change of temper. A burden, a weight of melancholy and foreboding seems to have been dissipated. The poems of *The Narrow Place* were all composed during a crucial period of Muir's life and *The Return of Odysseus* reflects the most profound and positive experience he had at that time. To say that he became a Christian would not represent it properly: for though he became convinced that 'Christ is the greatest figure who ever appeared in the history of mankind' and though, as he later said, he had 'a vague sense during these days that Christ was the turning point of time and the meaning of life to everyone, no matter what his conscious beliefs' (p. 247), his own conviction was not of a kind to place him unequivocally within Christian faith and practice. He never joined a church, felt theological dogma to be an obstacle and described himself in 1940 as 'a sort of illicit Christian, a gate-crasher, hoping in my own way to slip in yet'. This was a year after the crucial illumination – the phrase represents what happened as well as any other. He had been going through a particularly lean time: his wife ill, himself dissatisfied with the endless and increasingly meaningless translating of German books, good and bad, into English, he was 'more unhappy in St Andrews than I had been since the time of my obscure fears and the course of psychoanalysis that dispelled them' (p. 244). He began around this time to keep a diary 'as a sort of judgement of myself' and it is there that he records the turning point of which, on the surface anyway, there had appeared to be no chance. It was indeed an illumination as unaccountable and as authentic as those saving lines in *The Human Fold*:

Last night going to bed alone (Willa being in Cottage Hospital) I suddenly found myself (as I was taking off my waistcoat) reciting the Lord's Prayer in a loud emphatic voice – a thing I have not done since my teens – with urgency too, and deeply disturbed emotion. As I recited it I grew more composed; my soul, as if it had been empty and needed replenishment, seemed to fill: and every word had a strange fullness of meaning, which astonished and delighted me, and gave me not so much hope as strength. It was late; I had sat up reading; I was sleepy; but as I stood in the middle of the floor half undressed reciting the prayer over and over, the meanings it contained, none of them extraordinary, indeed ordinary as they could be, overcame me with joyful surprise, and made me seem to realise that this petition was always universal, always adequate, and to life as it is, not to a life such as we long for or dream of: and for that reason it seems to sanctify common existence. Everything in it, apart from the Being to which it is addressed, refers to human life, seen realistically, not mystically. It is about the world and society, not about the everlasting destiny of the soul. 'Our Father which art in Heaven' means merely 'Our Heavenly Father', not our earthly father. 'Hallowed be thy name', defines our human relation to him. 'Thy kingdom come', means 'Thy kingdom come here on earth', so that God's will may be done on earth as in heaven. It means that we should desire that human society might be directed in accordance with the perfect laws of heaven. 'And forgive us our debts as we forgive our debtors.' Excuse our failings, and our offences against You, as we excuse those who offend against us. 'And lead us not into temptation but deliver us from evil: For thine is the kingdom, and the power, and the glory, for ever. Amen.'

I never realised before so clearly the primary importance of 'we' and 'us' in the prayer: it is collective, for all societies, for all mankind as a great society. 'After this manner therefore pray ye.' Not 'My Father which art in heaven', not 'Give me this day my daily bread', not 'Forgive my debts'; not 'Lead me not into temptation' – as Protestantism almost succeeded in persuading us. And this collective form of prayer was the form enjoined by Jesus. It would be called now, in the jargon of the fashionable revolutionaries, political.[7]

It was not until much later, in Rome, that he became aware of 'the splendours of Christendom' and one wonders whether the tentativeness of his comments on Christian belief and his lack of interest in the Church have to be put down to his deep-rooted hostility to Protestantism in its Calvinistic garb. His poems about Scotland, his reflections in *Scottish Journey* and his early book on John Knox (1929) all complain of a general impoverishment of religious life for which he felt the main culprit was Knox himself. In *Scotland 1941*, the responsibility is squarely placed on individual leaders; from their narrow vision has sprung our present desolation:

> But Knox and Melville clapped their preaching palms
> And bundled all the harvesters away,
> Hoodicrow Peden in the blighted corn
> Hacked with his rusty beak the starving haulms.
> Out of that desolation we were born.

In an appendix to his book on Knox, Muir wrote: 'What Knox really did was to rob Scotland of all the benefits of the Renaissance.'[8] Whatever the truth of the matter, his letters at this time show him unable to feel that illumination can be accepted unconditionally. On the one hand he expresses his dismay that with his autobiography nearing completion, he has 'no philosophy', a 'lack which I must share with several million people' and that all he has is faith; 'and I think my faith is a little too easy, considering the enormity of things'. On the other hand, he consoles himself with the thought that when St Paul spoke of the three things needful 'he did not call them philosophy, hope and charity' (4 January 1940). His distrust of theology is probably related to his feeling that he prefers the mystery of evil 'to any explanation of it I know'. He would seem to me to have the disposition of the true contemplative: explanations, deliberations, words, threaten to destroy the always fragile and evanescent sense of mystery, of God. The reaching after certainty, however, is natural too; he wants a 'rounded conception of existence and all I can see is a flash here and there, which tells me that such a conception exists perhaps outside of Time, I don't know' (3 February 1940). With the mystery comes apprehension:

I am happier now than I have been, in spite of the state of the world, for I have had something like a sense of the presence of God, a sense which I have never been consciously aware of before, though I am now 52; it is too new and strange for me to write about it, and so inexperienced that I am afraid of writing about it. I have believed for a long time in the immortality of the soul, but this is something different: I tremble to lose it again by my own fault (28 February 1940).

I have used the words 'contemplation' and 'contemplative' before in this study and I think it is in considering the nature of Muir's faith as it is expressed in these quotations that they come to seem particularly apposite. He had from the beginning valued his art as 'the only way of growing, of becoming myself more purely'; in his art is his life and his life becomes more conscious, more known to himself through his art. It is through that that he contemplates the nature of human life, not through the constructions of the ranging intellect. Instinctively, as a man and as a poet, he obeys the injunctions of the medieval author of *The Cloud of Unknowing*, a work of mysticism to which one feels sure Muir could at many points have given his assent:

So pay great attention to this marvellous work of grace within your soul. It is always a sudden impulse and comes without warning, springing up to God like some spark from the fire . . .
For whoever hears or reads about all this, and thinks that it is fundamentally an activity of the mind, and proceeds then to work it all out along these lines, is on quite the wrong track. He manufactures an experience that is neither spiritual nor physical. He is dangerously misled and in real peril. So much so, that unless God in his great goodness intervenes with a miracle of mercy and makes him stop and submit to the advice of those who really know, he will go mad, or suffer some other dreadful form of spiritual mischief and devilish deceit. Indeed, almost casually as it were, he may be lost eternally, body and soul. So for the love of God be careful, and do not attempt to achieve this experience intellectually. I tell you truly it cannot come this way. So leave it alone.[9]

Muir 'trembles to lose' his newly gained sense of God through his own fault. He had in that moment of illumination during his wife's illness received what the medieval author calls 'a shaft of spiritual light, which pierces this cloud of unknowing between you [i.e. you and God] and shows you some of his secrets, of which it is not permissible or possible to speak'.[10] I think Muir knew instinctively that what he calls 'a flash here and there' and the author of *The Cloud of Unknowing* a 'shaft of spiritual light', was the most that a man could hope for. The medieval book, though it takes man's impotence as axiomatic – only through grace can he even become aware of his need for grace – stresses throughout the obligation to work at the discipline of contemplation, to create in oneself a readiness for those moments of special seeing which redeem a fallen world. Some of the poems in *The Narrow Place* volume work in that direction, notably *The Letter* and *The Good Man in Hell*.

I have spoken of Muir's sense of growing through his art. Looking over his life's work one sometimes has a vivid sense of that movement of growth, of intuitions deepening with time and experience but keeping their nature. Although he speaks of his sense of the presence of God as something different from his long-held belief in the immortality of the soul, they are surely in his own terms 'forms of [the same] experience'. Similarly, his knowledge that no man can attain 'an image one and whole' for more than a moment – a knowledge now *experienced* and grasped with a new intensity – had been with him at some level throughout his adult life. It informs and humanizes his early literary criticism. It is for instance made plain in the essays in *Latitudes* on Dostoevsky, Ibsen and Nietzsche. These essays were originally reviews of books on those authors by his friend, Janko Lavrin. Despite his general approval of the books, the criticism Muir makes of each of them is that Lavrin asks too much of these great men. Lavrin is too concerned by their shortcomings, their various failures, and not sufficiently appreciative of how hardwon and precious are their positive achievements. Muir cannot accept his criticism of Ibsen and Nietzsche for their failure to 'attain a synthesis'.

'In what human figure', he asks, after reading Lavrin on Dostoevsky, 'has belief not been more of a will to believe than anything else?'[11] In Muir's poetry, the characteristic expression of this will to believe is a curiously oblique one: the passion and the aspiration have their existence in a kind of vacuum left by the disappearance (or rather, in this case, the non-appearance) of traditional dogma and iconography. Blackmur suggests Muir is 'like George Herbert without a parish or a doctrine or any one temple to construct',[12] and this is an apt comparison. But it is in the contrast between the two writers that the peculiar dilemma of a certain kind of modern religious sensibility is made clear. Herbert's supplications, self-abasements and affirmations are always contained within the unquestioned Christian story, an unquestioned allegiance to Christ. Muir, on the other hand, has to find his own stories or pictures within which to express a sense of the possibility of man's salvation. In defending and praising Dostoevsky he had all those years ago said that 'the cause, the centre and the meaning of his struggle was that intuition, that fleeting but unshakeable realization of truth which is the most inviolable mark of human greatness'.[13] In *The Narrow Place* some such fleeting realizations are seized upon and made into poems, a creative response to the inducements of evil such as they are most horrifically expressed in *Then* and *The City*. In those poems 'the mute maternal presences' of the one and 'the simple fields' of the other offer small and pathetic resistance to the might of evil. Two other poems in the first section of *The Narrow Place*, *The Letter* and *The Good Man in Hell* make their own answer to that might through personal affirmation, an act of the imagination spurred on by the will to believe. Both poems were published before the 'joyful surprise' of the Lord's prayer, in November 1937 and January 1938 respectively, and they can now be seen to prefigure it. Each is a determined meditation from a sure centre. I use the word ' determined' because there is nothing in the least easy about the aspiration each expresses and the comfort they draw from their visions. The kind of determination *The Letter* represents may perhaps be seen the more clearly by contrasting it with *The Face*, which appropriately appears in the *Collected Poems* close to *The City* and *The Wheel*. Speaking of *The Face* in the chapter of *An Autobiography* that records the slough from which he emerged in the revelation of the Lord's Prayer, he relates it to his obsession with 'animal traits flitting across human features'. The beginning of that obsession is vividly remembered earlier in the book. It was part of his Nietzsche phase, when he had dismissed immortality 'as an imputation on the purity of immediate experience'. He had been travelling in a tramcar in Glasgow. It had been crowded with people returning from work. He had suddenly become conscious of something having 'fallen from them and from me and with a sense of desolation I saw that they were all animals' (p. 52). This had indeed been a desolating experience, a remorseless proof of the gap at that time between his intuitive belief in immortality and the 'ideas' that denied it. And it seemed to stay with him, to surface at times of depression as a reminder of the price of ignoring the humanity of man. In that tram he had been 'outside time without being in eternity; in the small, sensual, momentary world of the beast' (p. 53). In *The Face* we are in the same territory, in the land of 'that perfectly up-to-date gang of Renaissance adventurers' that for him disfigure the legendary world of King Lear and whose equally sinister successors were even then despoiling Europe:

The Face

See me with all the terrors on my roads,
The crusted shipwrecks rotting in my seas,
And the untroubled oval of my face
That alters idly with the moonlike modes
And is unfathomably framed to please
And deck the angular bone with passing grace.

I should have worn a terror-mask, should be
A sight to frighten hope and faith away,
Half charnel field, half battle and rutting ground.
Instead I am a smiling summer sea
That sleeps while underneath from bound to bound
The sun- and star-shaped killers gorge and play.

Indeed an image of the human face fit for a Iago or an Edmund, those deniers of the soul. It is an image Muir knew he could not live with since, as he says in another entry in his diary from around that time, 'I can see men and women as really human only when I see them as immortal souls' (p. 246). Yet the poem steps out of its background to challenge our sense of who we are by its very monstrousness, its heightening of a part of our nature which, if we are honest, we recognize as ever active, ever threatening to take over and reduce our human selves to the shape of our 'natural' instincts. The 'I' of the poem is an impersonal 'I'. This is hell again but without hope.

'The world of imagination is the world of Eternity', says Blake. In the country from which *The Face* comes there is no imagination, no seeing beyond the fulfilment of rage and desire. *The Letter* takes us beyond rage, uses and commands the use of the imagination and finally, urgently, sees in it salvation. The urgency of the poem seems more than personal. The poet seems to speak for us all, to draw attention in tenderness and certain knowledge to the inevitable facts of ageing. The gloom that dominates those poems where he obsessively rehearses the destructive powers of time is gone, though; instead, those powers are felt as the occasion for fresh discoveries within the self. It is an injunction to compassion, a plea for the recognition of our common humanity; it is a very moving poem because it has that simplicity that Muir himself recognized as the hallmark of good art: rhythm, diction, every aspect of the poem's form seems natural to the expression of its statement. Through the first few lines there is called up an unrelentingly soured view of life; and then the measured, not to be contested statement of what unites us all, including those who so rage:

Tried friendship must go down perforce
Before the outward eating rage
And murderous heart of middle age,
Killing kind memory at its source,
If it were not for mortality,
The thought of that which levels all
And coldly pillows side by side
The tried friend and the too much tried.

The second stanza, with its urgent appeal to fix the eye on our transitoriness, is followed by a conclusion in which one feels the touch of a poet arriving at a maturity where words come with that effortless control that is a sign of emotional honesty and can affect us so directly.

But should this seem a niggardly
And ominous reconciliation,
Look again until you see,
Fixed in the body's final station,
The features of immortality.
Try to pursue this quarrel then.
You cannot. This is less than man
And more. That more is our salvation.
Now let us seize it. Now we can.

The louring polysyllables of the first two lines here make the sense of release in the rest more emphatic. Almost, indeed, the effect is one of elation, prevented from rising so high only by the anxiety that the 'features of immortality' are not (in this age, no doubt) sufficiently obvious and compelling. Hence the determination, the urgent deliberateness of the last four lines. Muir is with Blake in the words that follow Blake's identification of imagination and eternity: 'The world of imagination is infinite and eternal, whereas the world of generation and vegetation is finite and temporal. There exist in that eternal world the eternal realities of everything which we see reflected in the vegetable glass of nature.' The truth of this is acknowledged in the last stanza; but the urgency is a sign of the difficulty of holding to it. There is so much that threatens to betray it.[14]

The hell of *The Good Man in Hell* is a fiction, obviously fed by the traditional imagery that attaches to the word but not constrained by theology. It is a poem about how hell might 'be a place like any other place' – obviously not a Christian idea. Hell, damnation, the devil, Eden – all these words carry their expected charge but the poem locates them all within the possible field of action open to man. It is, I think, Muir's most affirmative poem so far and it grows from a sense of the reality of freedom of moral choice. It is a powerful imagining of evil and an attempt through the imagination to recover the reality of grace from a past to which it has apparently been consigned by an age that has stripped 'the altar bare'. 'If a good man were ever housed in hell' is a first line that starts a sentence that builds powerfully through four quatrains, imagining the terrible pressure that would beset the good man in hell, almost inevitably forcing him to self-damnation. Almost but not quite; the last two stanzas meditate on the strength of faith and hope and, tentatively at first, then with a sudden onset of joyous conviction, proclaim the powers of those Christian qualities:

One doubt of evil would bring down such a grace,
  Open such a gate, all Eden would enter in,
Hell be a place like any other place,
And love and hate and life and death begin.

The alternative to Hell is not Heaven; it is normality, a ground on which the impulse of good men can exercise itself alongside the normal, human facts of 'love and hate and life and death'. Life is, naturally, conflict. Only the mystic and the visionary can glimpse the ground on which these elements are reconciled, are shown to be necessary. (*The Trophy* in this volume meditates on such a synthesis, evil and good 'in deep confederacy'.) That synthesis is beyond most men; but faith is not. Just as all men may be thought in some way responsible for the hellishness of the temporal world, of contemporary Europe, so they may be held responsible for laying hold on the powers of resistance that lie with them. The eye that here creates the image of the good man outfacing Hell would later find it reflected in the literal world of the postwar years. In chapter twelve of *An Autobiography* Muir describes the journey into Czechoslovakia during which he and his companions witnessed the dreadful devastation of Cologne, a vast graveyard. And yet, in that terrible scene, the eye alights upon the saving grace. Muir's imagery transfigures the scene:

It was a lovely late summer evening, and the peaceful crowds in that vast graveyard were like the forerunners of a multitude risen in a private resur-rection day to an unimaginable new life. It was moving to see a simple courteous inclination of the heart so calmly surviving, upheld by nothing but its own virtue after the destruction of all that had nourished it (p. 252).

What *The Letter* and *The Good Man in Hell* have to say about good and evil will not date; but, in no limiting way, they bear the mark of the particular evil of the times in which they were written. The poems grouped under the heading of 'Postscript' (in the *Collected Poems* they begin at *The Return of Odysseus* and conclude with *The Day*) do not bear that mark; they are poems *of* any time *for* any time. To know the circumstances of their composition is to see the achievement of the poems for the remarkable thing it is. It was a period of enforced rest, on doctor's orders, a low point in his life. But withdrawal made him realize that 'I had been rushing on like a madman, past my true self, living my own actual unique life as if it belonged to anyone at all, or to someone whom I had no concern with'. In June 1941 he wrote to Alec Aitken:

The result of my tranquillity – or rather one of the results – has been a little freshet of poetry: I'm enclosing some of it, not knowing how you will like it, for it seems to me different from most of my poetry: there is no effort in it, for at present I'm unable to make such things as efforts; and I'm afraid it lacks intensity, but it may have some other quality that makes up for that: I don't know. The war I've put behind me as much as possible, along with my personal worries; it's a justified precaution, indeed almost a duty: though I confess it's a duty I rather take to, unlike most duties (12 June 1941).

The poems Muir sent were *The Finder Found* (later called *The Question*) *The Guess*, *The Prize* and *The Old Gods*.

Do these poems lack intensity? Certainly they do not possess the intensity of a man conscious and torn by the sense of division that animates some of the earlier poems in this collection. It is a deeper, meditative intensity that we find in *The Prize*. The bitter immediacies of *The Narrow Place* and *The Human Fold* have retreated, leaving not a solution of the problem they pose but a calmer awareness of where it may be found. There is a feeling of wonder in the first four lines, of the fascination rather than the anguish of the problem which remind me of what Muir later said about 'religious explanations': 'I would rather have the problems themselves, for from an awareness of them and their vastness I get some sort of living experience, some sense of communion, of being in the whole in some way, whereas from the explanations I should get only comfort and reassurance and a sense of safety which I know is not genuine' (21 March 1944).

> Did we come here, drawn by some fatal thing,
> Fly from eternity's immaculate bow
> Straight to the heart of time's great turning ring,
> That we might win the prize that took us so?

There pass through his mind those ordinary sights within which the prize may be won; or is it more likely to be found in

> one sole thing, a certain door
> Set in a wall, a half-conjectured scene
> Of men and women moving as in a play,
> A turn in the winding road, a distant tower,
> A corner of a field, a single place
> Apart, a single house, a single tree,
> A look upon one half-averted face
> That has been once, or is, or is to be?

In his childhood there had been 'no great distinction between the ordinary and the fabulous' and the life he recalls in *An Autobiography* was one in which insignificant, even routine occurrences could be unaccountably charged with a kind of glory. This poem was written soon after he had finished the 1940 version of the book and he may have been the more conscious of that childhood blending of the mysterious and the commonplace. However that may be, the questions that he asks here look back to that time and forward to the conviction of such late poems as *The Transfiguration*. His poems regularly celebrate that corner of a field (*The Little General*, for instance), the single house (*The Great House*), the look upon one half-averted face (*The Confirmation*), but here – and this surely is what the last stanza expresses – is a wondering realization that, could we but see them, such things lie about us:

> all around each trivial shape exclaims:
> 'Here is your jewel; this is your longed-for day',
> And we forget, lost in the countless names.

We forget: we arrived with the knowledge but are bemused and misled by the sheer intensity of distraction. Paradoxically it is language, 'countless names', the very stuff of the poem, which deflects us from sight of the jewel, the deepest spiritual reality.

We live in forgetfulness, can easily spend our entire lives looking away from ourselves. But our natural goal is union with a deeper reality, a permanent ground of being whereon personal identity will be subsumed and we shall have found ourselves in the only sense that matters. Such a struggle is the stuff of *The Question*:

> Will you, sometime, who have sought so long and seek
> Still in the slowly darkening hunting ground,
> Catch sight some ordinary month or week
> Of that strange quarry you scarcely thought you sought –
> Yourself, the gatherer gathered, the finder found,
> The buyer, who would buy all, in bounty bought –
> And perch in pride on the princely hand, at home,
> And there, the long hunt over, rest and roam?

It is one long sentence, the continuity seeming – like the long, four-stanza sentence with which *The Good Man in Hell* began – to follow the aspiration of the soul in its exalted journey towards a natural resting place. The poet addresses himself, implicitly he addresses his reader, and in the deliberate succession of compact and paradoxical phrases uniting the finder and the found, he addresses his God. The exaltation contradicts the formality of the questioning: the passion and the yearning are themselves half an answer to the question, an active testimony to the possibility of grace. And yet – here Muir is, as it were, orthodox – the framing of the poem in the form of a question acknowledges the simple truth that permeates the poetry of Herbert and Vaughan. 'God ordered motion but ordained no rest', says Vaughan; and Herbert, in *The Pulley*, explains man's restlessness while praising God in man. What was left in the 'glasse of blessings' 'when God at first made man' was Rest.

> For if I should (said he)
> Bestow this jewell also on my creature,
> He would adore my gifts instead of me,
> And rest in Nature, not the God of Nature.
> So both should losers be.
>
> Yet let him keep the rest,
> But keep them with repining restlessnesse.
> Let him be rich and wearie, that at least,
> If goodnesse leade him not, yet wearinesse
> May tosse him to my breast.

The seventeenth-century parson and poet can explain God's action; this twentieth-century poet can only accept it, must do so indeed without invoking God at all. What stays in the mind is the impersonal strength of the feeling. The quality of this strength can be best illustrated by a comparison with a poem nearer to Muir's own time. Matthew Arnold's melancholy poem, *The Buried Life*, is a lament over the distractions that are placed in the way of man's self-realization, of 'his genuine self'. 'Fate', Arnold's locution for God, ensures that despite this, the unregarded river of our life nonetheless flows through 'the deep recesses of our breast'. Suddenly in the midst of our uncertainties we become aware of that buried stream.

> But often in the world's most crowded streets,
> But often, in the din of strife,
> There rises an unspeakable desire
> After the knowledge of our buried life,
> A thirst to spend our fire and restless force
> In tracking out our true, original course;
> A longing to enquire
> Into the mystery of this heart that beats
> So wild, so deep in us, to know
> Whence our thoughts come, and where they go.
> And many a man in his own breast then delves,
> But deep enough, alas, none ever mines:
> And we have been on many thousand lines,
> And we have shown on each talent and power,
> But hardly have we, for one little hour,
> Been on our own line, have we been ourselves;
> Hardly had skill to utter one of all
> The nameless feelings that course through our breast,
> But they course on for ever unexpress'd.
> And long we try in vain to speak and act
> Our hidden self, and what we say and do
> Is eloquent, is well – but 'tis not true:

Such poetry 'has no power to distil its own alleviation'.[15] I quote this at length not to dismiss Arnold but rather to point up the difficulty of writing of the presence of God. There was no living tradition – as of course there had been for Herbert and Vaughan – to support Arnold in expressing such a presence. The language is consequently enfeebled, inadequate to what is demanded of it and Arnold seems overwhelmed by that inadequacy: the dominant emotion of the poem is not so much that of an aspiration towards 'tracking out our true original course' as of a melancholy inspection of a failed religious sensibility. One can sympathize with Arnold but my purpose is to point to Muir's achievement. For him also there was no language available in which to express the kind of assent that we find in *The Question*. That poem has no obvious background; it is created out of an inner search, a discipline of the imagination that has yielded a language adequate to its highly uncontemporary purpose.

The exalted tones of *The Question* arise of course from a private region; but for one of the sources of this new confidence and spiritual ease I think we need look no further than the three beautiful love poems printed together in 'Postscript': *The Annunciation, The Confirmation, The Commemoration*. Taken together with *The Prize* and *The Question*, they seem to give body to the general spiritual strength and direction expressed in *The Bird*, with its obvious affiliations with Hopkins but its own independent life:

> The wide-winged soul itself can ask no more
> Than such a pure, resilient and endless floor
> For its strong-pinioned plunging and soaring and upward and upward
>   springing.

The Narrow Place had been produced in and bears the pressure of 'this iron reign'. *The Annunciation* is the first poem of unqualified triumph, of escape from that reign; the anguish, the yearning, the meditations have given way to a simple joy, a song of celebration. The emotional strength and directness of each of these three love poems is not just a matter of feeling; it is an intellectual strength too. *The Annunciation* celebrates love the creator, the natural source of that defiance which individuals offer to 'this iron reign'. It is the simplest, most natural answer to the deterministic philosophies that make to extinguish the life of the soul. That life is only life when it is called out, created. The wonder of that creation is what is celebrated in the poem:

>   each awakes in each
> What else would never be,
> Summoning so the rare
> Spirit to breathe and live.

In the third and fourth stanzas there is a serious playing with ideas that in some of its images recalls Donne's poem, *The Extasie*. It is an echo though, not a borrowing. Muir is his own man. The note is of wonder in humility, of humility before wonder:

> Whether the soul at first
> This pilgrimage began,
> Or the shy body leading
> Conducted soul to soul
> Who knows?

Willa Muir talks of Muir's art aspiring to ecstasy rather than domination; and what better text to show it? The vision of the great poet and mystic is at best evanescent but what such a poem argues through its very existence is that spiritual wholeness has other forms and this love is one of them.

>   This is the most
> That soul and body can,
> To make us each for each
> And in our spirit whole.

A great poem, a beautiful lyric. As a poet, says Blackmur, Muir 'is singularly little in love with words'. Despite the strong mould of thought in which the ecstasy is held, there is no sense of effort, of the words being asked to do more than they naturally will. As I have already said, Muir trusts words, trusts them as carriers of what matters to men, and he here calls upon them to give their natural shaping to a natural emotion. 'Soul', 'grace', 'spirit', 'pilgrimage': the ancient words are remade with a total absence of self-consciousness, a total faith in their power to express the nature of love between man and woman in an iron reign whose principal feature is that it denies the realities of which those words speak.

The same can be said of *The Confirmation*. The opening line, 'Yes, yours, my love, is the right human face', is startling; that simplicity one might have expected to find banal or mannered. But it is not so at all. The excitement of discovery, of sure recognition, is what it expresses and the rest of the poem fully justifies the use of the word 'right'. The rightness belongs to that 'jewel within the maze' whose paradoxical nearness and remoteness Muir had contemplated in *The Prize*, a jewel eventually found, in *The Confirmation*,

> as a traveller finds a place
> Of welcome suddenly amid the wrong
> Valleys and rocks and twisting roads.

It is an arrival that is being celebrated here; and there comes tumbling out on the current of feeling that is released a whole catalogue of symbols to mark the quality of the lover and the love. Each is appropriate, none totally adequate:

> Your open heart,
> Simple with giving, gives the primal deed,
> The first good world, the blossom, the blowing seed,
> The hearth, the steadfast land, the wandering sea,

The final two lines are masterly, again without a hint of bathos descending from this high and noble praise to a rare simplicity of statement. As with Donne (*The Good Morrow*) his image of the true has become the real and it is because he can believe in the given quality of that reality that he can with such dignity describe his love as

> Not beautiful or rare in every part,
> But like yourself, as they were meant to be.

The Annunciation and *The Confirmation* are beautiful poems but I think *The Commemoration* is even finer. This is surely Muir at the height of his powers: formal perfection seems the inevitable outcome of integrity of feeling. Through love something new has been created (as in *The Annunciation*), intangible, beyond demonstration, but joyously real. The buoyancy of the poem is paradoxically in its demonstration of what apparently cannot be known, a triumph of the creative imagination in the shaping of the unshapeable. The 'idea' of the poem is that there is no way of proclaiming 'my faith enshrined in you'. But the poem becomes the way. There is a new serenity, an inward peace that is the prize of the journey that led to the right human face. He can contemplate with ease the passing of time, secure in the knowledge that in personal terms at least, it doesn't matter. That peace yields the beauty of this:

> Material things will pass
> And we have seen the flower
> And the slow falling tower
> Lie gently in the grass,
> But meantime we have stored
> Riches past bed and board
> And nursed another hoard
> Than callow lad and lass.

And it yields the metaphysical felicity of this:

> Invisible virtue now
> Expands upon the air
> Although no fruit appear
> Nor weight bend down the bough,
> And harvests truly grown
> For someone or no one
> Are stored and safely won
> In hollow heart and brow.

And the magical beginning of the final stanza:

> How can one thing remain
> Except the invisible,
> The echo of a bell
> Long rusted in the rain?

Yeats's speculation on the real origin of our emotions and actions is perhaps the best comment:

We should never be certain that it was not some woman treading in the wine-press who began that subtle change in men's minds, that powerful movement of thought and imagination about which so many Germans have written, or that the passion, because of which so many countries were given to the sword, did not begin in the mind of some shepherd boy, lighting up his eyes for a moment before it ran on its way.[16]

Thus is tradition given a metaphysical dimension; the elation of the poem is born of a faith in the reality of that tradition, at once intimate and impersonal, creative and immortal.

Chapter 6

The Three Mirrors

The Narrow Place collection closed with a prayer, *The Day*. It is a poem that could with equal appropriateness have opened the 1946 volume, *The Voyage*. Written during the same period of enforced tranquillity as produced *The Question*, *The Day* looks forward to a new spiritual freedom that is indeed the feature of the later volume. And just as *The Question* had seemed to spring from a feeling that the answers for which it sought were almost within reach, so in *The Day* one feels that Muir is able to frame his prayer in the way he does because already in sight of the transformation for which he sues. The 'eternal recurrence' and other versions of determinism are implicitly dismissed even while, on the surface, the poet accepts them as possibilities with which he must come to terms.

> If, in the mind of God or book of fate,
> This day that's all to live lies lived and done,
>
>   *   *   *
>
> Oh give me clarity and love that now
> The way I walk may truly trace again
> The in eternity written and hidden way;
> Make pure my heart and will, and me allow
> The acceptance and revolt, the yea and nay,
> The denial and the blessing that are my own.

The Christian words carry in themselves the assurance of deliverance from the static, determined day; the last three lines are a familiar paradox: the acceptance and the revolt, the denial and the blessing, are within my power, and yet that power is not mine unless it first be given. Tentatively it seems, Muir refrains from making his prayer explicitly Christian. The power to which it is addressed is not God; it is nothing specific. The Christian vocabulary evokes associations and would seem to imply a belief that the form of the poem and the juxtaposition in the first line are careful *not* to espouse: the power which may have gone before him to make 'a region and a road where road was none' is God *or* fate. The mood is one of aspiration and acceptance, the remaining tentativeness a natural reflection of that hesitancy to commit himself in the terms of explicit Christian belief that we see in his letters.

The equanimity and hopefulness of *The Day* are fully justified by the

1946 volume. One way of describing the range of Muir's achievement in *The Voyage* is to say that the poems aspire to and express the clarity and love for which he had sued in *The Day*. It is a clarity of spiritual recognition. At the deepest level his preoccupations do not change: the problem and the challenge are in the everlasting conflict of good and evil and the temper with which we approach it. What is new, and the change makes itself felt as one reads this volume as a whole, is the feeling that Muir has reached a place of rest from which, with a new calmness and faith, he can survey the confusions that at one time were a source of so much anguish and despair. There are troubled and troubling poems in *The Voyage* but the volume seems to have been planned to open and close with strong affirmations: *The Return of the Greeks* at the beginning and *In Love for Long* at the end. In between is a variety of tone and content that indicates the spiritual and artistic freedom to which Muir has won through. The problem of evil is in the nature of things still an acute and necessary preoccupation; but whether it be a source of personal doubt and unease (as in *Sorrow*, *Comfort in Self-Despite* and *The Covenant*) or of a more philosophical, generalizing concern (*The Castle*, *The Window*, *The Fathers*), the prevailing tone of the volume is not represented by any of these poems. On a personal level, it is best represented by the more gentle, domestic, lyrical verse such as *On Seeing Two Lovers in the Street*, *Suburban Dream*, *Song* ('*Why should your face so please me*') and *For Ann Scott-Moncrieff*; and, on a philosophical level, by *Twice-Done*, *Once-Done*, *The Three Mirrors* and *The Myth*. The range of the new work is the proper outcome of Muir's growth as a man. He is not dominated by any one impulse or preoccupation as he tended to be in *Journeys and Places*; there is not the deliberateness, the determination to hold off and disavow evil that there was in the first part of *The Narrow Place*. The sense of freedom comes from the acceptance and the revolt having been made real for him. There will be times of appalled incredulousness at the death of innocence, as in *The Covenant*, and times when 'clarity' seems desperately difficult, as in *Sorrow*. But these moments assume their proper proportion against a deepening awareness that 'The in eternity written and hidden way' is real. The struggle is to make that awareness ever more real, through the imagination 'to gather an image whole' which will put us in touch with the ultimate synthesis of which *The Three Mirrors* speaks. That synthesis of good and evil is forever unattainable, but through 'clarity and love' we may eventually come to feel its reality and, as a consequence, peace.

For Muir, the truth of that ideal was – as it must be for anyone – simply given or, as *The Day* has it, 'allowed'. But the clarity with which he came to see it arose partly through the reflection upon and ordering of his past life from which *An Autobiography* arose. There is the closest relationship between the writing of that book, *The Three Mirrors* and *The Myth* ('My childhood all a myth'). For the first time in his poetry, Muir sets down his childhood with an objectivity that shows it in relation to the rest of his life, accepts it as being in a fundamental way the beginning and end of the road. That the power and beauty of these two poems is intimately bound up with the active remembering of *An Autobiography* is clear from Muir's article, 'Yesterday's mirror: Afterthoughts to an autobiography', which he wrote soon after completing it. He says in the article that it was only after finishing the book that he became fully aware that the 'three ways of seeing life . . . are all related in some way to childhood, positively or negatively'. His main metaphor in describing these three ways is identical to that of the poem, *The Three Mirrors*, and indeed the prose is virtually a paraphrase of the poem. Briefly, a man may look in the first mirror and see the unqualified triumph of greed and selfish illusion and the stifling of generosity and good will; in the second he may, remembering his childhood, see 'an indefeasible rightness beneath the wrongness of things' and life as an unceasing conflict between the two. He will sense that 'the rightness of human life has a deeper reality, a more fundamental appositeness, than the evil, as being more native to man'.[1] This is our normal view. In the third mirror, could he but look, he would see a world in which 'good and evil have their place legitimately'; in the words of the earlier, less successful treatment of the same idea, *The Trophy*, his vision would embrace 'king and rebel . . . irreconcilables, their treaty signed'. But vision indeed it is and denied to all but the greatest poets and mystics; and to them, too, except in their greatest moments.

It is interesting that in this article Muir explicitly compares such a vision with Nietzsche's idea of being beyond good and evil. So often in reviewing Muir's life and work, one has the feeling of his earlier experiences and thoughts being inadequate approximations to an ideal he had always been instinctively in search of. From the vantage point of *The Three Mirrors* and Muir's commentary in 'Yesterday's mirror', we can see that Nietzsche offered an escape from conflict that was inadequate in being fundamentally at odds with Muir's deepest but unacknowledged sense of reality. We might say of it, as he said himself of his conversion to Socialism at the age of twenty-one, that 'it was false in being earthly and nothing more'. It was bound to be displaced as he recovered his hold on life. For Muir now, to be beyond good and evil in Nietzsche's interpretation is to be cut off from one's own humanity; to accept it, on the other hand, as the characteristic power of the mystic, makes for a deeper humanity, a reaching out to life rather than a withdrawal.

In *The Three Mirrors* we encounter the familiar paradox of Muir's poetry: that a diction and imagery by now so familiar can be so urgently charged. It is not easy to demonstrate that urgency. 'The fenceless field', 'the slowly twisting vine', 'the hunting roads' and 'the quarry' of the first part; 'the house with its single tree', 'the little blade and leaf', 'the child at peace in his play' in the second, sound unremarkable enough in isolation. But there is a cumulative power in the way the phrases are deployed. Muir's handling of the short line is masterly throughout – flexible and responsive to shifts of feeling and perspective. The movement between the black view in the first mirror, the mixed, normal view in the second, and the visionary third, is precisely responsive to the feeling with which each section is charged: we move from the pitilessness of

> The mountain summits were sealed
> In incomprehensible wrath

to the sad inevitabilities of

> The crack ran over the floor,
> The child at peace in his play
> Changed as he passed through a door,
> Changed were the house and the tree,
> Changed the dead in the knoll,
> For locked in love and grief
> Good with evil lay.

to the inspired and inspiring imagining of

> If I could look I should see
> The world's house open wide,
> The million million rooms
> And the quick god everywhere
> Glowing at work and at rest,
> Tranquillity in the air,
> Peace of the humming looms
> Weaving from east to west,
> And you and myself there.

This mastery can be illustrated many times over from *The Voyage*. It is of a piece with that surer grasp of the meaning of the past to which the writing of *An Autobiography* led. Expanding his statement that all three views can be related to childhood, he says 'there is most of childhood in the third; and when I realised this a great number of forgotten impressions rose up in my mind. I remembered suddenly how right and fitting I had felt the world and everything in it to be when I was a child.'[2] This, we remember, was after the completion of the book. Those impressions do not make their way into the poetry; there is no increase in circumstantial detail in the poems that deal with childhood. The opposite is the case. There is a gain in symbolic intensity, an increased power in the use of generalizing poetic statement. The intimate interrelation of childhood vision and adult intuition is imagined with fresh immediacy. Muir's language seems possessed of an inner radiance answering to an irresistible conviction of life's underlying unity and expressing the more than earthly peace that it brings with it. *The Myth* draws a thread across from childhood to approaching old age and conjures forth a profound metaphysical unity. The simple signs of flower, wave and wood join to summon an unnameable beauty in which there is no distinction between seer and seen, the 'watchers' and the watched:

> My childhood all a myth
> Enacted in a distant isle;
> Time with his hourglass and his scythe
> Stood dreaming on the dial,
> And did not move the whole day long
> That immobility might save
> Continually the dying song,
> The flower, the falling wave.
> And at each corner of the wood
> In which I played the ancient play,
> Guarding the traditional day
> The faithful watchers stood.

After childhood had come the 'tragi-comedy' of youth and manhood. And

> Now past the prime
> I see this life contrived to stay
> With all its works of labouring time
> By time beguiled away.
> Consolidated flesh and bone
> And its designs grow halt and lame;
> Unshakeable arise alone
> The reverie and the name.
> And at each border of the land,
> Like monuments a deluge leaves,
> Guarding the invisible sheaves
> The risen watchers stand.

This is Muir's most perfect, most mature expression of his intuitions about childhood. From the first poem in the collected edition, *Childhood*, he had been acutely responsive to the mystery of his 'seven years Eden' ('Yesterday's mirror'). But the difference between that early venture and *The Myth* is fundamental. *Childhood* recreated the tranquillity and security of that state, but it had nothing to say of its relations to adult life. *The Myth* reinterprets that tranquillity as one emanation of a spirit that will in the course of life undergo the transformations of experience while remaining essentially itself. It is in this sense that the child has the true vision of the world and that the mystic's gift of seeing into that third mirror attests its truth. *The Myth* does not express or illustrate the 'deep confederacy' of good and evil and the deep familiarity of childhood and adult vision. That is beyond language. Instead, the poem creates, powerfully persuades us of, the potentiality of such a vision.

The power, then, of *The Three Mirrors* and *The Myth* is one of spiritual clarity and imaginative power. The final section of each of these poems takes on that most difficult and elusive of tasks: the creation of a spiritual reality that *can* only be imagined and that, for a gauge of its authenticity, we can refer to nothing beyond itself. For that we can only look into ourselves. Otherwise we are thrown back on those genuine but inadequate complimentary words like 'intensity' and 'imaginative conviction', indeed 'authenticity'. Nonetheless, if we need to convince ourselves that such compliments are warranted, there is the evidence of the rest of the 1946 volume. The inner assurance and balance of these two poems is reflected in the way the operation of evil is evoked in others. I would guess that the nearer Muir came to such an inner balance, the more imaginatively rich was the poetic result. So that even when, as in *The Window*, he writes of the activating of evil, there arises a sense of possible redemption through the fineness of the imagining. (*Merlin* was an earlier example of such a poem). *The Window* describes a catastrophic fracture in the 'changeless ground' of these opening lines:

> Within the great wall's perfect round
> Bird, beast and child serenely grew
> In endless change on changeless ground
> That in a single pattern bound
> The old perfection and the new.

The serenity and wholeness of the state Muir describes is called up in this finely controlled verse. It is the by now familiar evocation of Eden, of innocence. Despite the familiarity, this poem has the stamp of the deepest knowledge made into metaphor. We forget that it *is* metaphor. The serenity and changelessness is displaced by menace and uncertainty. We can say that the images record the end of childhood, the end of innocence, the discovery of corruption within the apparently perfect and dependable, the loss of traditional certitudes, as well as a personal sense of loss and fear. The latter part of the poem contains, or rather condenses, all these meanings, but the more potently for being limited to none of them:

> Then turning towards you I beheld
> The wrinkle writhe across your brow,
> And felt time's cap clapped on my head,
> And all within the enclosure now,
> Light leaf and smiling flower, was false,
> The great wall breached, the garden dead.
>
> Across the towering window fled
> Disasters, victories, festivals.

It would be sentimental and a misrepresentation of what I have called Muir's inner assurance to think of it as leading to simple joy, to a fading away of the sense of evil and the elimination of conflict. Conflict is fundamental, inescapable; what is not constant is the temper with which we view it. The gain from Muir's confidence in the 'risen watchers' 'at each border of the land' is felt as an increase in imaginative clarity. Generally, the equanimity of *The Day* and the unanxious reflectiveness of *The Myth* enable him to see the problem of evil more frequently with that secure objectivity that he had early on noticed as the hallmark of great art. Both *The Castle* and *The Fathers* are achievements of this kind.

The Castle is a much anthologized piece and so probably as well known as any of Muir's poems. But to see it in the context of his work as a whole is to know more clearly what kind of achievement it is. I think we can see how the preoccupations and representative imagery of much of his early work have in this poem been transmuted in the light of that greater clarity which his work in this volume displays overall. In his early novel of the Reformation, *The Three Brothers*, the main character, David – obviously modelled on Muir himself, though he has very little reality as a separate creation – is fascinated and appalled by the murder of Cardinal Beaton: his father, coming home one night with the news, tells him of the Cardinal apparently safe and strongly guarded within a sturdy castle, beyond reach except through an inconspicuous little gate, 'a wee thing that ye would hardly notice, a weak, wicked-looking, wee gate'. Although the story does not take on the symbolic resonance that Muir may have intended for it (the novel was not his métier) it is clearly one more expression of that preoccupation with the insidiousness of evil and the helplessness of individuals that marks so much of his work. Its harshest, least relenting expression in his poetry is probably the early *Betrayal* where time 'slays her (beauty) with invisible hands/And inly wastes her flesh away'. Evil tangible but beyond control, terrifyingly visible in its effects but pointless, incomprehensible; Muir's imagination was tortured by its manifestations in the last illnesses of his brothers. In *An Autobiography*, we remember, he speaks, describing his brother Willie's last illness, of 'that invisible, deadly, and yet peaceable enemy quietly working beyond our reach'.

The Castle was first published in 1945 when Muir was fifty-eight. He had said in *An Autobiography* that the years in Glasgow 'seemed like a heap of dismal rubbish' that he had to climb out of and that the 'rubbish still encumbered me for a long time with post-mortem persistence'. Just how persistent in their effect were those years can be felt in this poem. But of course they have by now come under imaginative control, so that though the poem obviously draws upon those early, dreadful experiences of the impersonality of evil in its physical shape, they have become assimilated within a picture that gives them a kind of logic. For the watchers in *The Castle* are not innocent victims, beauty haplessly awaiting the knife. Their security has bred complacency, a too ready trust in the comfortable depths of their stronghold. The confident and generous feeling, the expansive ease of summer, is in the second stanza:

> For what, we thought, had we to fear
> With our arms and provender, load on load,

> Our towering battlements, tier on tier,
> And friendly allies drawing near
> On every leafy summer road.

When the unthinkable happens it has not in any way been predicted; it is no matter of the enemy climbing walls, securing footholds. It is simple, deadly, almost, indeed, ridiculous. The playing with words here is neither indulgent nor childish; it is a sickly indication of that deadly simplicity.

> There was a little private gate,
> A little wicked wicket gate.
> The wizened warder let them through.

It is a 'shameful tale'. But the shame has nothing to do with the insidiousness of the enemy. It has to do with slothful ease and delusion – the delusion that evil can be defeated by external means. It cannot; the price of security is watchfulness and self-knowledge. These men ignore the unignorable, the enemy within the gates, and they pay their price. In the bathos of the conclusion is the unrecognized truth of the matter. Theirs is the ingenuousness of childhood but without childhood's excuse that it could not know the real enemy and that the arms to fight it with were within:

> How can this shameful tale be told?
> I will maintain until my death
> We could do nothing, being sold;
> Our only enemy was gold,
> And we had no arms to fight it with.

In *The Castle*, then, the imagery that once expressed a private anguish now does service for a fundamentally altered view of life. There has been no reduction in the activity of evil. What has changed is Muir's view of man's relation to it. He had said that he could recognize 'one or two stages' in the 'fable': 'the age of innocence and the fall and all the dramatic consequences which issue from the fall'. An important aspect of the advance in imaginative clarity that I have stressed as the outstanding feature of this volume is the conspicuousness of these two stages; which is to say that Muir's belief in them has deepened and his power to give them poetic reality has increased. The men of *The Castle* idle in false innocence, avoidable immaturity. In *The Fathers* 'we' suffer not from lack of self-knowledge but from too much. 'All these (stages), lie behind experience, not on its surface; they are not historical events; they are stages in the fable' (p. 49). The distinction of *The Fathers* is that it imagines a stage in the fable that is more real than any historical event. The fall is the protagonist of this poem, a permanent active presence in men's minds, calling them back to themselves when they strain for self-forgetfulness, as inevitable as life itself. These men – 'we' – are in some ways like those of *The Castle*. They were at ease, with apparently nothing to fear; these have 'careless brows' and their blood courses through 'unhurried veins'. The difference is that the fathers cannot be put aside; complacency cannot disguise their presence. However much we try to lose ourselves in good, healthy living we cannot continue to deceive ourselves; it is not in us to do so.

> Archaic fevers shake
> Our healthy flesh and blood
> Plumped in the passing day
> And fed with pleasant food.
> The fathers' anger and ache
> Will not, will not away
> And leave the living alone,
> But on our careless brows
> Faintly their furrows engrave
> Like veinings in a stone,
> Breathe in the sunny house
> Nightmare of blackened bone,
> Cellar and choking cave.

In this disturbing section we have an example of Muir's poetic imagination at its most distinctive, touching on present and past, conscious and unconscious, the willed and the unwilled, the new and archaic. All are brought into relation in a way that expresses their deep and necessary interdependence: this is what being human means. In these few lines we move from the recognizable region of ordinary, material, forgetful living – the feeling of sickliness and surfeit in the mutually echoing 'plumped' and 'pleasant' immediately qualifying the description of our flesh and blood as healthy – through the frustration of impotence ('will not, will not away') to the nightmare imagery of the archaic fevers themselves. It is the irresistible advance of the past into the present that we are watching in this poem – how sinisterly apt is the word 'faintly', with its normal suggestion of delicacy coming sharply up against the insidiousness of the implication it is made to carry here. This is the world that awaits the children of Muir's earlier poem about the pain of maturity, *The Gate*. They in their innocence were 'cherished with gentle hands' by guardians who

> in grave play put on a childish mask
> Over their tell-tale faces, as in shame
> For the rich food that plumped their lusty bodies

But while in that poem the journey from innocence into experience was conceived as pure loss, the exchange of security for shame and self-indulgence, in *The Fathers* the picture is subtler, more comprehensive. Our 'healthy flesh and blood' is the outward symbol of a life lived, or an attempt to live life, in a continuous present, 'the passing day'. This middle part of the poem records the inevitable failure and the frustration of the attempt. But the final part is in a different mood: we must accept the anger and the ache as we must accept everything else in our inheritance. We have no choice. With the realization, a surprising calm:

> We hold our fathers' trust,
> Wrong, riches, sorrow and all
> Until they topple and fall,
> And fallen let in the day.

In *The Fathers*, then, Muir accepts Original Sin: these fathers belong to no time or place. They are as much of the present as the past, a condition of existence, as elemental as the fighting shadows of *Then*. They are also as sad and as sinister. The anger and the ache of *The Fathers* would seem, in its inexorable, tenacious persistence, to be of a piece with that unassuageable Wrath which Muir had identified as the common element in Calvinism and Communism. So that while it is a poem for all time, calling us back from the temptation to immerse ourselves in the passing day, in the conception of evil there is something desperately gloomy and nightmarish. There is, I think, no indication in the poem that Muir dissociates himself from it: it belongs more to the visions of nameless terrors that we find in his later volume, *The Labyrinth*, than it does to his eventual reading of the place of evil in human life.

I have said that *The Myth* and *The Three Mirrors* come out of a new equanimity, a confidence that there is a deep confederacy of good and evil, even though we can for the most part do no more than remind ourselves that it is occasionally within men's power to glimpse it. But that confidence, though hard-won and cherished, is precarious. In our day-to-day living the promise of those two poems may seem too shadowy and remote to be of any use; all too often the world will be too much with us. And then the world is simply out of joint, opaque. In *The Covenant* and *Sorrow*, the exulting aspiration of *The Three Mirrors* – 'evil and good/Standing side by side/In the ever standing wood' – has thinned into an acceptance of this eternal synthesis as a mere theory; a theory, moreover, that in *Sorrow* he rejects. Earnestly in that poem, he insists that he will learn from sorrow 'Wealth joy would toss away'; in other words, not see them in the normal everyday way as opposites but as necessary aspects of our human nature bringing their peculiar good. By the time of *One Foot in Eden* (1956) and his deepening knowledge of the Incarnation, such a view will be possible. But now, it is not – for all the will to accept that it is:

> If it were only so . . .
> But right and left I find
> Sorrow, sorrow,
> And cannot be resigned,
> Knowing that we were made

By joy to drive joy's trade
And not to waver to and fro,
But quickly go.

Muir has been compared to Herbert. In an earlier age the doubts and
unease would have been declared before God and, as with Herbert,
solace gained through supplication and prayer. Here, though, we feel
God by His absence. Muir wrestles with the inadequacy of his faith, his
failure to believe deeply enough and his feelings can go nowhere but
abortively back into himself. *Sorrow* arises from a despairing conflict
between the way he wants to see life and the way he actually does
see it. *The Covenant* expresses an appalled dismay at the fate of
'innocence, innocence past defence or cost'; just as it is impossible to see
how we can 'wring from sorrow's pay/Wealth joy would toss away', so
in this poem there is no hint that the loss can be meaningful in the way
promised in *The Three Mirrors*.

> What jealousy, what rage could overwhelm
> The golden lion and lamb and vault a grave
> For innocence, innocence past defence or cost?[3]

The anguish of these poems is real enough but they are equalled in
conviction by others with a more resigned and hopeful attitude to
experience. And this is what we should expect in a poet who, if he cannot
himself look into that third mirror, at least believes in its reality, 'Teach
me to believe, for to believe's to be', he asks in *Twice-Done, Once-Done*;
and this will surely be the prayer of any 'believer'. A sense of
inadequacy, of backsliding, of positive aberration – these are some of
the impelling emotions of Herbert's poetry, as are the sense of joy,
gratitude and ease in the presence of a God who can forgive them. Faith
need not narrow the emotional range of poetry and we would expect
Muir's 'secular' faith to issue in a variety of tone and gesture similar to
that of Herbert. The frustration of *Sorrow* and the melancholy
alienation of *Dejection* (a return of the 'enemy indifference') are no
doubt less supportable than Herbert's consciousness of ingratitude or
neglected duty. Herbert's penitence is expressed before a Christian God;
Muir looks over an abyss. On the other hand, when it is given to him to
return to his 'solidest foundation', he can speak of failure and of making
amends, of self-disgust and fresh aspiration, with a sweetness worthy of
Herbert himself:

Comfort in Self-Despite

When in revulsion I detest myself
Thus heartily, myself with myself appal,
And in this mortal rubbish delve and delve,
A dustman damned – perhaps the original

Virtue I'd thought so snugly buried so
May yet be found, else never to be found,

> And thus exhumed into the light may grow
> After this cruel harrowing of the ground.
>
> For as when I have spoken spitefully
> Of this or that friend, piling ill on ill,
> Remembrance cleans his image and I see
> The pure and touching good no taunt could kill,
>
> So I may yet recover by this bad
> Research that good I scarcely dreamt I had.

We must feel the poignancy of this the more keenly for knowing the spiritual deserts that have been crossed to reach this point. That is true, too, of the lyrics in this volume – *Song* ('*Why should your face so please me*') stands comparison with the exquisite love poems of *The Narrow Place*. *The Voyage* concludes with three more beautiful lyrics (*A Birthday*, *All We* and *In Love for Long*) in which Muir recognizes that the journey, or a certain kind of journey, is complete, and expresses his gratitude for the peace he has been granted. The nature of the peace is most fully expressed in the final poem, *In Love for Long*. Yet to speak of expression might be misleading since it is of the essence of this peace that it is beyond understanding, beyond full utterance. Story, emblem, image – all are contrivances for laying hold on the ineffable:

> I've been in love for long
> With what I cannot tell
> And will contrive a song
> For the intangible
> That has no mould or shape,
> From which there's no escape.

In Love for Long deliberately affirms the unutterable, glancing at meanings beyond expression, affirming through negatives and finally through emblem:

> This love a moment known
> For what I do not know
> And in a moment gone
> Is like the happy doe
> That keeps its perfect laws
> Between the tiger's paws
> And vindicates its cause.

It would be wrong to say that good and evil are reconciled here in an encompassing vision; rather, the poem celebrates the joy that is still to be found despite the lack of such a vision. Sorrow and suffering are not extinguished, not reconstituted by 'this happy, happy love'. Indeed, this love

> Is seized with crying sorrows,
> Crushed beneath and above

Between todays and morrows;
A little paradise
Held in the world's vice.

The memorable closing couplet of this stanza catches the character of
the joy as precisely as one could hope. The rare pun, on 'vice', suggests
the surrounding evil and the stubbornness of its hold on life; but the
following stanza makes it clear that evil has its limits. Ultimately there is
a stasis within which the spirit thrives and rejoices:

And there it is content
And careless as a child,
And in imprisonment
Flourishes sweet and wild;
In wrong, beyond wrong,
All the world's day long.

Many of the motifs and recurring images of Muir's poems are drawn
into this accommodation of the facts of evil. There is the old valuing of
childhood ('all a myth') as the truest measure of our spiritual wholeness;
there is the notion of a permanent, irrefrangible resistance, a natural
faith before the omnipresent corruption – 'sole at the house's heart,
Penelope'; there are echoes of those poems in which Muir had yearned
for the experience of just such a stillness and joy as he celebrates here, a
yearning that yielded the image of Merlin 'deep in the diamond of the
day', the image of the 'prize/that far within the maze serenely lies', the
image of the 'strange quarry you scarcely thought you sought' (*The
Question*). None of Muir's poems is more affirmative than this. It is one
of those poems, rare surely in any poet, where the calm of the spirit
seems effortlessly to create its own voice, where every phrase seems the
right one in the right place:

It cannot part from me;
A breath, yet as still
As the established hill.

In none of Muir's poems, in the event, is the word 'contrive' less apt.
'Now', in the words of *A Birthday*,

that I can discern
It whole or almost whole,
Acceptance and gratitude
Like travellers return
And stand where first they stood.

There is never a trace of irony or self-consciousness in the way he uses
words such as 'gratitude', 'constancy', 'bliss', 'paradise'. When they
occur they do so to call up realities that have been *achieved*. Behind the

'acceptance and gratitude' of *A Birthday*, the 'constancy' of *In Love for Long*, the 'pure and touching good' of *Comfort in Self-Despite*, is the record of a spirit for whom these qualities have at one time or another been called severely in doubt. One thinks of Muir's poems at times as a continuous meditation, a continuous effort to fix his whole being on a still centre of life and in so doing bring the chaotic whirl of affairs into intelligible relation with it. Many of the poems record the difficulty and the frustration; *In Love for Long* celebrates an arrival.

That 'arrival' is a figure of speech. In *The Return of the Greeks* it is a fact. Maybe it is a happy coincidence that these two poems respectively close and open the 1946 volume. Whether accidentally or deliberately it is significant that they do. It is that still centre of life which the returning Greek soldiers must learn to know again. The poems in *The Voyage* record Muir's own return to such a centre, to a place where the 'faithful watchers' of his childhood rise again to round out and bless the arrival at old age. For the Greek soldiers too it is a return to 'a childish past'. Their return is, as it were, a metaphor for Muir's own and his for theirs. 'My childhood all a myth', he had said; *The Return of the Greeks* re-enacts that myth, drawing its strength from Muir's own struggle but composing a picture in which there is no trace of the personal story. It is a perfect example of that art which 'raises no echo in our ordinary subjective emotions', yet nonetheless makes its enduring connection with our lives. Willa Muir says in *Belonging* that 'the European wartime flavour can be found in Edwin's poems of these years, such as *The Refugees* or *The Escape*, even *The Return of the Greeks* who were an image of the homeless soldiers who turned up in Edinburgh with their terrible stories.'[4] Willa Muir's closeness to the poet no doubt justifies the word 'flavour'; but with *The Return of the Greeks* it is precisely its lack of anything so limiting, so occasional, that partly accounts for its success. It is an astonishingly assured and moving use of myth. Indeed to employ the word 'use' here is to misrepresent the quality of the assurance. We don't have the sense of a deliberate recourse to the currency of the educated European mind, to a source of analogy and comparison. Instead we sense the fusion hinted at in the last stanza of *Twice-Done, Once-Done*:

> For first and last is every way,
>   And first and last each soul,
> And first and last the passing day,
>   And first and last the goal.

In *The Return of the Greeks* these warriors returning from the siege of Troy bemused and frankly disappointed at the flat ordinariness of their homelands are soldiers of any time, any war. The key figure is of course Penelope. She in her tower speaks for a quality of life that is temporarily beyond the understanding of the returning warriors. The intensity of their action at Troy –

Reading the wall of Troy
Ten years without a change
Was such intense employ

– should, they feel, have been acknowledged by some conspicuous, some dramatic change in the contours of their homeland and the lives of those they left behind. The triteness, the strangeness, the banality are however in them; their lives around Troy have diminished their awareness of what their lives in peace can be: 'the peace, the parcelled ground'. It seems a dismissive description. But Penelope knows that they will rediscover the proper values of their lives when they have got over the hesitancies of their initial steps. She

saw within an hour
Each man to his wife go,
Hesitant, sure and slow:
She, alone in her tower.

Penelope looks 'down upon the show'. From her tower – frequently in Muir the point from which to look at life whole (see, for instance, *The Window*) – she surveys a typical warriors' return and is serene in her knowledge of its outcome.

This is surely Muir at his best. Stories are our major access to the 'fable' and in choosing to compose within the ancient legend of the Trojan war Muir avoids the distractions that attend a contemporary setting and at the same time represents to us the deeper realities of warfare in any age. The soldiers are presented sympathetically; the 'intense employ' from which they have come is invigorating, but it is narrowing too. The singlemindedness has been a condition of survival and a source of dignity but it has cut them off from quieter and more real joys:

How could they understand
Space empty on every hand
And the hillocks squat and low?

Hence they have to relearn the message of these hillocks,

a childish scene
Embosomed in the past,
    *   *   *
A child's preoccupied scene.

'Childish' is of course used here in no patronizing or whimsical manner. The 'preoccupation' of the child allows no consciousness of a fracture of past and present, no questioning of the meaning of experience:

never a change!
The past and the present bound

In one oblivious round
Past thinking trite and strange.

But of course the soldiers are not returning, uncomprehending, to a merely ideal childhood. They have to learn to understand and love a 'triteness' that only their long absence makes them see as 'strange'. The peace they cannot understand is immemorial and – surely this is the burden of the poem – 'past thinking trite and strange'. The 'fable' inheres in 'the peace, the parcelled ground'. Those for whom they are daily familiar and unquestioned are not conscious of the fable, though it is no less real for that. It is 'past thinking'. The show that Penelope looks down upon is, one sees, by the very word, an embodying of a recurrent movement in human affairs: it is given to us every so often to arrive at the 'solidest basis' of ourselves though we may be bewildered when we do. Mostly we are like the returning soldiers, engaged in 'business', intense activity that allows us to forget or ignore the grounds of our existence. The poem, still and contemplative within its narrative form, is a profound act of faith: faith in the capacity of human beings to recover their sense of those grounds. The men go to their wives, both 'hesitant' and 'sure'. The paradox is resolved when we realize that the basis of the eventual reconciliation is the inherent capacity for recovery. It may be slow, surrounded by doubt and bewilderment, but its sureness is in human nature itself.

The pressure on Muir's imagination was to produce narratives and constructions that would 'gather an image whole' (*Reading in Wartime*), that would give the timeless a shape within time. When he is successful the poem is an intimation of the 'fable'. Both *The Return of the Greeks* and *The Return of Odysseus* are such intimations, each presenting a narrative within which one has the sense of 'the miscellaneous dross of experience' having fallen away. What is revealed is an indestructible core – a core obscured by that dross in the messy continuity of everyday life. The passions that are an indissociable aspect of that continuity are stilled, leaving an image of the whole suffused by what one can only call love – a love springing from faith. Without being in any strong way pictorial, Muir's best narratives often have the quality of a series of images somehow arrested and held up for our contemplation. These images do not confront us with the immediacy of felt experience. Any personal experience lies well behind the images; the charge they carry sends us back into ourselves, there to discover our relation to the subject of the poem.

Chapter 7

The Journey Back

Muir's essay, 'The natural man and the political man', was first published in a literary magazine, *New Writing and Daylight*, in 1942. Looking back on it nearly twenty years later, John Lehmann described it as 'one of the most remarkable I ever published – in fact one of the most important published anywhere during the war'.[1] His enthusiasm was justified. That essay, like almost everything else in the 1949 collection, *Essays on Literature and Society*, possesses the pre-eminent virtues of Muir's mature prose writing. In some ways it is suggestive of T. S. Eliot at his best: each essay is concise, lucid, illuminating, its forte the trenchant generalization rather than the prolonged analysis. We are persuaded as we read that the generalized perceptions about literature, politics and society have arisen from and distil the results of a wealth of observation and experience. And, of equal importance, they stand in the closest relation to his own poetic art. This volume, his best collection of critical essays, was published in the same year as *The Labyrinth*, the collection of poems which Muir felt – rightly, I think – was 'the best I have done yet'. (8 September 1948) T. S. Eliot said of the best of his own critical work that it had 'consisted of essays on poets and critics who have influenced me . . . it is a by-product of the thinking that went into the formation of my own verse'.[2] Broadly, though he would have expressed it differently, that was true of Muir. In whatever he wrote, whether criticism, autobiography, social comment, or poetry, his writings are at one with each other in this central respect: that they all bear upon what he saw as man's inevitable calling in life – to know himself. And this is not at all incompatible with giving an honest account of other men's work. Only, indeed, by reckoning as honestly as he can with the work of others can a man decide wherein they have something out of the ordinary to offer us and to offer himself as a writer. In reading Muir's criticism I am reminded of D. H. Lawrence's description of the good critic and the way he goes to work:

He must be a man of force and complexity . . . emotionally alive in every fibre, intellectually capable . . . and skilful in essential logic, and then morally very honest. . . . We judge a work of art by its effect on our sincere and vital emotion. And a man who is emotionally educated is rare as a phoenix. The more scholastically educated a man is generally, the more he is an emotional boor.[3]

Muir passes the tests of these sentences. Indeed, one senses that his lack of formal education might have been an advantage since it left him more free to know and respect his 'sincere and vital emotion'. What is so pertinent in Lawrence's view is the acceptance of a critic's natural gift, of the necessity of a natural depth of character. I imagine that by 'skilful in essential logic' Lawrence intends the capacity to see and make clear the natural relation between one form of experience and another. (The obvious example in his own criticism is in the essay on Galsworthy from which those sentences come: he makes the connection between a failure in morality, in imaginative insight and in artistic achievement.) Muir's best criticism shows him to have this power. Whether commenting on the ballads, on the writings of Hemingway or Huxley or indeed of Lawrence himself, he exercises an acute sense of their deep relations with other realms of experience. To use a phrase of his own, he 'divines the connected relations' between one part of life and another. The job of the critic, as of the poet, is to clarify those relations – a moral business since it entails judgements from one's 'sincere and vital emotion'. Like Lawrence, Muir is impatient with 'critical twiddle-twaddle, all this pseudo-scientific classifying and analysing' (D.H.L.) because it ignores the larger questions.

Lawrence says, too, that 'a good critic should give his reader a few standards to go by' and instances Sainte-Beuve as 'setting up the standard of "the good man"'. Muir's standards arise from those qualities that should in Lawrence's eyes make him a good critic: they flow naturally from a trust in his vital feeling: judgement with him is, we feel at every turn, intimately a matter of trust in native intuition, of experience illuminated through intuition and of intuition made good through experience. He has, again in Lawrence's terms, 'the courage to admit what he feels, as well as the flexibility to know what he feels'. That being so – and consistently so – there is a vital, reciprocal relation, an 'essential logic' binding the prose writings and the poetry. Through the prose, Muir reaches out to and describes whatever seems to his 'vital feeling' to be most real, most human. In so doing he clarifies what is most real both for us and for himself. In other words, as surely with every good critic who is also a poet, there is a reciprocal relation between the discursive work and the 'creative', the interest of this relation for the reader being the insight it gives him into the integral nature of the life of the mind. The more powerful and controlled that mind, the more consistent the one form of writing with the other. The 1949 volumes – one of prose, the other of poetry – display such a consistency.

The unity of such essays as 'The natural man and the political man', 'Oswald Spengler', 'The political view of literature' and 'The decline of the novel' is that they arise from and articulate Muir's reading of the 'image of modern man' as it may be found in art, in political systems, and attitudes towards religion and the life of the imagination. Broadly, this reading suggests that the idea of inner conflict as a central principle of human life has given way to that of a continuous development and improvement in man's estate; that, in consequence, the 'historical view', banishing the natural belief in a transcendent reality, is at odds with the 'religious view' that depends on it; that, in short, we are witnessing an impoverishment in our conception of human nature that is both reflected in and furthered by much of the art of the time. There is an obvious consistency between these views and the character of Muir's poetry at any stage. 'To seek the meaning of human life in itself is to seek its meaning in time; and the conception of life which prevails today is a conception of life purely in time' ('The decline of the novel'). Like everything else in these essays, such a statement is not an opinion; its truth has been known on the pulses. In this instance, it comes as part of an answer to a question about art and normal life:

Is there any universal mark by which we can recognise a conception of human life that is complete and in a high sense normal to mankind? I shall hazard the assertion that all such conceptions postulate a transcendent reality and recognize man's relation to it, and that human life must always stop short of meaning if we seek its meaning merely in itself.[4]

The particular essay explores the value of such a formulation in considering the relationship between the history of the novel and changes in the order of thought and belief from which it arises. But behind it, as we can see well enough, is another history: Muir's own creative endeavour to arrive at a description of the 'normal'. In the forties he had through his own poetry finally vindicated what intuitively he had always known: that in the imagination lies the mysterious power of calling up a transcendent reality and that it is only in the imagination that it can be known. What is even more important to the critical work – and it is, I think, not at all to be readily expected of a modern critic that he should make so unreserved and confident an assertion as the one quoted – is that such a discovery was more than personal; that, in giving form to what was timeless in one man's experience, his own art confirmed the naturalness of the timeless in all good art.

From so clear and sure a basis, then, Muir is able to go decisively to the centre of such alternative readings of human life as that of Spengler. The inhumanity of Spengler's view of history, his reduction of man to a mere beast of prey, is set sharply against a view that reminds us of all that Spengler's universe omits and leaves us in no doubt about the essential connection between the 'historical view' and the basis of Nazism. Spengler is not anymore a fashion; the particular dismissal is no longer necessary. But it is the virtue of Muir's work that the generalizations within which he reviews the particular case continue to remind and challenge us. As he says in 'The natural man and the political man': 'The idea of man current at any one time is not a homogeneous one; old conceptions linger on; new ones tentatively appear.'[5] Spengler is, as it were, one passing manifestation of a strong current in modern feeling. And just as we can re-read that essay with profit because in it Muir arrests the current and leads us firmly towards good judgement, so in

'The political view of literature', the writing as surely survives its occasion. That essay is a review of David Daiches's book, *The Novel and the Modern World*. Muir uses it to censure some contemporary misreadings of the nature of literature of which he sees that book to be typical. The kind of misreading that the book exemplifies and the kind of objection that Muir brings to it are evident in the case of T. S. Eliot. Eliot's Anglicanism is interpreted in the book as having been adopted 'to compensate him for his wounded sense of order'. 'The difficulty of dealing with criticism of this kind', says Muir, 'is that it entirely ignores the nature of the things it is treating.' His defence of Eliot concludes with a judgement that in its characteristic mixture of firmness and lucidity well represents the tone of this whole volume. Muir is never exaggeratedly severe; he does not need to be:

Words like 'compensation' are two-edged; Mr Daiches' interpretation of Mr Eliot's experience may be a compensation for not understanding it. The first condition of any genuine criticism of Mr Eliot's religion is that it should be understood; the critic may then decide that it contains truth or contains nothing but error; but he is not entitled to transform it into something else and then assess it as something else. I do not know whether Mr Daiches would deny that there have been men who have been genuinely religious in the past and that there may be men who are genuinely religious now; the interpretative method of criticism, which deprives everything of its individuality, changing it into something without individuality, can become so strange that one does not know what to expect.[6]

It is not the untruthfulness but the 'inadequacy' of such a view that troubles Muir. (His criticism seems to warrant his use of this word more than Matthew Arnold's does: it springs from a clearer understanding of the nature of art and its relation to society.) As if, obliquely, commenting on its inadequacy as an account of his own art, he points out that the notion of the best modern literature as a variety of 'adjustments' to a transitional society can hardly do justice to Proust. It can hardly be an adequate term for the experience described by Proust in *Le Temps Retrouvé*, which drove him to devote the rest of his life to the resuscitation of the 'Eternal Man'. The enduring value of Muir's argument here is that it is literary criticism of a central kind: implicitly it is part of a critique of contemporary values. The objection, developed in other essays in this volume and given point throughout Muir's work, is to a devaluing of imaginative experience. Difficult though it may be to trace the tendency to its source, 'this assumption is founded ultimately upon some such hypothesis as dialectical materialism which simplifies everything on a vast scale'. I think Muir saw that such a simplification is deeply attractive in one sense: it offers a prospect of control, of understanding a fearsomely complicated world. It is deeply unattractive, on the other hand, because such an understanding must be at the expense of those mysteries that traditionally art exists to serve. It produces the illusion of control and understanding, offers a coherence resting on a misrepresentation of human nature. It is perhaps the most powerful distortion to which modern men are prone, whether they live in East or West. For just as Fielding or Jane Austen 'lived in an order in which everybody possessed without thinking about it much the feeling for a permanence above the permanence of one human existence', so modern men are subject to this simplification even when they are unaware of its actions or its origins.

This is the burden of the outstanding essay, 'The natural man and the political man' and it is the reason why it still has so much to say to us. For Muir the 'new species of the natural man' departs radically from the natural man of religion in that while the latter has need of regeneration, the new man is capable only of indefinite improvement. Traditionally, man was not regarded as 'human in the complete sense until he put on the spiritual man' and the inescapable condition of human life was 'a moral struggle in the centre of the individual'. To Dante, Shakespeare, Milton, Pascal, Balzac and Tolstoy, such a struggle was axiomatic. But lately, 'for the separate autonomous drama of mankind we have gradually substituted a natural process'. 'The result has been a reduction of the image of man, who has become simpler, more temporal, more realistic and more insignificant.' What particularly engages Muir in this essay and remains so relevant to our own day is the political implications of such a reduction. With the stress on the practicability of continuous all-round improvement – Darwin's idea of evolution applied to the individual – there have, in Muir's eyes, followed major political consequences: if man's life was a development to be seen not in moral and religious but in political and sociological terms, then such a conception was 'bound to lead to the conclusion that this development could be controlled, and that human life could be conditioned to a great extent, given the power and the equipment'. The reduction of man is a matter of ignoring the fact of his inner life, of seeing him purely in environmental terms, responsive 'in a more or less calculable way to certain things such as encouragement, suggestion, the carefully thought out system which is called propaganda, intimidation, display, rubber truncheons and in general all the varieties of greed and fear'.[7] What is particularly impressive about this essay is its breadth: Muir understands that when the natural man becomes the political man, he does so in the direction of either Communism or Fascism, to both of which the inward struggle of the individual is irrelevant. But he also sees the phenomenon he is describing as more pervasive than this would suggest. Broadly, Muir accepts Denis Saurat's generalization, tracing 'the graph of the modern fall of man': that French writers of the seventeenth century exalted reason, the nineteenth-century Romantics emotion, and certain contemporary writers sensation. He tests this generalization in the comparison between Dickens and Hemingway that I quoted earlier and in brief analyses of the work of Aldous Huxley, Henri de Montherlant and D. H. Lawrence. He acknowledges the genius of the last two and because they are great writers sees it as part of their value to us that 'they draw with exceptional honesty the consequences of a belief in the natural man'. I can do no more here than offer this inadequate sketch of the essay but I think it indicates its breadth of implication. Its rareness is a matter of integrity – if we can recover something of the fading resonance of that word: that it offers to reinstate a *whole* image of man and succeeds through analysis and persuasion. It is certainly a text for today in all sorts of ways. The loss of the notion of an inward struggle and thus of the primacy of the individual has, as Muir sees it, been displaced by a religion of development. Its first article is 'the primacy of things, and it finds its fulfilment in the theory that men can be conditioned by things'. I cannot pursue the continuous implications of all this but we do not have to look far, for instance, to see them in the fields of educational planning, sexual mores and political debate. In education, successive improvements in environment and opportunity continue to fail to produce the millennium to which it so recently seemed the key: so little were the will and nature of the individual child regarded and so much hope invested in the power of better and better provision to mould him, that bewilderment and cynicism are inevitable. With 'sexual behaviour', the very term suggests the character of the reduction suffered in the traditional language of passion and conflict: on the one hand the imagery of the age advertises the diminishing capacity to see sexuality as an element that must in the nature of things be related to 'a moral struggle in the centre of the individual'. On the other hand, it promises this attenuated version of sexuality as a birthright and a guarantee of happiness. (This is one definition of pornography and one way of registering the objection to it. Pornography pretends to be the real and is in fact only its poor relation.) In political debate, the reduction is startlingly obvious and increasingly more pronounced. The 'primacy of things' is axiomatic: man has become economic man and the language of politics consequently impoverished. Here the doctrine of continuous material improvement issuing in general fulfilment has run into the ground: the doctrine is untrue but the conventional wisdom and the language that goes with it makes it almost impossible to admit the truth. When a politician invites the electorate to consider the folly of paying ourselves more than we can afford, he has no other conception of the good life with which to suggest a perspective and an alternative.

It would not be difficult to draw out the further implications of Muir's essay in other directions – in various kinds of modern art, for instance. But I hope I have suggested what a fertile source it is, how suggestive its generalizations remain almost forty years on. I have already suggested in my earlier discussion of *The Combat* how the essay can help us to understand the basis of Muir's view of human life and the character of that poem. And, indeed, it would make an excellent preface to *The Labyrinth*. For, like *The Combat*, many of the poems in that volume challenge the reduction in the image of man that is the theme of the essay. Many of them were written in 1947, the year before the Communist putsch in Czechoslovakia. But others are from the year of the putsch itself and contain within them Muir's response to the events of the period. The penultimate chapter of *An Autobiography* – 'Prague Again' – is an account of that time. After the 'revolution' men became, in the familiar course of these things, 'suspicious even of their friends' and Muir found himself lecturing students at Prague University in the company of two communist agents taking down everything he said. The teaching that had begun as a pleasure, albeit a demanding one (there being hardly any English books in the university library after the German occupation, he had had to teach English literature from memory), now became impossible. The atmosphere was one of fear and foreboding.

Most memorable in this chapter, though, are the stories of suffering that the new system imposed on the Czech people. One of these stories illustrates the ghastly logic of the natural man become political. The truth of Muir's analysis of Communism in the essay of six years ago could hardly be more cruelly shown. A Czech lady had been receiving a small government pension which helped her to support her invalid parents. Now, she was told that the pension would be withdrawn and she would lose her job unless she joined the Communist party. Her choice was an impossible one: if she became a Communist her parents – like herself, Catholics – would never speak to her again; if she did not, they would starve. This horrible dilemma troubled Muir. (He left Prague without knowing the outcome.) Its authors, like the Nazis before them, 'called up a vast image of impersonal power, the fearful shape of our modern inhumanity'. The most sinister part of this was that the Communists did not hate or dislike her. What they asked her 'must, I think, have appeared quite reasonable, since their theory did not take the soul into account. . . . Freedom to them was a strange aberration, almost a nothing; for real freedom was necessity; and so what they offered the lady was necessity.' (A kind of hell indeed: In *The Good Man in Hell*, Hell would only 'be a place like any other place' when 'love *and hate* and life and death' had found entrance.) Moreover the thinking of these men was on a grand scale. Private affections and duties were as nothing compared with the great and 'inevitable' impersonalities overtaking people's lives, fulfilling history, bringing on (supposedly) the dictatorship of the proletariat and 'the final utopia when, at the great halting place of history, the state would wither away and all be changed'. Such men usurp an ancient tradition, a tradition so deeply rooted that it fully warrants the statement that 'it is unnatural for human beings to act impersonally towards one another'. They are, surely, 'the usurpers' – men for whom the dark places of the imagination and the freedom that grows from them must not be admitted to exist. *The Usurpers* first appeared in July 1948. The 'we' of the poem are the new men, deniers of the Fable, 'self-guided, self-impelled and self sustained':

> When night comes
> We drop like stones plumb to its ocean ground,
> While dreams stream past us upward to the place

Where light meets darkness, place of images,
Forest of ghosts, thicket of muttering voices.

The voice that speaks in this poem comes from no specific location and enunciates no creed. But it is an authentic voice, its tones defining a way of seeing man's place in the world and in history that permeates enterprises large and small, political and personal. The first section gives us the conceit of nihilism, its easy assurance that the 'ancestral voices' were not 'hard to still', the new liberty that 'no-one has known before' a simple question of 'our thoughts' being 'our deeds'. But while the authenticity of the tone is beyond doubt, the irony grows as the repeated affirmations of self-sufficiency both use the language of the traditions from which the usurpers are supposedly free – 'our kingdom', 'world without end', 'our home' – and acknowledge the existence of the 'place where light meets darkness'. The acknowledgement grows throughout the latter section of the poem in which what we might broadly call 'the pathetic fallacy' is described, admitted to be faintly troubling, but eventually dismissed as mere 'imaginations'. Though the dismissal is expressed throughout by these same usurpers, their 'argument' carries its refutation within itself:

Sometimes we've heard in sleep tongues talking so:
'I lean my face far out from eternity
For time to work its work on: time, oh time,
What have you done?'

These lines, recalling the end of *The Human Fold*, are haunting in unaccountable ways – ways that have no place in the 'deepening silence' that the usurpers claim to inhabit. Through this poem we have more clearly what in *The Solitary Place* was somewhat obliquely and less confidently expressed: Muir's faith in the existence of a reality outside this 'I and not I'. The final assertion of the poem, 'We are free', is thus deeply ironic and touches our own lives in all those aspects in which questions of freedom and responsibility are paramount. The 'world' which is here allowed to speak for itself at its most transparent, and is found wanting, is a recognizable world of our time: the world of brutal, reductionist political philosophies, of those varieties of progressivism fuelled by a hatred and contempt for everything past, of all those forces, indeed, that narrow man's image of himself to a creature of the hour, a bundle of appetites no longer even in search of a soul:

Archer and bow and burning arrow sped
On its wild flight through nothing to tumble down
At last on nothing, our home and cure for all.

Such an image has a potency that reminds us of the difficulties faced by artists in our own time. The art of our time is pervaded by images of desolation and spiritual bankruptcy, at its best commending itself to us for its refusal to flinch before the challenge of those images, at its worst self-indulgently exploiting both its object and its audience. To go beneath the characteristic imagery of the age, the artist presumably needs a quality of self-discipline that will enable him to distinguish the provisional from the permanent, contemporary fact from future possibility. He needs to be aware of the provenance of the 'characteristic imagery' – its moral and spiritual foundations – and to have the imagination to reach out for alternatives. We have already seen that Muir was peculiarly well placed to carry out the necessary analysis and to envisage possible alternatives. These alternatives are in the end a matter of faith, faith informed by the witness of the past. That witness will not allow '1984' to become a conceivable future.

After 1984, printed in the *Collected Poems* as one of the 'Poems not previously collected', envisages a time in which men's minds are no longer their own:

> Our fetters locked so far within,
> And not a key in the world to fit;

It is the familiar nightmare of brainwashing and programmed existence. But the poem takes its stand on a mystery not normally allowed for by those who plan or those whom we imagine planning the nightmares. It puts its faith in the ground of our being, a mystery ultimately inaccessible to doctrine, persuasion, torture. It is perfectly in accordance with its being a matter of faith that the second stanza should be largely in the form of questions:

> The secret universe of the blind
> Cannot be known. Just so we were
> Shut from ourselves even in our mind;
> Only a twisting chaos within
> Turned on itself, not knowing where
> The exit was, salvation gate.
> Was it chaos that set us straight,
> The elements that rebelled, not we?
> Or the anguish never to find
> Ourselves, somewhere, at last, and be?
> We must escape, no matter where.

The release will come as inexplicably as a poet's inspiration. 'Where traveller never went' was his 'domain'. So, here, 'ourselves' are shut out from the mind, dwelling in a country to which there must always be the possibility of access but which we can never come consciously to know. With a poet for whom belief in immortality is impossible such a statement of faith would probably be facile. Muir's poem, on the other hand – even, one suspects, without the support it has from his other poems – has the force that comes with genuine conviction: one doesn't imagine for a moment in reading *After 1984* that he is having to convince *himself.*

Muir of course did not need the experience of the Prague putsch to convince him of the unnaturalness of modern Communism. His analysis had been made many years before. Events were merely confirming its accuracy. He had studied Communist theory in his twenties and been repelled by it then. Hampstead in the early 1930s had, in Willa Muir's words, been 'well furnished with Communists and near-Communists' and Muir's objection had crystallized at that time. Contrasting the Socialism of his youth with the Communism of the 1930s, he concluded that an impulse of love and compassion for 'misshapen humanity in all its forms' had been overtaken by a massively impersonal system: 'Communism presented itself as a strange, solidly made object, very like a huge clock, with metal bowels, no feelings, and no explanation for itself but its own impenetrable mechanism.' As we have seen, Muir had not the slightest interest in writing the kind of poetry that attachment to such a system called for. In the 1930s an instinctive distrust of abstractions made it impossible for him to accept what he called the political interpretation of life. 'It stopped at the reality of categories.' And when, as in Prágue in 1948, the Communists' 'moral judgements were judgements of their categories' – the working class, the capitalists, the bourgeoisie, and so on – the essential inhumanity of such an interpretation was once more attested. The distrust of categories and abstractions was doubtless native to Muir and ratified by his early years in Orkney. It is associated with that intense responsiveness to the concrete that I have indicated as a unifying feature of his poetry: the capacity to detect or, rather, to illuminate a meaning inhering in a situation or a picture. Here, indeed, we touch the essence of Muir's hostility to impersonal political systems and the character of the response that he made to them in his poetry. The key to that character is, I think, Kafka.

People who know nothing else of Muir probably know of him and his wife as the translators for the standard English editions of Kafka's work. Kafka's importance to him as a poet is not so obvious. In July 1929, while translating *The Castle*, he wrote about it to Sidney Schiff in terms that prefigure the kind of poetry he was to write himself and that made clear the nature of Kafka's appeal for him: 'It is a purely metaphysical and mystical dramatic novel; the ordinary moral judgements do not come in at all; everything happens on a mysterious spiritual plane which was obviously the supreme reality to the author; and yet in a curious way everything is given solidly and concretely' (8 July 1929). To try to establish how far Kafka 'influenced' Muir is fairly fruitless but at the very least he must have been encouraged in the discovery of an imagination so much akin to his own. In an article written soon after Muir's death, Michael Hamburger coined the happy phrase 'absolute fictions'[8] to suggest a quality of some of his work that links him with Kafka. Incidentally defending him against the charge that his work lacks 'striking imagery', he said 'no prominent image or metaphor is needed where the whole poem goes beyond analogy, beyond allegory, to render absolute fictions like *The Combat*'. And, in a footnote, he recalled that in a 1947 Czech publication Muir had corrected his previous view that Kafka's fiction was allegory (a view to be found in the introduction to the translations) and 'stressed the purely imaginative character of Kafka's works'. Although Hamburger says that this important correction was never noticed in England, the change in view is implicit in Muir's essay on Kafka in *Essays on Literature and Society*. It is clearer still if we read that essay together with the one on Henryson that opens the book. 'Henryson, like Chaucer, exists in that long calm of storytelling which ended with the Renaissance, when the agreement about the great story was broken.'[9] What Muir means by the great story is clearly that order from which the natural and political man of the later essay has so disastrously departed, one where 'everything, in spite of the practical disorder of life, seems to have its place; the ranks and occupations of men; the hierarchy of animals; good and evil; the earth, heaven and hell'. While that story lasted, allegory was 'a perfectly natural convention'; but 'the allegory is a form which the modern taste finds stilled and unreal, because the great story as Chaucer and Henryson knew it is dead'. Muir, one feels sure, had the quality of imagination that would have made him perfectly at home when the 'great story' held sway. Now, however, that kind of imagination must work as it can, without the support of such a convention as allegory; there is a premium on invention. Muir's essay on Kafka makes this point abundantly clear and guides us to the centre of *The Labyrinth*.

It is a short essay but it makes an excellent and provoking introduction to Kafka's work. In addition, the key formulations touch on Muir's work so centrally that it might have been put down to make an introduction to parts of that. For Muir, Kafka is 'a great story-teller, because there is no story for him to tell; so that he has to make it up . . . he has to create the story, character, setting and action and embody in it his meaning.' 'The scenes and figures and conversation seem to rise out of nothing, since nothing resembling them was there before.' Kafka's stories 'are not allegories. The truths they bring out are surprising or startling, not conventional and expected, as the truths of allegory tend to be'.[10] Such, too, are the qualities of Muir's 'absolute fictions'. We encountered them earlier in such poems as *The Enchanted Knight*, and *The Good Man in Hell*, but it is in this volume that they most powerfully show the time its form and pressure. The mark of Prague and the European terrors of the last ten years is upon poems such as *The Combat, The Helmet* and *The Bridge of Dread*, as is Muir's response to all that is threatened in the triumph of 'political man'. As we have seen, Muir found in Kafka a perfect and mysterious commingling of the spiritual and the concrete. One might not describe these poems in quite this way but they seem at one and the same time to inhabit yet to stay outside the world of material objects; to describe the hidden contours of our awareness so that we know them for what they are. The self-sufficiency of these pictures is, we feel when reading, not due to conscious shaping.

They seem to come at us with the inevitability of those 'forms of experience' that he records and discusses in *An Autobiography*. And to speak of their self-sufficiency is to be reminded again of the ballads. The difference, of course, is that Muir's, while unconditional in the sense that we don't find ourselves striking analogies with contemporary events, nonetheless touch contemporary nerves. The dreads and terrors to which they give shape are palpably those of our time; they call up 'the fearful shape of our modern inhumanity'.

Many of Kafka's stories begin 'in the midway of life, at a point decided by the chance of the moment, and yet at a decisive point'. Muir's poem, *The Interrogation*, is such a story – 'we could have crossed the road but hesitated'. That incident actually happened to Muir himself (it is recorded in *An Autobiography*) during the Russian occupation of Czechoslovakia. *The Bridge of Dread* likewise begins 'at a point decided by the chance of the moment' but, as in *The Combat*, the location of that point cannot be plotted on any map we know. There is much in the poem that seems to belong to the iconography of modern torment. It isn't difficult to feel the relation of the first two stanzas to the known facts of Belsen and Auschwitz:

> But when you reach the Bridge of Dread
> Your flesh will huddle into its nest
> For refuge and your naked head
> Creep in the casement of your breast,
>
> And your great bulk grow thin and small
> And cower within its cage of bone,
> While dazed you watch your footsteps crawl
> Toadlike across the leagues of stone.

The pathos of the flesh forced to want to deny itself, the dislocation of mind and body, the one a spectator of the ghastly contortions of the other – we sense the pressure of the age within these images: the very namelessness of the place and the indeterminateness of the terrors it holds belong to familiar modern nightmares: the dislocations of war, the prevalence of torture and oppression in modern States. These things are there and yet the vision here connects with deep and nameless fears that belong to men at any time. This is indeed one of Muir's absolute fictions; its images have the unconditional quality of dream images: they are alarmingly real in their fantastic unreality. We don't find ourselves asking for an explanation of their meaning. They connect with our deepest forms of awareness. But *what* they connect with we can know in no other way than through the images themselves. The shock of recognition that one experiences in reading *The Bridge of Dread* (as with *The Combat*) is an intuitive token of their accuracy. The poem continues:

> If they come, you will not feel
> About your feet the adders slide,

For still your head's demented wheel
Whirls on your neck from side to side
Searching for danger.

Contemporary and traditional references link to produce an image that
locates the horror everywhere and nowhere. 'If *they* come' – a modern
locution for the nameless and menacing; at the same time the menace is
old, deeply known – 'adders slide'. But this kind of exposition cannot
account for the power of the synthesis and the weird evocation of the rest
of the stanza:

> Nothing there.
> And yet your breath will whistle and beat
> As on you push the stagnant air
> That breaks in rings about your feet
> Like dirty suds.

The images have a logic of their own which we shall certainly not
penetrate by intensive local analysis. It will do no good to interrogate
the stanza for the 'consistency' of the notion of air that can break
around your feet. What we can say is that their power is of a part
with the vision of torment and dread that has been building in the
poem from the start: a broth that contains the unnameable and
infects the ordinary – those 'dirty suds'. The unnameable terror is
indeed the worst:

> If there should come
> Some bodily terror to that place,
> Great knotted serpents dread and dumb,
> You would accept it as a grace.

The Bridge of Dread is not a nihilistic poem; rather, like all Muir's
mature poetry, it calls up the evils of human existence from an
increasingly assured sense of their relativity. If this poem is strikingly
successful in giving expression to the horrors that lie in wait for us, it
nonetheless accepts the promise of deliverance as equally natural:

> Until you see a burning wire
> Shoot from the ground. As in a dream
> You'll wonder at that flower of fire,
> That weed caught in a burning beam.

I think the image of release has less power than the images of torture and
oppression: the 'burning wire' does not lock into one's imagination with
the same inevitability as the earlier pictures do. Perhaps this is not
surprising. It is in the nature of the deliverance that Muir says awaits

mankind that it can normally only be guessed at: there are those rare moments when its form stands before us. This poem, however, does not re-create such a form. It concludes by reminding us that though evil and good come upon us unbidden, deliverance from evil is a moral imperative. It has happened to you and you must live by that fact.

> And you are past. Remember then,
> Fix deep within your dreaming head
> Year, hour or endless moment when
> You reached and crossed the Bridge of Dread.

The appropriate kind of comment on such a poem is surely one that takes account of its complexity in the sense explained by Kathleen Raine in her criticism of Empson:

There is one type of complexity which he fails to consider, that resonance which may be present within an image of apparent simplicity, setting into vibrations planes of reality and of consciousness other than that of the sensible world: the power of the symbol and of symbolic discourse.[11]

The Labyrinth collection echoes to Muir's description of Kafka's work:

The image of a road comes into our minds when we think of his stories; for in spite of all the confusions and contradictions in which he was involved he held that life was a way, not a chaos, that the right way exists and can be found by a supreme and exhausting effort, and that whatever happens every human being in fact follows some way, right or wrong.[12]

The echo in the poem that opens the volume, *Too Much*, is a very precise one. Just as the bleaker poems of *The Voyage* had been placed between affirmations – 'the crying sorrows' besieging 'this happy, happy love' – so here *Too Much* and the title poem that follows it, *The Labyrinth*, help us to see the desolations of *The Combat* and *The Bridge of Dread* in proportion. Briskly, almost jauntily, *Too Much* opens with a declaration:

> No, no, I did not bargain for so much
> When I set out upon the famous way
> My fathers praised so fondly – such and such
> The road, the errand, the prize, the part to play.

The 'such and such' suggests the conventionality, the predictability of the talk of parents and elders, the catalogue of the fourth line composing the standard language in which their expectations are expressed. But how has it been in the event?

> For everything is different. Hour and place
> Are huddled awry, at random teased and tossed,
> Too much piled on too much, no track or trace,
> And north and south and road and traveller lost.

The language of those expectations seemed to promise a straight road and a clear goal, simplicities there for the embracing. But these lines record the facts of experience; those facts crowd in upon us without apparent relation or meaning. And yet, the second change of pace in the poem, the abrupt settling into the quietness of these rhythms, lays the disquiet that such incoherence might once have aroused:

> Then suddenly again I watch the old
> Worn saga write across my years and find,
> Scene after scene, the tale my fathers told,
> But I in the middle blind, as Homer blind,
>
> Dark on the highway, groping in the light,
> Threading my dazzling way within my night.

'Saga', 'scene', 'tale': the words have come to possess connotations of permanence. They speak of echoes of the one great story or fable that each man occasionally hears in his own life. And when he does hear them, he knows there is that within him that Homer – and, by implication, all great artists – heard. One recalls Muir's statement about the poetic imagination having advanced not at all since the time of Homer. It cannot 'advance' in the linear manner that the word denotes; it can only thread its way within the 'night' that remains the same as it has always been. By invoking Homer, Muir seems to be implying that the ordinary individual and the great artist are at one in the nature of their search. Neither possesses the unconditional power of total understanding; even the very greatest await the partial revelation. The paradoxical act of watching from within a state of blindness is explained by the involuntariness with which it comes upon us. There are moments – 'suddenly' – when the pattern, the assurance of meaning, declares itself; we are acted on, cannot choose to see. Indeed our normal condition is one of blindness, the 'watching' an inward mode of apprehension rather than an active process which we are at liberty to set in motion or curtail. ('I watch the old/Worn saga write across my years.') In the terms of the poem, 'my night' surrounds me and though the light is there all the time – 'my dazzling way' – I can only grope, seeking, seeking all the time.

The conceit of the final couplet is no mere trickery, a teasing paradox; it is a statement of faith. Condensed and at first bemusing, it expresses Muir's conviction that the 'famous way' exists though we can never know it in a direct and constant way. My way is 'dazzling', not to me but potentially to the eye of the imagination, always to God; the way is guaranteed, but my poor self must stumble and wander. By the end of the poem, the conventional language of the generations, the standard imagery of roads and prizes, has been enriched to a depth such language could only hint at. Set the important lines against one another and the transformation is obvious:

                              such and such
    The road, the errand, the prize, the part to play.

and

    Dark on the highway, groping in the light,

The casual and the ordinary are transformed into a vision.

Too Much is a masterly poem. The changes of tone and pace reflect the
motions of the spirit. The restlessness, the serenity and the eventual
vision are indeed 'contemplated with passion'. We are not simply
reading about Muir's progress through those various states; we relive
that progress with him during the course of the poem and at the same
time participate in the assurance with which it moves towards the
outcome of that final couplet. The assurance of the poem is no merely
formal matter; it is a natural part of the spiritual resolution that it
records: in other words Muir's recreation of his story is undertaken in
the confidence of its meaning having already declared itself. He can
contemplate the feelings that attached to its various scenes with a
detachment that is reflected in the easy control of the verse form. The
poem is proof that immediacy is not the prerogative of poets who deal
in the sensuous and the concrete. The striking feature of *Too Much* is that
it so convincingly expresses the soul's progress without recourse to
anything of the kind; to say it expresses it through the *movement* of the
verse is true but inadequate. The movement is only what it is because, as
so frequently, the pressure of Muir's imagination has enabled the other
elements of the poem to gather a richness they don't separately possess.

There is then, a right way and 'it can be found by a supreme and
exhausting effort'. In their different ways, the three outstanding
'visionary' poems of the 1949 volume – *The Labyrinth, The Transfiguration* and *The Journey Back* – evolve from such an effort and
describe the outcome. These poems are the fullest answer to that
reduction of the image of man that Muir traces in 'The natural man and
the political man'. In the essay the coherence and persuasiveness is that
of discursive argument. In the poems it is the 'truth of a vision' that we
are witnessing, the kind of truth which, in concluding the essay, Muir
had claimed for the poetry of Wordsworth. What he said there comes as
close as anything he wrote to defining the character of his own journey
and the reason why it can never be complete. Wordsworth's poetry
'records a moment of mystical co-operation between reason and
impulse, man and nature; it does not describe a process, or make a
general statement about life which can be embodied in a theory. It is
rather the outline of a possibility, and the record of moments in which
that possibility was realised'.[13] Such possibilities are outlined and
realized in *The Labyrinth, The Transfiguration* and *The Journey Back*.

'Great poetry', said Jung, 'draws its strength from the life of
mankind, and we completely miss its meaning if we try to derive it from
personal factors'.[14] Muir would agree with that. Whatever knowledge

we may possess about his time in Czechoslovakia, whatever the political circumstances that might seem to make the central image of *The Labyrinth* so appropriate to our time and to unite it with *The Bridge of Dread*, it is not the nature of the poem to make us conscious of such things as we read it. In a broadcast in 1952 Muir spoke of the poem having 'started itself'. 'Thinking there of the old story of the labyrinth of Cnossos and the journey of Theseus through it and out of it, I felt this was an image of human life with its errors and ignorance and endless intricacy.'[15] Yet the 'I' of the poem is not Theseus and it has no personal flavour; it is nonetheless full of urgency. The experience of the labyrinth is real enough. The 'I' that it has happened to is you and me. Rather than compelling us to recognize the basis of the poem in an individual life, the 'I' remains a narrative convention through which a universal 'form of experience' is transmitted. The bemusing power and menace of the labyrinth is not simply recollected; the writing of the poem is itself the occasion, one of those 'times when I have heard my footsteps/Still echoing in the maze.'

> Since I emerged that day from the labyrinth,
> Dazed with the tall and echoing passages,
> The swift recoils, so many I almost feared
> I'd meet myself returning at some smooth corner,
> Myself or my ghost, for all there was unreal
> After the straw ceased rustling and the bull
> Lay dead upon the straw and I remained,
> Blood-splashed, if dead or alive I could not tell
> In the twilight nothingness (I might have been
> A spirit seeking his body through the roads
> Of intricate Hades) – ever since I came out
> To the world, the still fields swift with flowers, the trees
> All bright with blossom, the little green hills, the sea,
> The sky and all in movement under it,
> Shepherds and flocks and birds and the young and old

– and so it goes on; the first thirty-five lines are one sentence. (Harvey Gross, in his book *Sound and Form in Modern Poetry*, has pertinent things to say about Muir's masterly handling of the verse here, the careful pacing of rhythmic movement, the 'gentle curve from steady iambic to prose statement.')[16] The long, disjointed, parenthetical movement reflects the experience of the maze as it was and still is. It is a past experience and a present fear or – in terms more suitable to a work so entirely nourished by myth and dream – it is a permanent feature of human life. Having said which, it is the more surprising that before the description of the saving 'dream or trance' in the second part of the poem, Muir can say of the labyrinth:

> I could not live if this were not illusion.
> It is a world, perhaps; but there's another.

The power of the 'illusion' has been acknowledged; its presence in the poem is of a strength to deny the word itself. Do we then have a limp contradiction of that power, a hopeful assertion of faith in the existence of that other world? No. The power of an illusion does not convert it into a truth. Our 'bad spirit' (the subject of *The Intercepter* in the same volume) may sneer and say

> you'll end where you are,
> Deep in the centre of the endless maze

but that is not the only source of persuasion. From other sources come the kind of dream or trance described in the final part of the poem. In contrast to the restlessness of the movement in the maze – that maze woven of Greek myth, the life of the mind and 'all the roads/that run through the noisy world' – there is the alternative vision of a still life. It is a picture with the serene finality of a Breughel landscape: human activity is multitudinous, but in a blessed pattern. Everything has its place but only the gods see the pattern:

> While down below the little ships sailed by,
> Toy multitudes swarmed in the harbours, shepherds drove
> Their tiny flocks to the pastures, marriage feasts
> Went on below, small birthdays and holidays,
> Ploughing and harvesting and life and death,
> And all permissible, all acceptable,
> Clear and secure as in a limpid dream.

We might say, oversimplifying, that in *The Labyrinth* Muir has invoked Greek myth by way of asserting the truth of his own vision. The myth of the labyrinth is 'a form of experience' that speaks of certain potentialities in human nature. It is a metaphor for the multitudinous confusion of motive and action. The dream of the 'spontaneous syllables bodying forth a world' is another such metaphor, this time for the order that confusion disguises. Ultimately we declare our belief in one or the other as being the more complete, the more truthful. Hence the explicit declaration of 'I could not live if this were not illusion'. There is no alternative to this explicitness, no possibility of *exploring* the validity of these contradictory images. The relative conviction each carries is decided according to criteria that we have no means of knowing. And yet, though the poem embraces the dream as the 'real world' which, having once 'touched' it, the poet will know always, this is no easy resolution. Myth and dream here figure permanent states of the spirit; the tension between those states is one from which we can never be entirely free. Good and evil are eternally in conflict; the most we can hope for is occasionally to touch that 'real' world in which the deepest harmony of all is attained. 'That my soul has birdwings to fly free' is the guarantee of that hope; it is to its precariousness, though, that Muir returns at the end:

Oh these deceits are strong almost as life.
Last night I dreamt I was in the labyrinth,
And woke far on. I did not know the place.

It is a perfect ending. Two phases in the life of the spirit have been made
known to us; the conflict will continue and though we may know the
'deceits' for what they are, their power is permanent and disturbing.

As so frequently with Muir's poetry, brief quotation can give no
accurate indication of the quality of what is before us. As with much of
Wordsworth, the authenticity of the vision grows in the development of
the narrative. Phrases, lines, indeed whole sequences, seem unremarkable out of context. And yet, with a line such as

But they, the gods, as large and bright as clouds,

– in itself apparently unremarkable – we do not find ourselves resisting it
because of its lack of 'concreteness', its failure to refine our conception
of the gods. In the event it takes its place in a sustained meditation on the
dream of 'another world' about which it is difficult to give an account
save to say that it impresses us as a natural statement of faith. In a most
uncontemporary way Muir trusts words; they have a history and a
reason for existing. In themselves they are evidence of the spiritual life. It
seems as though the authenticity of the myth and the dream here
naturally call forth the right words in the right order. The words do not
strain after the inexpressible; the history they bear is, as it were,
illuminated from within by the particular experience they express:

But they, the gods, as large and bright as clouds,
Conversed across the sounds in tranquil voices
High in the sky above the untroubled sea,
And their eternal dialogue was peace
Where all these things were woven, and this our life
Was as a chord deep in that dialogue,
As easy utterance of harmonious words,
Spontaneous syllables bodying forth a world.

'He approached the mystery of time and eternity through the
imagination. He attacked it directly; the mystery itself, not any
particular manifestation of it, was his theme'[17] (Muir: 'Hölderlin's
Patmos').

More than once in his prose writing Muir refers to von Hofmannsthal's
claim that 'great imagination is always conservative'. Pondering the
implications of those words in his essay, 'The poetic imagination', he
provides us with the thread which may lead us into his great poem, *The
Journey Back*, the most extensive of his attempts in poetry to arrive at
'the outline of a possibility' of vision. Among the variety of implications
in Von Hoffmansthal's words may be this:

In the past only is the human pattern complete . . . there is the place to which the present turns back to find its finished and timeless pattern. So that the present is a question perpetually running back to find its answer at a place where all is over.[18]

The search for that place – never to be found, ever to be sought – is the matter of *The Journey Back*. It is probably the most ambitious, complex and elusive poem that Muir wrote. It is ambitious in the sense that here, perhaps for the last time, he is attempting a comprehensive understanding of the problems and experiences that have over the years both distressed and fascinated him: time and eternity, present and past, the individual and mankind. He had said in *An Autobiography* that 'our minds are possessed by three mysteries: where we come from, where we are going, and, since we are not alone, but members of a countless family, how we should live with one another'. It is the achievement of *The Journey Back* to attend to those mysteries with memorable seriousness, to leave us feeling that the simple verbs of his sentence – 'came from' and 'are going' – disguise an unfathomable spiritual condition before which the necessary response can only be acceptance and gratitude. I use the word 'achievement' with deliberation because the acceptance and the gratitude are not merely enjoined upon the reader; they arise naturally through the kind of thing that the poem is. It is a work in which the conventional categories of thought and feeling, intuition and reflection, seem inadequate to describe the character of what takes place. For it is exploratory in a fundamental sense: that the poet calls upon all the resources of the mind that he can command and simultaneously contemplates their virtue and their insufficiency in what they are called upon to do. *The Journey Back* treats of the 'Many in One' – a phrase with an ancient lineage that in one way or another represents the aspiration of the major religions. Indeed, the poem is unambiguously Christian in occasional reference and allusion while, in the fourth section, as it approaches the limits of language in an attempt to express what never can be expressed, it has something of the elusive beauty of the Upanishads.

The complexity, then, is a necessary one. Muir's is a 'high and difficult theme'. And though Christianity is in the poem, it is not there in any explanatory fashion; it becomes a voice amongst the many voices that the poem calls up and attempts to interpret. Because of its complexity it may be useful to begin by offering a brief description of the poem's various sections and the way in which they compose a sequence.

The first stage of the 'journey back to seek my kindred' is the remembered and loved landscape of boyhood, the 'I' observing and describing the scenes that allowed his heart to 'beat in surety'. Already, though, this place 'most strange and familiar' is 'pined and shrunken'; the mind can recover the features of the landscape and its people but it is losing its sense of their solidity. He is very quickly up against the limits of observation and ordinary memory. Now, through the imagination alone, he must enter an unknown area in which already he senses the unity that underlies the variously distressing, inspiring and banal 'I's in which the One has manifested itself – neighbour-hater, miser, simpleton, hero, murderer:

> In all these lives I have lodged, and each a prison.
> I fly this prison to seek this other prison,
> Impatient for the end – or the beginning

There would seem to be no point in that endless chain of identities except that he knows that he will find the man one day who will be 'Image of man from whom all have diverged'. Such a man will unite in one image those various ancestral identities, those selves that include in the speaker the 'random self/That in these rags and tatters clothes the soul'.

The deliberate, attentive, back-tracking of this first section gives way to a song of wandering. Section one was meditative, largely at home in familiar country. Here the song is not of separate human identities but of archaic phases in the long story of man's beginnings; of an unimaginably ancient life, a different cosmic order:

> I wear the silver scars
> Of blanched and dying stars
> Forgotten long,

Then, there was no distinct humanity but a homogeneous life in an age which surely is the one of which Muir says in *An Autobiography* that 'our unconscious life goes back into it'; when

> The well-bred animal
> With coat of seemly mail
> Was then my guide.

The laws that he obeyed then were none that could be put into words; for there were no words. This was before the word was spoken, so that he lived in the way of the animals in the later poem, *The Animals* (*One Foot in Eden*) – 'as a sleep my wandering was'. The search for 'the secret place/Where is my home' is thus of a different kind from that of the first section. The 'random', meditating, developed, fully human psyche, conscious of its desire to know its beginnings and of the way it must approach them, gives way to an ancestral psyche instinctively 'threading the shining day' (like the fully human 'I' of *Too Much*), bewildered, 'dizzied' by the wild road, trusting that it will come to 'the ground for which I was born'.

In the third poem of the sequence (as in the fifth) Muir stands aside to see where his meditations are leading: here to a grieving for the 'poor child of man', 'shut in his simple recurring day', knowing nothing of eternity and the freedom of the spirit. With the fourth poem we approach the region of pure spirit which, because of its purity, must use the sensuous earth and with it the rhythms and images of poetry to make itself known. I want to comment on this beautiful section later. It may though be useful to have it here:

> And sometimes through the air descends a dust
> Blown from the scentless desert of dead time
> That whispers: Do not put your trust
> In the fed flesh, or colour, or sense, or shape.
> This that I am you cannot gather in rhyme.
> For once I was all
> That you can name, a child, a woman, a flower,
> And here escape
> From all that was to all,
> Lost beyond loss.
> So in the air I toss
> Remembrance and rememberer all confused
> In a light fume, the last power used,
> The last form found,
> And child and woman and flower
> Invisibly fall through the air on the living ground.

Once, child, woman and flower had no separate existence as things we can name. They were one with spirit. But that is no longer so. The spirit is not now identical with but separate from those things. Nonetheless, humanity – 'rememberer' – can dimly realize that child, woman and flower are essentially forms of the spirit. In the realization, the 'remembrance', is the knowledge of our spirituality. Both 'rememberer' and 'remembrance' attest the life of the spirit. Beyond understanding though it is, one truth we may glimpse: that they are one form – 'the last form found' – in which the spirit makes itself manifest.

After the unutterable mystery of that fourth section, the next acknowledges the need for a blessing, for a grace without which we, 'wild for prophecy', are dumb; while the sixth is an unearthly evocation of a peace beyond understanding that belongs to the unidentified 'they' who 'pace their tranquil round/That has no end, whose end is everywhere', the world of pure spirit whose intangibility the fourth section had glanced at. The sequence concludes with a meditation on the world as having no end but whose end is everywhere. In the lines

> And the tumultuous world slips softly home
> To its perpetual end and flawless bourne.

is embodied the realization that 'what might have been and what has been/Point to one end, which is always present' (T. S. Eliot: *Burnt Norton*). And that there is a deep and incomprehensible unity of the world, ourselves and our thoughts.

The variety of verse forms in *The Journey Back* is important – we find, for instance, blank verse, sonnet, terza rima, irregular rhyming verse, the short two or three stress line. The variety is intrinsic to the poem's theme and intention. The One is, as it were, approached through the Many: each of the sections and each of the verse forms may be seen as an alternative route, another entrance to the same domain. Muir's poem is a journey back from the personal self to that universal Self of which the Upanishads speak. It is an attempt to evoke the transformations of the spirit through the various guises in which it is made known to us, to come within reach of pure spirit. The work is full of paradox: there is a feeling of real freedom in the ranging of the imagination; yet we come to see that the further it ranges, the more abundant its inventions, the clearer will become the elusiveness of the spirit. In reach and aspiration the poem reflects back its own insufficiency: each of the sections represents – and each qualifies the others – a provisional route to a description of the nature of the spirit. But that never can be described: it can, instead, be endlessly and in endlessly varied ways called up and contemplated. And we come to a point in the reading of *The Journey Back* where we sense the paradox that though – or, perhaps, because – the gift of language is indispensable to the contemplation, so in its turn it becomes a part of the whole which the sequence attempts to describe. Since 'all is in all' the mystery deepens and the challenge becomes more acute; for the very aspiration to understand, to bring into momentary focus one aspect of the truth, is itself part of the all. In section 7 this is condensed so:

> We and the world and that unending thought
> Which has elsewhere its end and is for us
> Begotten in a dream deep in this dream
> Beyond the place of getting and of spending.

Explicitly here, and implicitly throughout, we touch this most fundamental mystery: our very imagining is part of, impossible to conceive of apart from, a whole creation, a dream that makes it possible. And in understanding *that*, we must in turn reflect that our understanding is likewise made possible, is, too, included in 'that unending thought'. We touch here the essence of subjectivity but it is experienced and called up not as a condition of irksome confinement but as a liberty. The echoes in the lines quoted are Wordsworthian. But the poem draws strength from – or, at least, is in sympathy with – that other great spiritual tradition that we know Muir was acquainted with, the tradition embodied in the Upanishads. Many passages in the Upanishads are possessed of the mystery of which Muir's poem speaks. The mode of expression is different but the knowledge of the unbridgeable gap between the reality of the spirit and any way we can figure it to ourselves is the same:

That which cannot be expressed in words but by which the tongue speaks – know that to be Brahman. Brahman is not the being who is worshiped of men.

That which is not comprehended by the mind but by which the mind comprehends – know that to be Brahman. Brahman is not the being who is worshiped of men (Kena Upanishad).[19]

'That unending thought', Brahman, can never be known; it can only be acknowledged in whatever ways human weakness allows. To acknowledge that is to accept man's need of grace. Only through grace can we attain the peace that passes understanding:

> Without the blessing cannot the kingdom come.

The line comes from the fifth poem in the sequence, 'I have stood and watched where many have stood', one of the two sections in which the 'I' stands aside and seems to make its comment on the more elusive statements of the others. In the other one – the third, 'And I remember in the bright light's maze' – through the 'poor child of man', 'shut in his simple recurring day', that lasting obsession with time is vigorously rejected, the vigour well warranted by the imaginings of the rest of the poem. That 'recurring day' simply is not true; and to be in thrall to it, to rest content with its close spiritual horizons is an unnecessary and pathetic impoverishment. The picture in *The Journey Back* (section 3) might be taken as Muir's own comment on himself in the days of his most anguished detachment:

> And I remember in the bright light's maze
> While poring on a red and rusted arrow
> How once I laid my dead self in the barrow,
> Closed my blank eyes and smoothed my face,
> And stood aside, a third within that place,

The confinement that he imagines himself observing is like that of *The Enchanted Knight* or like that of his early days when he so often had the sensation of looking in on himself from the outside. And they of course were the days of his deepest enthralment to Time. Now the outright rejection of so inhuman and narrow a 'philosophy' is spurred by the sublime, time-redeeming Christian words borrowed here to describe the 'poor child of man'

> Not knowing the resurrection and the life,
> Shut in his simple recurring day,
> Familiar happiness and ordinary pain.
> And while he lives content with child and wife
> A million leaves, a million destinies fall,
> And over and over again
> The red rose blooms and moulders by the wall.

The beauty of the rose is not the vulnerable, pathetic thing of the early *Betrayal*. The beauty of the red rose is as depthless, as immeasurable as the spirit that reveals itself through it; its blooming and mouldering are material facts for the man shut in his recurring day, but in the vision that the poem aspires to they become inconceivably more real, with that ideal reality that belongs to the spirit alone.

The Journey Back communicates an unmistakable sense of urgency. These matters are being considered deeply and there is rigour and great force in the expression. But that urgency is not on the surface. It is in the nature of the poem's theme that it demands the subjugation of the personal, would indeed be a quite different theme were that not so. Muir may begin by journeying back to seek his kindred, but 'kindred' rapidly expands its meaning to take in the all, the known and the unknown, the material and the spiritual, the seer and the seen. So that the mere personality of the poet (and one recalls Muir's animadversions against 'personalities' in *An Autobiography*) becomes a minute part of the total picture, a conduit through which can emerge various intimations of the Whole. If we see *The Journey Back* this way, then its structure becomes the proper expression of the nature of the search and the lesson of the discovery: the first poem in the sequence begins with the personal reflection, the exhortation to think back through the generations, while the last sees and endeavours to make clear the reflection and the exhortation, the search and the discovery, as aspects of the Whole. So that *The Journey Back* becomes a metaphor – or a series of metaphorical forays – in search of the real, the soul, the Self, spirit. And that is Beauty.

The 'real' is the beautiful. The fourth poem in the sequence (quoted whole a little way back) conjures beauty out of the very impossibility of our coming to know the spirit. As we read we are conscious that the mysterious relations between spirit and matter, mind and memory, past and present, are being pondered and fleetingly realized. The sensation is as of momentarily understanding the relationship between two truths about our condition: first, that the form of eternal life is that of the unknowable spirit, the material world its imperfect reflection: and, second, that it is a source of joy that we are nonetheless able to *realize* this first truth in both senses of the word: on the one hand it is given to us to know that the All, the spirit, exists; on the other hand, we can endeavour to call it up in words, partially to realize it through contemplating child and woman and flower and gathering them up in rhyme. This rhyming poem partially confutes the impotence that the spirit claims for it: 'This that I am you cannot gather in rhyme.' 'Plato's is the truest poetry', Muir was later to write (in the last poem printed in *Collected Poems*). It is Plato's poetry that we are listening to in these lines, intimating to us the reality of 'that which cannot be expressed in words but by which the tongue speaks' and of those 'fleeting moods of shadowy exultation' that Wordsworth describes in *The Prelude*, in which

> the soul,
> Remembering how she felt, but what she felt
> Remembering not, retains an obscure sense

Of possible sublimity, whereto
With growing faculties she doth aspire,
With faculties still growing, feeling still
That whatsoever point they gain, they yet
Have something to pursue.[20]

That something yet to be pursued is the infinite theme of *The Journey Back*. If Muir's 'absolute fictions' elsewhere in *The Labyrinth* volume tend to outline the darker figures on his unchanging ground, there are exceptions. The ethereal sixth poem in the sequence is one of them. Here is a land where no man ever set foot nor ever will, a triumph of pure imagination in which a state of the spirit is created for our contemplation. We cannot identify or characterize the 'they' of the poem; they have no more personal weight than the whispering dust 'Blown from the deserts of dead time'. They are pure being, in the element of pure being, music – only this is no earthly music; it is a universal unheard music to which the poem can only allude through the subtle delicacy of its movement, leaving us with the knowledge that, still, there is 'something to pursue'.

There they like planets pace their tranquil round
That has no end, whose end is everywhere,
And tread as to a music underground,

An ever-winding and unwinding air
That moves their feet though they in silence go,
For music's self itself has buried there,

And all its tongues in silence overflow
That movement only should be melody.
This is the other road, not that we know.

Chapter 8

Something to Pursue

> But to apprehend
> The point of intersection of the timeless
> With time, is an occupation for the saint –
> No occupation either, but something given
> And taken, in a lifetime's death in love,
> Ardour and selflessness and self-surrender.
> For most of us, there is only the unattended
> Moment, the moment in and out of time,
> The distraction fit, lost in a shaft of sunlight,
> The wild thyme unseen, or the winter lightning
> Or the waterfall, or music heard so deeply
> That it is not heard at all, but you are the music
> While the music lasts. These are only hints and guesses,
> Hints followed by guesses; and the rest
> Is prayer, observance, discipline, thought and action.
> The hint half guessed, the gift half understood, is
>   Incarnation.
> (T. S. Eliot[1])

. . . nothing is wholly real until it finds an image as well as a formula for itself. For the image is a record that a conception has been steeped in the unconscious, and there accepted by the deeper potencies of the mind. Because it was once accepted in this way, the cosmogony of the Bible is still in one sense more real than that of modern science; for while we no longer accept it, we cannot but visualize it.[2]

In 1926 Muir was discussing the problem of writing poetry in an age of science. With hindsight, we can see this quotation from *Transition* as a comment on the nature of his own pursuit of the 'real'. In his life as in his poetry the real and the Fable come to mean much the same thing: the story is of a search for an image that has been 'accepted by the deeper potencies of the mind'. Much of *An Autobiography* is concerned with those occasions when 'the miscellaneous dross of experience' 'has fallen away to reveal' 'a few glints of immortality', a reality beyond the moment. Those moments come in a variety of forms and they indicate an essential truth about the Fable: that it is known not in one but in many ways, some more adequate than others, some distorted and misleading, but all giving expression to a fundamental and usually inarticulate knowledge. The two 'purifications' Muir describes – the boyhood religious 'conversion' in Kirkwall and the socialist conversion in Glasgow – were times when he seemed 'to become for a little while part of the fable'. They, as we have seen, were impure 'purifications', too earthbound to be of enduring value. In their most elemental form, Muir had thought, they would occur in dreams, 'for dreams go without a hitch into the fable, and waking life does not'. Yet there are many moments recorded in *An Autobiography* when in waking life he was conscious of a kind of transfiguration of the ordinary and – again, with hindsight – we may justifiably see them as stages on the road towards that comprehensive transfiguration of which he wrote in the poem to which it gave its name. His first visit to Italy in the 1920s 'was a curiously external affair'; but though it was not the revelation of the later visit, he describes occasions when he encountered a quality of life that had for him a kind of transparency. These were experiences within which he sensed the larger continuing life of the spirit, always there within the dross of circumstance but rarely as immediate as, for instance, in the gentleness and dignity of the Italian family in the Carrara mountains. Muir and his companions had taken shelter from the rain in a lonely farmhouse. It is a poetic eye that recalls the experience of the scene:

The gentleness and dignity of that family in that lonely place, the veil of flies hanging from the walls, bemused us as we walked on, and I became dimly aware of a good life which had existed there for many centuries before medicine and hygiene identified goodness with cleanliness. The veil of flies seemed to throw into relief the delicacy and purity of these faces bred by a tradition so much older than ours, and embodying virtues which we had forgotten.

Following this he recalls 'another glimpse of that more real Italy when we attended the annual celebration of the Black Christ at Lucca'. Note, again, it is the artist's use of the word 'real'. Here the reality was in the shape of the

old peasant women kneeling in prayer, their faces streaming with tears as they gazed at the statue of their Lord. At the same time, not far off, a fair was in full swing, with booths displaying giants and dwarfs, clowns and conjurors. This was an immemorial part of the solemn day, and it seemed to us in no way incongruous (pp. 212–13).

On the whole, though, he had not come alive to Italy on that first visit.

I could have had little sense of form at that time. At any rate I saw many fine buildings in Pisa and Florence and Lucca, but except in Lucca every palace or church was irrecoverably cut off from the part of myself in which I could feel as well as see it (p. 210).

He had clearly not been free of that impulse to turn away from the physical shapes of his surroundings that he had developed out of self-protection in his years in Glasgow and 'Fairport'. There was still in him something of *The Enchanted Knight*:

When a bird cries within the silent grove
   The long-lost voice goes by, he makes to rise
And follow, but his cold limbs never move,
   And on the turf unstirred his shadow lies.

When they did not come through dreams, the 'glints of immortality' came from encounters with individuals: from such as his friend, John Holms, (commemorated in the poem, *To J.F.H.*) whose company always 'brought a sense of abundance . . . all things gladly fulfilling the laws of their nature . . . and was like a return to Adam's world'; from a meeting in the 1920s with 'an impoverished Junker, Ivo von Lucken' whose 'style of life' was 'created out of a complete lack of pettiness and a refusal to recognize the existence of time. . . . I cannot remember that he had any views. I think he had only devotions.' In Prague just before his departure for England after the Communist coup of 1948 it was again in the peasants and in immemorial ceremony that he found an image of hope. He and his wife had walked out to a church on the outskirts of Prague and inside had seen 'peasant women kneeling before the image of their Lord':

one of them, just in front of me, with a worn, kind, handsome face, knelt motionless, and my eyes came back again and again to the worn and patched soles of her boots, a battered image of her own constancy and humble faith. I did not feel that this ancient humanity could ever be destroyed by the new order (p. 272).

Some such image surely lies behind the late poem, *The Cloud*. In that and in many more of the poems in his final volume, *One Foot in Eden*, lies one kind of response to his earlier feeling that 'the images of universal purification' that he had known 'stick out from my workaday existence . . . do not go into life'. And this, as we shall see, was directly to do with 'the gradual revelation of Italy' during his period there as Director of the British Council Institute. There at last, it seems, he discovered a full image of the real, a culmination and justification of an intuitive understanding that had previously come to him through a variety of forms of the fable – through myth, emblem, story and personal relationship. Such a culmination had been foreshadowed in *The Transfiguration* (included in *The Labyrinth* collection) and there is a certain imaginative aptness in Muir's misrecollection of having written this poem in Rome.'[3] For although it was actually written in Czechoslovakia, it belongs to the temper of mind that produced *One Foot in Eden*.

Very aptly, *The Transfiguration* is placed in the collected edition immediately after *The Visitor*. It is not only that it turns on a moment of unsolicited vision of which *The Visitor* speaks; in addition, the very writing of the poem had for Muir something in the nature of a discovery. Replying to a lady who had written to thank him for the poem, and had drawn his attention to its 'links with orthodox Christianity', he said:

I know nothing of the literature of the Transfiguration, and in writing the poem probably did not see where it was leading me. On the other hand I have always had a particular feeling for that transmutation of life which is found occasionally in poetry, and in the literature of prophecy, and sometimes in one's own thoughts when they are still . . . I seem to have blundered into something greater than I knew (23 July 1948).

He says in the same letter that 'the idea of Judas going back into innocence has often been with me', but what we must imagine, I think, is a long period of time during which the various 'transmutations' he had experienced had as it were coalesced and were awaiting formal recognition, a single embracing statement of meaning. A later comment suggests that Muir himself saw it this way and, moreover, that his own psychic history was an image of mankind's, a representative story issuing in a climactic revelation to which the whole world could give assent: 'Perhaps in the imagination of mankind the Transfiguration has become a powerful symbol, standing for many things, and among them those transformations of reality which the imagination itself creates.'[4]

At two points in *The Transfiguration* the disciples are made to question the vision. But for them and for us, the question is rhetorical, a concession to conventional scepticism. For the poem itself answers the question. It is easier to register one's sense of its genuineness negatively rather than positively: there is here no hectoring, no special pleading, no wrestle with meaning, no sense of the personal at all. As if effortlessly, the vision seems to choose the words for itself, so that from the start we are drawn directly to the stillness within which all is purified, renewed:

> So from the ground we felt that virtue branch
> Through all our veins till we were whole, our wrists
> As fresh and pure as water from a well,
> Our hands made new to handle holy things,
> The source of all our seeing rinsed and cleansed
> Till earth and light and water entering there
> Gave back to us the clear unfallen world.

The genuineness of the vision redeems the everyday language (just as the language of the vision speaks for the redemption of the world); 'virtue' here grows in meaning as the effects of its branching are described; 'Holy', too. As we know, Muir never became an orthodox Christian, but his imagination here is deeply enmeshed with Christian beliefs. Paradoxically, a traditional vocabulary much soiled by rhetoric and various kinds of abuse is here made good and usable. So that when, later in the poem, after the detailed description of the transfigured world, we read that now, afterwards, 'all that radiant kingdom lies forlorn', the shop-soiled, Sunday-school-suggestive 'radiant' has itself been rescued from its contemporary tawdriness and given its proper meaning. Such a restoration cannot be accounted for except by reference to the commanding vision which it helps to express. Muir's imagination works with greatest ease and expressive effect when in touch with myths and traditions most closely in tune with what he is seeking, what he is 'blundering' into. There are echoes of Milton in parts of the poem's syntax; there are, more obviously, the cadences of the authorized version:

> For he had said, 'To the pure all things are pure.'
> And when we went into the town, he with us,
> The lurkers under doorways, murderers,
> With rags tied round their feet for silence, came
> Out of themselves to us and were with us,

But such features do not enter the poem as intrusive special voices, lending weight to an otherwise doubtful story. They are natural elements in that skein of traditional symbolism and imagery – that language, indeed, of revelation – upon which Muir's conviction authorizes him to draw. 'All was in its place', making this world 'unreal'; the language removes everything from its provisional, temporal perspective, bestows a stillness and a grace such as there was on 'the starting day':

> The painted animals
> Assembled there in gentle congregations,
> Or sought apart their leafy oratories,
> Or walked in peace, the wild and tame together,
> As if, also for them, the day had come.

The anguished search whose beginnings were recorded in *The Stationary Journey* ends – or, rather, reaches one of its ends – in *The Transfiguration*. There the desire to read in 'transmutation's blank' seemed a cruel burden, a hapless thing beyond all realization; the imagination might exercise itself in pursuit of it but in *The Stationary Journey* it remained

> A dream! the astronomic years
>   Patrolled by stars and planets bring
> Time led in chains from post to post
>   Of the all-conquering Zodiac ring.

In fact, as Muir's reference to 'one's thoughts when they are still' suggests, the very effort of the imagination that *The Stationary Journey* records comes from that level of the mind on which the eventual resolution of the problem of time will be discovered. Like the Eden of *The Transfiguration*, transfiguration is 'everywhere and nowhere'; but we have to learn to see. For Muir the learning was not entirely, perhaps hardly at all, a conscious thing; the eventual revelation came as a summation of the visionary experiences that he records in *An Autobiography* and upon which his poetry so often draws. (In this case, one of the 'sources' is a dream he had had over a quarter of a century earlier at the time of his psychoanalysis. It is described in *An Autobiography*.) The movement of the last section of this poem threads its way back through the labyrinth as it were (*The Labyrinth* began with a seemingly endless, meandering sentence of thirty five lines; *The Transfiguration* ends with one of ten) to a state of innocence. The broken rhythms of the earlier stages give way to the fluidity of the final statement that describes the prophesied second coming and the transmutations it will bring with it:

> But he will come again, it's said, though not
> Unwanted and unsummoned; for all things,
> Beasts of the field, and woods, and rocks, and seas,
> And all mankind from end to end of the earth
> Will call him with one voice. In our own time,
> Some say, or at a time when time is ripe.
> Then he will come, Christ the uncrucified,
> Christ the discrucified, his death undone,
> His agony unmade, his cross dismantled –
> Glad to be so – and the tormented wood
> Will cure its hurt and grow into a tree
> In a green springing corner of young Eden,
> And Judas damned take his long journey backward
> From darkness into light and be a child
> Beside his mother's knee, and the betrayal
> Be quite undone and never more be done.

The Transfiguration appeared in *The Listener* in February 1948, the month of the Communist takeover in Prague. In July of that year Muir returned to Britain and suffered a nervous breakdown, undoubtedly a direct consequence of the stress of Prague. We might have thought that the poem represented a point from which he could survey life with some equanimity. But it was never to be so simple. Back in England, in Cambridge, he 'fell plumb into a dead pocket of life which I had never guessed at before'. The consequences were those that follow when a man takes 'the drug that Helen knew' (*The Charm*):

> while the drinker, wide awake,
> Sat in his chair, indifference grew
> Around him in the estranging day.

Under the deadening enchantment, a man will look out on life as a mere passing show, 'all storyless, all strange'. (To be insane and 'storyless' is the fate of Oedipus in *The Other Oedipus*, the poem that precedes *The Charm*). Such a detachment is spiritual death: it is free of agony but knows no joy. The withdrawal into insensibility that Helen's drug induced in her victim was in Muir the outcome of the denial of humanity that he had witnessed in Prague. Yet, there is always hope. Locked into indifference he may be

But far within him something cried
For the great tragedy to start,
The pang in lingering mercy fall,
And sorrow break upon his heart.

For Muir the cure was – fortuitously – quick. He moved to Rome in the following year and made a complete recovery. To Rome, it may be said, we owe many of the best of his later poems, for it was there that he knew for certain for the first time in his life that 'Christ had walked upon the earth'. In Prague everything that had happened in the months preceding the putsch had made that a nonsense. Inevitably Muir had felt the challenge to his idea of humanity in a personal way. *The Cloud* (from the second part of *One Foot in Eden*) lets us in to his own feelings at that time; but that is, as it were, an incidental benefit. What we are reading about in *The Cloud* is the challenge to our own humanity that the events of Prague represent. Seen against that challenge, the faith of many of the poems in *One Foot in Eden* is the more impressive. The speakers in the poem are driving to the 'Writers' House'; they lose their way, see a 'young man harrowing, hidden in dust'. They arrive, listen to a 'preacher from Urania' preaching that God is dead, and drive back, 'teased'

> By the brown barren fields, the harrowing,
> The figure walking in its cloud, the message
> From far Urania.

The disturbance we experience in reading *The Cloud* grows from the maturity of Muir's powers having been brought to bear on distinctively contemporary tensions and fears that he shares with us. The poem's strength is not that of an attitude forcefully and challengingly expressed. It is not a question of our being moved to think out a position, moral or political, though politics and morality are here of the essence. As in so much of Muir at his best, *The Cloud* presents through a simple narrative an image that expresses the relations between our present anxieties and our deeper intuitions in a way impossible in discursive forms. 'The young man harrowing, hidden in dust' is an immemorial figure; a figure unchanging, unspectacular, but with his own dignity and grace. 'He seemed

> A prisoner walking in a moving cloud
> Made by himself for his own purposes;
> And there he grew and was as if exalted
> To more than man, yet not, not glorified.

As the repeated negative insists, and the following line no less, he is

> A pillar of dust moving in dust; no more.

The setting is one in which, particularly if we are sensitive to the various resonances of the 'road' images in Muir's poems, this man is the only sign of life in an otherwise anonymous and arid landscape. The 'little winding roads' lead to 'nothing but themselves'.

The poem opens casually enough, seemingly anecdotal, and yet with startling effect we are quickly in a 'country of the mind' where alienation and mystery are simultaneously present. This ambivalence in which the young man is both 'exalted' and a 'prisoner' prefigures the content of the second part of the poem. The 'preacher from Urania' is a figure through whom the ambivalence of the young man is illuminated and our age thus most impressively shown 'its form and pressure'. As the word suggests, the 'preacher's' message is conveyed in the language of religion though the message portends its eclipse:

> And there a preacher from Urania
> (Sad land where hope each day is killed by hope)
> Praised the good dust, man's ultimate salvation,
> And cried that God was dead.

Our time is familiar with materialistic and nihilistic creeds that appropriate the very vocabularies they exist to extinguish. Muir is alive to the ironies of a situation in which the stance and the promises of the new men can only be expressed in a language, a tradition, that they hate. But the irony is not exploited, and for a very good reason: the poem does not simply repudiate the speaker's message and its image of humanity. The world it describes is vulnerable to the strident ideologies that threaten to overturn its traditional values; and the poet is part of that world – more perceptive and sceptical no doubt, but aware that a challenge has been issued that will not be lightly put off. The battle will be in men's minds, and who knows the limits of the mind's capacity to discover the truth and to hold on to it once it is known? The image of the young man and the memory of the message fuse in the poet's mind; the result is a world out of joint, a feeling of bewilderment and lost directions. The 'winding roads' have led to this:

> Image and thought condensed to a giant form
> That walked the earth clothed in its earthly cloud,
> Dust made sublime in dust. And yet it seemed unreal
> And lonely as things not in their proper place.

Magnificently, this image condenses the opposing values and world-views of traditional Christianity and modern materialistic ideologies such as Communism. The form is 'giant', a thing of irresistible power, whatever the end to which that power is put; it has the earthliness of a creed that sees man as nothing *but* dust, and yet it is 'sublime', a word whose reach and association is denied to such a creed. Hence the unreality, the loneliness as of a creature disinherited – or, alternatively, of a being set on adventures of the spirit as yet beyond understanding. The vulnerability of the speaker here is given in the narrative sequence; it is he who experiences the fusion of disparate images of man, he who suffers the anxiety of displacement. The greatness of the poem is that Muir to a degree accepts the challenge and is aware of the difficulties of withstanding the apparent flood of alien ideologies: the fusion acknowledges the power of their message. And yet there is a deep reluctance to accept them, a longing for assurance that the life of the spirit is real and enduring. Without it, what is there?

> And thinking of the man
> Hid in his cloud we longed for light to break
> And show that his face was the face once broken in Eden
> Beloved, world-without-end lamented face;
> And not a blindfold mask on a pillar of dust.

One could not call this a desperate longing; to be able to use the language of these few lines is surely an earnest of the spiritual realities it represents. But the language is under threat and thus so are those realities. *The Cloud* is a more troubled and troubling poem than Hardy's *In Time of the Breaking of Nations* or of Edward Thomas's *As the Team's Head Brass*, both of which it in some ways resembles. Those poems express a faith in the enduring simplicities of life; these, they say, will survive catastrophe, however terrible. We can see, however – and Muir's poetry helps us to see it the more clearly – that Hardy's and Thomas's views belong to a world with a still traditional sense of possible catastrophe. However extensive and terrible the physical suffering and dislocation caused by the First World War, it did not for them figure as a metaphysical event – that is to say, as a war that threatened to work a fundamental change in man's idea of himself. The possibility of nuclear war is surely one of the pressures telling in Muir's poem, as it so obviously is in *The Horses*, the poem that follows *The Cloud* in *Collected Poems*; but the war that gives the poem its impetus and its disturbing imagery is of a more radically consequential kind: it threatens to rewrite the story of mankind, to deny the existence of the Fable. For Hardy and Thomas there would always be acts of a simplicity and predictability that would guarantee the survival of values. By the time of *The Cloud*, with its apparent allusion to the world of 1984 (Urania) the enemy had become so much more subtle and persuasive.

First published in 1955, *The Cloud* of course looks back to a time before the revelation of Italy. What that 'gradual revelation' meant to Muir is clear both from the final chapter of *An Autobiography* and from his letters written from Italy in 1949 and 1950.

You feel the Gods (including the last and greatest of them) have all been here, and are still present in a sense in the places where they once were. It has brought very palpably to my mind the theme of Incarnation and I feel that probably I shall write a few poems about that high and difficult theme sometime (20 December 1949).

'Rome is supposed to give you a scunner at Catholicism, or a temptation to join. I haven't any scunner (except at some of the politics) or any temptation to join (I couldn't) but what a religion it is, how much it takes into itself, and how much more human Catholics are at least in Italy, than Protestants anywhere. I'm immensely impressed with Romanism, on the whole I like it, and the carelessness of it, and all the imaginative richness and ritual of it; but I could no more join it than fly to the moon' (19 May 1950).

It is perhaps not surprising that Muir should have delighted in the imaginative ritual and richness: it surely appealed to that part of him which had earlier applauded the Scottish ballads for the 'sheer unconditionality of their vision and . . . that something materialistic in the imagination of the Scots which is one of their qualities'. In that part of himself he had always been deeply repelled by the action of Knox and the Reformation in turning 'the grand conception of life as a thing of sin and enjoyment into a theology and a set of intellectual principles'.[5] The tentativeness of his allusion to Christ and his care to speak simply of incarnation rather than of *the* Incarnation belong with the suspicion of dogma and principle. But they also belong with a developed intuitive knowledge that all art incarnates imaginative truth; that with myth, emblem and religious iconography, it offers us a way into that reality of which for Western man the figure of Christ is the least easily denied. 'The cities of Tuscany and Umbria . . . looked like new incarnations sprung from the source of inexhaustible felicity and though they had witnessed violence and crime, they rose above it into their own world and their own light.' One is reminded of that passage in the first chapter of *An Autobiography* where he talks of looking across to the neighbouring island of Egilsay and to 'the black chapel with a round, pointed tower, where St Magnus had been murdered in the twelfth century': 'It was the most beautiful thing within sight, and it rose every day against the sky until it seemed to become a sign in the fable of our lives.' The distance between Wyre and Rome was only the distance between two signs in the fable, one in childhood simple, the other in maturity inexpressibly rich and various, but both existing on a common ground uniting the different stages of a man's life. Each was an incarnation and an image of life. In a letter to Aitken written in 1951 Muir says of such an image that it is 'humanly necessary and can never be complete. It has to be visual, sensible, and as far as it comes from participation in life, as far as it shows understanding, spiritual at the same time' (28 June 1951). Such an image will call out to and express the aspiration of all our faculties, every level of our being. The appeal of Catholicism and of the Incarnation was for Muir in the fullness of their imagery. Like Goethe before him 'his troubled soul found calm and repose among the antiquities of Italy'.[6] 'But it was the evidence of another Incarnation that met one everywhere and gradually exerted its influence.' As a boy attending the United Presbyterian Church in Orkney he had been 'aware of religion chiefly as the Sacred Word . . . it did not tell me by any outward sign that the Word had been made flesh'. He had come to feel that Protestantism (Knox especially) was a key factor in Scotland's winter, estranging a people from themselves in some ways as violently as purely material philosophies had done with other peoples. So that the summoning of an image of life, whether through art or religion, becomes for him a reaching out for the real; or, alternatively expressed, an assimilation of the real, so that one shall know one's humanity. Now is the day of the 'abstract man'; in his ascendancy is to be read the decline of Scotland.

'Scotsmen', he had written in *Scottish Journey*, attempting to explain 'the myth of Burns', 'have an exceptionally powerful myth-making faculty. The history of Scotland is filled with legendary figures, actual characters on which the popular imagination has worked, making them its own and by doing so, transfiguring them'.[7] *The Incarnate One* is about everything in Scottish history that despises or condemns such a faculty. Muir's anti-Calvinist feeling had always been intense but the experience of Rome and the visible incarnations that surrounded him there clearly strengthened the feeling further and provoked him to a directness of expression that earlier would have worried him as being too 'minatory'. *The Incarnate One* is an indictment and a prophecy; an expression of outraged incredulity that 'our race' could 'betray/The image and the Incarnate One unmake' and a prediction that the unmaking, life-denying ordinances of King Calvin's 'iron pen' will for generations to come continue to work their way 'invisibly in brain and nerve and cell'. It may be that Muir could find it in himself to accept so strong a poetic expression of his distaste because, angry and saddened though it is, the poem arises from a very firm basis of experience and conviction: behind it lie not only the overwhelming immediacies of Rome but a clear understanding of what it is in the modern world to which they issue so strong a challenge. We have seen that to Muir Calvinism and Marxism were equally grounded in Wrath, equally insensitive to the struggle within the individual. In that similarity they express that most characteristic feature of modern societies, the tendency analysed in 'The natural man and the political man' as leading to a reduction of the image of man – 'who has become simpler, more temporal, more realistic and more insignificant'. The reduction is given in the poem in the contrast between Giotto with his picturing of 'Christ, man and creature in their inner day' and Calvin 'with his iron pen'; between 'the archaic peoples in their ancient awe' and 'those who can/Build their cold empire on the abstract man'. The universal sign of the degeneration, the ice age of the spirit, is announced in the first lines of *The Incarnate One*:

> The windless northern surge, the sea-gull's scream,
> And Calvin's kirk crowning the barren brae.

and is condensed in the radical contrast of Word and word:

The Word made flesh here is made word again,
A word made word in flourish and arrogant crook.
See there King Calvin with his iron pen,
And God three angry letters in a book,
And there the logical hook
On which the Mystery is impaled and bent
Into an ideological instrument.

The Word of St John's Gospel has here become the ordinary word of human speech and that in turn has become the death of meaning, imprisoning rather than restoring the spirit. The unusual physicality of the last three lines here, where we feel the cruel disnaturing of the Mystery, is not melodramatic: in implicit answer to and denial of the abstract man on whose behalf ideologies are constructed, the very word 'ideological' is invested with a muscularity, a deliberate awkwardness that well renders the unnaturalness of the process it is there to describe. Just so, the conclusion of *The Incarnate One* –

The generations tell
Their personal tale: the One has far to go
Past the mirages and the murdering snow.

– arrives with a prophetic intensity fully justified by the sustained conviction of the whole: we know – and we know it the more completely if we have read the poems in the first section of *One Foot in Eden* – that the reading of past, present and future which it gives us has been lived, not just observed. Despite the personal antagonisms and deprivations that we know are at the root of the poem, it does not have the character of a case made out so much as of an experience rendered. These things have been true for Muir and now so clear is the truth that it stands forth with an objectivity that frees it from its connection with personal circumstances.

The Incarnate One spells out the meaning of disinheritance and in its story we read more than the decline of Scotland. 'Muir', says Kathleen Raine, 'possessed a birthright rare in the modern world, and perhaps irrecoverable, in being able to write for his tribe, to speak with the voice of the ancestors.'[8] The 'I' and the 'we' of many of his poems do not signify (as they would with many modern poets) fundamental differences in the focus and direction of the writing. Frequently, each is a form of the other. For the personal journey of the spirit is in the individual life analogous to that of the tribe, the race, of humanity itself. That is perhaps clearest in *The Journey Back* where the personal quest 'to seek my kindred' quickly leads to the inescapable realization – 'I must in other lives with many a leap/Blindfold' – and thence, eventually, to the knowledge hinted at in the question: 'How could we be if all were not in all?' All men make the same journey. The difficult thing for modern men is to realize that truth with the immediacy it once possessed. Kathleen Raine's feeling that Muir's birthright in this respect is 'perhaps irrecoverable' suggests how we should see that difficulty. Muir's early years, as we have seen, introduced him to a life that was communal in the richest sense: a life that through its art, its customs, its rituals and its general piety, confirmed the continuity of present and past and the naturalness of the individual's place within both. Muir's upbringing in such an environment and his subsequent wanderings strongly disposed him both to feel it as the norm of human society and to see much in the modern world as a falling away from it. Sometimes, that disintegration became the image of the very first Fall: 'Long since we were a family, a people,/The legends say' (*The Ring*). In *Scotland 1941*, it is seen as a historical reality, an avoidable disaster:

> We were a tribe, a family, a people.
> Wallace and Bruce guard now a painted field,

In the light of this we can understand that Muir should have been drawn to the stories of Moses and 'legendary Abraham/The Old Chaldean wanderer', patriarchs who undertook their journey in the name of a promise much more than personal. Abraham, in the poem that bears his name, dies 'content and full of years' and though Moses' vision is shattered in history, the 'holy bread of the land crumbled and broken . . . gnawed as offal', that vision is a reality; 'it stands becalmed in time for ever', a source of strength and a symbol of a heritage in which the individual and the race are one. Modern Scotland, its inheritance blighted, hill and altar stripped bare, the 'ancient oak of loyalty' (*Scotland 1941*) felled, is the very winter of the spirit. In *Scotland's Winter*,[9] 'Kingless . . . songless', its 'powerless dead'

> Listening can hear no more
> Than a hard tapping on the sounding floor
> A little overhead
> Of common heels that do not know
> Whence they come or where they go
> And are content
> With their poor frozen life and shallow banishment.

It seems that in his poetry at least Muir could not write of Scotland except in palpable anger uncharacteristic of his work as a whole. He seems temporarily to lose sight of that larger view in which men continue to resist the attempt to destroy their inheritance. Elsewhere in the poetry 'we' or 'they', when not journeying but at rest, are often conceived as persisting, in simplicity and modesty, with a life of ancient and unspectacular virtue, a guarantee of continuity in the face of disaster and betrayal. They 'lead in their harvest still' in *Outside Eden*; they are the people 'not sad nor glad' but in 'an order natural and wise' in *The City*; they know and regret that 'old bad world that swallowed its children quick/At one great gulp' in *The Horses*; they are the people who, in the bleak accusation of *Scotland 1941*, lived where 'A simple sky roofed in that rustic day'. These are the people – and we may at the same time say that they are that part of ourselves, since 'I' and 'we' fuse in Muir's reading of man and tribe – who keep alive the prospect of a humanity that goes beyond the intense and intent individualism that has displaced the traditional harmony of individual and race. They do this faithfully, but under difficulty. *The Difficult Land* is, as it were, their poem. This is at once an ancestral land and a country of the mind. The poem seems to draw upon a pervasive modern malaise, a sense of purposelessness, of fruitless effort, and yet to place it in a perspective of ages in which it becomes an 'outline of a possibility' that may be realized in any age. The physical detail of this difficult land aligns it with that of *The Cloud*:

> our fields
> Mile after mile of soft and useless dust.
> On dull delusive days presaging rain
> We yoke the oxen, go out harrowing,
> Walk in the middle of an ochre cloud,
> Dust rising before us and falling again behind us,
> Slowly and gently settling where it lay.

In other words the immemorial peasant landscape, anywhere. And the 'we' of the poem are as universal as that landscape: not the Jews, not the Scots, but humanity itself, ever subject to the barrenness for which the 'sad and senseless' earth comes to stand and to the 'men from over the border' who 'come trampling down the corn, and kill our cattle'. What answer can there be to these dull expectations of monotony and occasional violence? The answer comes in the latter part of the poem which amounts to an acknowledgement of those elementary gifts and accomplishments that sustain human beings even when all around threatens to destroy them:

> We are a people; race and speech support us,
> Ancestral rite and custom, roof and tree,
> Our songs that tell of our triumphs and disasters
> (Fleeting alike), continuance of fold and hearth,
> Our names and callings, work and rest and sleep,
> And something that, defeated, still endures –
> These things sustain us.

Despite that continuity – a less vulnerable inheritance than *Scotland's Winter* admits to – despite the 'something that, defeated, still endures' (with its echo of *The Combat*) despair and weariness is sometimes upon men when that very inheritance seems an imprisoning burden and the overwhelming desire is for union with 'the secrecy of the earth/ Furrowed by broken ploughs lost deep in time'. What is described is a mood or a temporary halting of ordinary faith that we all know. What follows, though, is one of those simple passages in which the ordinary virtues of 'honesty, kindness, courage and fidelity' are revisited in their natural home – 'faces of goodness'. In them the 'unremembered' dead 'who lodge in us so strangely' are remembered and the continuity and our obligation asserted in one of those beautiful figures that come to Muir when he is most possessed by the mystery of time:

> For how can we reject
> The long last look on the ever-dying face
> Turned backward from the other side of time?
> And how offend the dead and shame the living
> By these despairs? And how refrain from love?
> This is a difficult country, and our home.

This is what it means to 'write for his tribe, to speak with the voice of the ancestors'.

It is probably idle to wonder whether, with a different upbringing, Muir might have become a practising Catholic. It is puzzling to see on the one hand the intensity of response to the Christian story from which *The Annunciation* arose and, on the other, the unequivocal opposition to becoming a member of the Church. It may be that he could never altogether accept that a Church could avoid making 'God three angry letters in a book'. But I fancy that the reason for his holding back has much more to do with native sensibility, with that capacity described by Kathleen Raine of 'wedding the archetypal to the real as only those poets can do for whom the real is the signature of the Mystery'.[10] Imaginatively, Muir is an eclectic, discovering the fabulous in the ordinary, drawing upon a variety of traditions and approaching the truth under whatever transformations they contain. Such a hospitality was partly learned, but it was also inherited. In his late essay on the ballads, 'The natural estate', he says of the supernatural world of such poems as *Thomas the Rhymer* that it 'embodied for the peasantry their sense of the mystery surrounding them, in which they saw at one glance and with no sense of incongruity, Christian revelation and natural magic'.[11] Obviously Muir's hospitality is of a more conscious kind and has access to richer sources but I think that fundamentally he retained that instinctive peasant feeling for the unseen unity of different artistic and religious traditions. 'The picture', as he said in talking of our need for an image of life, 'is never complete.' 'The evidences of another Incarnation' are much felt in *One Foot in Eden* (1956) – though he rejected from *Collected Poems* the unequivocally Christian poems in that volume – but no myth or story dominates. Greek, Hebrew and Christian myth sort with familiar heraldic emblem to their mutual advantage. *The Emblem*, indeed – the poem that closes the first section of the volume – we may surely read as a commentary on the vitality of these various traditions, their continuing power to reveal the order within the dross of circumstance, the 'jewel within the day':

> For that scant-acre kingdom is not dead,
> Nor save in seeming shrunk. When at its gate,
> Which you pass daily, you incline your head,
> And enter (do not knock; it keeps no state)
>
> You will be with space and order magistral,
> And that contracted world so vast will grow
> That this will seem a little tangled field.

One implication of the picture never being complete is that a living tradition is always open to transformations that will reveal fresh meaning. Several poems in *One Foot in Eden* draw on the book of Genesis but it is no matter of modernizing the myth of the creation or of the Garden of Eden. In every case, the biblical story is transformed and a relation established with worlds not dreamed of at its conception. The mode of *The Animals* and *The Days* is typical Muir. In the first neither the 'animals' nor the 'world' with which their condition is contrasted are concrete presences. Each is an abstract and it is a feature of Muir's skill that the contrast is nonetheless strongly felt. It is a very compact poem, making its statements with an admirable economy. Initially the animals are accounted for largely through negatives; they are identified by what, negatively, distinguishes them from human beings. It is a life of unconsciousness and insensibility – no past, no future; above all, no resistance to offer earth's diurnal course through the creative force of language:

> No word do they have, not one
> To plant a foot upon,
> Were never in any place.

The world as we know it is a creation of language:

> For with names the world was called
> Out of the empty air,
> With names was built and walled,

Language is the resistance we can offer to 'deceiving death', to the blank unconsciousness from which for the animals there is no escape. The negatives return as if once again to signal man's fortune in being granted a way back 'into the memoried day'. But then, startlingly, the poem turns on itself and the effect is of a sudden expansion, a sudden recognition of the obvious, as the perspective shifts and, simply, we are made to see that

> All is new and near
> In the unchanging Here
> Of the fifth great day of God,
> That shall remain the same,
> Never shall pass away.

The insistent stresses of that third line call us away from the simple contrast in the earlier part of *The Animals*. That now appears almost self-congratulatory. Man's gift is unique; but so is that of the rest of His creation – in this case the gift of knowing that which is beyond change, beyond improvement, beyond self-induced catastrophe. That this is the reading we should give the poem is clear from the final line. It comes, as in a good many of Muir's poems, separated by double line spacing, with an effect of closing one argument and opening another:

> On the sixth day we came.

The line reverberates with the ambiguities that have come to light within the main body of the poem. What was the significance of man's creation? There is no simple answer. For all the creative energy that the power of language released, for all that it enabled an intelligible world to be built and walled, the mere unvarnished statement that 'on the sixth day we came' instantly provokes us into making our own qualifications. When we came, so did sin, destruction, disaster – all those things that keep us perpetually 'walled' *out* of 'the unchanging Here . . . that shall remain the same'.

In *The Days* deliverance from the evil heralded by the sixth day is envisaged as the longed for resolution of the seventh:

> Issuing from the Word
> The seven days came,
> Each in its own place,
> Its own name.

The 'Word', of course, is that of St John's Gospel; it is the source of all creation, not (as in *The Animals*) a human invention giving shape and purpose to our actions. The poem affects us as myth. We get nowhere if we ask *how*

> The stallion's tread
> Soundlessly fell on the flood, and the animals poured
> Onward, flowing across the flowing wave.

Water, night, shadow, the stallion, the lion, the flood, earth and heaven, the fish, all enter with their weight of traditional meaning and suggestion, the achievement of the poem being to incorporate them into a picture that proclaims their authenticity, their natural truth. When 'the shadow of man' falls upon the waters

> and earth and the heavens scrawled
> With names, as if each pebble and leaf would tell
> The tale untellable.

we are reading of that moment in creation when the Word gives birth to language, to the commanding facility for understanding and celebration. Pebble and leaf are more real once man has the words to describe them; the tale is still untellable but through the word man strives to discern and express it. It is the moment of glory, the acme of the Creation:

> And the Lord called
> The seventh day forth and the glory of the Lord.

The Days is in two parts and the above lines link them. The latter part of the poem presents a vision of humanity as glory fulfilled through the Word. The hard and rocky spring has given way to a pattern which can only exist because man is there to discern it.

> And now we see in the sun
> The mountains standing clear in the third day
> (Where they shall always stay)
> And thence a river run,
> Threading, clear cord of water, all to all:
> The wooded hill and the cattle in the meadow,
> The tall wave breaking on the high sea-wall,
> The people at evening walking,
> The crescent shadow
> Of the light-built bridge, the hunter stalking
> The flying quarry, each in a different morning,
> The fish in the billow's heart, the man with the net,
> The hungry swords crossed in the cross of warning,

The elements of this vision are archetypal, a collection of images that connect not with the sensuous objects to which the individual words normally refer but with their inward, gathered meanings. The wooded hill and the cattle in the meadow, the hunter stalking, the flying quarry, are figures constant in human life; they are not provisional, not temporal at all. And yet what we see in this vision – though it represents an order that we may celebrate and worship – is itself an imperfect representation of that higher order where 'the tumultuous world slips softly home/To its perpetual end and flawless bourne' (*The Journey Back*). That is what the women pray for. The day is 'fragmentary' and can never be anything else until

> the day where all are gathered together,
> Things and their names, in the storm's and the lightning's nest,
> The seventh great day and the clear eternal weather.

Though *The Days* was written in Rome, there is no hint in it of that 'inexhaustible source of metaphysical felicity' that Muir there felt to be all around him. The promise of that source is in another poem written around the same time, *Day and Night*. I have spoken frequently in this study of the direct relationship between imaginative clarity and technical assurance, of the way in which in Muir's best poems one feels the skill in handling verse forms to be intimately bound up with the sureness of the perception it expresses. In *Day and Night* Muir turns round upon his life and with something of that undismayed and relaxed clear-sightedness that distinguished *The Myth* recognizes that, as ever, there is 'something to pursue'. This, the characteristic attitude of the final volume, is made possible by a provisional arrival at a place from which, in the words of *The Question*, he can 'rest and roam'. In the paradox lies the provisionality; for the meaning is in the seeking. And the satisfaction is not in the arrival but in the certain knowledge that the goal, though unattainable, is real. We might thus pursue the metaphor of *The Question* to describe these final poems: the hunt (the Word used in that poem) continues and will always continue along those roads that keep recurring in Muir's poetry. The risk to the poetry is that it will become repetitive, that we will merely feel that the mystery is dissolved rather than affirmed through repetition. (Towards the end of his life Muir said he had been 'daunted in the last year or two by the fear that I keep on writing the same poem'.) And this does happen occasionally. Poems such as *Into Thirty Centuries Born* and *The Other Story* are examples. But the impressive feature of *One Foot in Eden*, as indeed of much in the earlier volumes of Muir's maturity, is the distinctive life of individual poems palpably arising from a common source. It is impressive, but it should not be surprising. The devotional poets of the seventeenth century rehearse a mystery and celebrate a faith with no anxiety about repeating themselves. For Vaughan, for instance, who loved 'to resolve the sad vicissitude of things', each poem expresses a continuous aspiration, attempts to give form to a spiritual truth that is never in doubt. Vaughan's familiar comparison of the soul to a flower or to a creature whose broken wings can be repaired only through prayer and God's intercession; his use of springs, fountain, water and streams to signify the source of eternal life; or of 'cell', 'seat' and 'room' to indicate the heart as the temple of the Holy Ghost or the body as the prisoner of the soul – the recurrence of these emblems is not a blot on his work. They recur because they have found acceptance with him and his reader as a proper reflection of an unquestioned truth. The true test of their acceptability is, however, in the poet's ability to prevent their decline into cliché: when the imaginative pressure is inadequate, when the familiar emblem recurs in the absence of the feeling that should animate it, the result is a stillbirth. In Muir's *Day and Night* the emblem of the road occurs yet again, but its life is that of the distinctive freshness of the poem as a whole. 'Night' here is the literal remembered night of childhood. It is more than that, though. Unlike the daylight with its

> Extravagant novelty too wild
> For the new eyes of a child

Night

> showed me only what I knew,
> Knew, yet never had been told,

It is also the more general darkness of archaic knowledge, of the ground whereon we know life as 'shapes too simple for a place/In the day's shrill complexity'; the child's night becomes symbolic of that more general darkness. I am reminded of Jung's description of himself as a young man: his 'No. 1' personality, the graspable social, conscious self; his No. 2 'no definable character at all . . . a *vita Peracta*, both, living, dead, everything in one, a total vision. . . . Number One regarded Number two as a region of inner darkness . . . but in Number two light reigned, as in the spacious halls of a royal palace whose high casements open upon a landscape flooded with sunlight. Here were meaning and historical continuity.'[12] Such a contrast is certainly there in *Day and Night* but the association that the poem makes is again Biblical. What from the night he 'knew, yet never had been told' was

> A speech that from the darkness grew
> Too deep for daily tongues to say,
> Archaic dialogue of a few
> Upon the sixth or the seventh day.

That 'speech' is the Word of St John – and of Muir's poem. The shapes that it calls up are native to us, known profoundly in childhood when we cannot know their significance, to be sought again now that we can understand. By the end of the poem, the two meanings of 'night' have been fused. He looks back, 'a man now gone with time so long' and tries

> to fit that world to this,
> The hidden to the visible play,

'That world' encompasses both childhood itself and the ancestral wisdom buried within us. The aspiration is to fully realize what faith tells us is true; to be true to that memory which for 'the few' in *Outside Eden* makes 'simple all that is', the memory that summons back that which we 'knew, yet never had been told'. He

> Would have them both, would nothing miss,
> Learn from the shepherd of the dark,
> Here in the light, the paths to know
> That thread the labyrinthine park,
> And the great Roman roads that go
> Striding across the untrodden day.

The expansive and solid sounding final two lines arise from a strength of conviction such as was expressed in *Too Much*. Those roads are real.

'The shepherd of the dark' is as close as Muir allows himself to get to a mention of Christ, but in imagery and emotional direction he echoes what Vaughan before him had said in his poem *The Night*:

> Wise Nicodemus saw such light
> As made him know his God by night.
>
> Most blest believer he!
> Who in that land of darkness and blinde eyes
> Thy long expected healing wings could see,
>   When thou didst rise,
> And what can never more be done,
> Did at mid-night speak with the Sun!

How should 'that world be fitted to this, the hidden to the visible play'? One answer, is, through Christ. In childhood 'nothing told me that Christ was born in the flesh and had lived on the earth'. *One Foot in Eden* says nothing of Christ but it is inconceivable without an acceptance of that truth. It makes no proclamations, issues no challenge.

> One foot in Eden still, I stand
> And look across the other land.
> The world's great day is growing late,
> Yet strange these fields that we have planted
> So long with crops of love and hate.
> Time's handiworks by time are haunted,
> And nothing now can separate
> The corn and tares compactly grown.
> The armorial weed in stillness bound
> About the stalk; these are our own.
> Evil and good stand thick around
> In the fields of charity and sin
> Where we shall lead our harvest in.

'At his best,' says Kathleen Raine, 'Muir achieved a poetic language at once powerfully mythological, yet concrete; symbolic, yet poignant with particular joy or anguish'.[13] *One Foot in Eden* is Muir at his best in the way Kathleen Raine indicates. The personal element, the 'I' that makes its calm and lucid profession is held in perfect balance with the emblems through which it is made. It seems right to use the word 'emblems' rather than symbols here (as in the related poem, *Outside Eden*) for the 'corn and tares', 'the armorial weed', 'the archetypal leaf' do not carry into the mind that charge of barely intelligible but nonetheless quite real significance that belongs to the symbolic. That is the mode of other poems in this volume such as *The Horses*. In *One Foot in Eden* emblems are the source of a generalizing precision of statement. They are not so intrinsically of course; the precision is not built into them. Like myth itself they await reanimation through the individual imagination. And the nature of that reanimation is not easy to point to. Just as in Muir's blank verse poems, the effect is a cumulative one, owing little to striking phrase or image, so in the poems that do their work in this other manner, one has to refer to an integrity of feeling at the core of the poem – an integrity that can be felt but hardly demonstrated save in quotation.

We know of course from Muir's other poems that such generalized emblematic language is not for him something that has to be enlisted to serve particular occasions. It is permanently present for him as a natural mode of understanding experience. Eden is, indeed, 'not an idea but an experience'. The beauty of the poem is in the commitment to, the belief in, that experience and in the other 'ideas' that are brought into relation with it. I have already pointed to the naturalness with which Muir can use words like 'hope and faith and pity and love', as he does here, and suggested how unusual that is. Here he makes a conclusive and comprehensive statement about good and evil that is similarly natural and rare. Why does one notice this so readily? It is I think because Muir's imagination was always in touch with ancestral notions of good and evil that were real for him in the way that for most of us now they never can be. It is not just the pervasive scepticism of the age that makes it difficult for our minds to come fully alive to the history in those words. It is, too, that we are in a different tradition from the one within which Muir grew up. Pre-eminently the mode in which the most vigorous and subtle thought of the last two centuries or so has expressed itself has been the discursive one. Broadly speaking, there has been a progressive decline in our ability to *feel* the reality of moral concepts. When Muir writes, in *One Foot in Eden*,

> Evil and good stand thick around
> In the fields of charity and sin
> Where we shall lead our harvest in

and

> Blossoms of grief and charity
> Bloom in these darkened fields alone.

the imaginative world from which such statements arise has much in common with the one from within which Shakespeare makes Duncan say (*Macbeth*)

> I have begun to plant thee, and will labour
> To make thee full of growing.

and Banquo to reply

> There if I grow
> The harvest is your own.

This is not, of course, to suggest that Muir's verse possesses the Shakespearean density to which in *Macbeth* the imagery of husbandry and fruitfulness so strongly contributes. But if the comparison seems extreme it may be useful to remember that Muir grew up in a tradition where the ballads 'handed down orally for hundreds of years' perpetuated just such an easy and fundamental intimacy of morality and metaphor. What is astonishing in Muir's case is that such an intimacy of understanding has survived in a modern world so hostile to it. From the rest of the poetry and from our knowledge of his life, we know what suffering and distraction lie behind *One Foot in Eden*. The serenity and finality are all the more moving for it. In '*I have been taught*,' the very last poem in the *Collected Poems*, he acknowledges, simply, that when everything else is taken into account he has learnt most from 'two mainly/Who gave me birth'. What he learnt from them is in this poem. It is as if everything that life has brought – the needless deaths in the family, the periods of personal despair and disillusion, the general European catastrophes of the present century – were allowed for in the understanding of good and evil that he drew in from parents, 'kinsmen, ancestors and friends'. In *One Foot in Eden*, now that 'the world's great day is growing late', that deep, traditional inarticulate understanding has been proved true.

> What had Eden ever to say
> Of hope and faith and pity and love
> Until was buried all its day
> And memory found its treasure trove?
> Strange blessings never in Paradise
> Fall from these beclouded skies.

'The road', says Muir in 'Yesterday's mirror', 'is a road which as it continues curves round towards its beginning, so that Traherne's description of his childhood is nearer to St Augustine's description of his ecstasy than any account of an intermediate stage of life could be.' It is in that essay that he talks of 'how right and fitting I had felt the world and everything in it to be when I was a child'. It was a time when in sharp distinction from the years of manhood,

Evil itself, when it entered that world, seemed to have work of its own to do; the Bad Man – my mother's mild designation for the devil – was a character playing his allotted part; the witches in my father's stories had as much claim to their place in the world as the farmer or the doctor or the ploughman.[14]

He still has one foot in that Eden. Now as he looks 'across the other land' it is to see, not the denial of that vision but a deepening and enrichment of it. The mystery remains, the why of it all. But – and this is the mood of the poem – that there is a reason for the existence of evil has come home to him not as a philosophical conclusion but as an imaginative truth.

One Foot in Eden is a personal statement. But not only does it achieve a power of generalization that takes it beyond the personal, it implicitly acknowledges the strength of the world where the faith that it expresses first took root. That world is fully acknowledged in *Outside Eden*, where the acceptance and the resignation, the fullest humanity, are seen as the features of a wise simplicity. The 'few' of *Outside Eden* are not Orkney people; as ever, the subjects of the poem are not characters, or even people in the normal way. 'They' represent a spiritual attitude, a possible condition. And yet pressing on their story, we do not doubt, is the memory of those 'kinsmen and kinswomen, ancestors and friends', from whom Muir learnt so much. These, now grown up, are the children who sat 'warm against the wall' (*The Gate*) until with the onset of adult consciousness, 'all seemed old/And dull and shrunken'. But those children grew up into a sullen travesty of humanity, eligible for the 'rich food that plumped (the) lusty bodies' of their guardians. Now, in *Outside Eden* their children in turn 'live where then they lay', but the picture of adult life is very different. These people belong to a clan (humanity in fact) sprung from Eden and now, after the fall, forever forbidden entrance to that lost domain. And yet it is so near:

> A few lead in their harvest still
> By the ruined wall and broken gate.
> Far inland shines the radiant hill.
> Inviolable the empty gate,
> Impassable the gaping wall;
> And the mountain over all.

These people continue to 'live in the land of birth/And count all else an idle grace'. They spring from a common root, but they are not simply to be identified with mankind now. For theirs too are negative virtues: they lack that insistent inquisitiveness that compels some men to 'browse in sin's great library' where 'learned enquirers look/And blind themselves to see their face'. (A dismissal of excessive Calvinist self-scrutiny and introspective guilt.) Theirs is a good order in which an instinctive trust in the ancestral memory and its image of life guarantees spiritual peace and invites the natural tribute:

> Their griefs are all in memory grown
> As natural as a weathered stone.
> Their troubles are a tribute given
> Freely while gazing at the hill.
> Such is their simplicity,
> Standing on earth, looking at heaven.

This is the 'order natural and wise' of Muir's earlier poem *The City*. Those who did not know it when they saw it and went on in fierce ambition to find only 'a dead land pitted with blind whirling places', are absent from *Outside Eden* except through the light allusion of the second stanza:

> Such is the country of this clan,
> Haunted by guilt and innocence.
> There is a sweetness in the air
> That bloomed as soon as time began,
> But now is dying everywhere.

Muir makes my point for me about the failing grasp of the language of the spirit: guilt and innocence haunt the few who 'lead in their harvest still', but the rest are committed to the search for the 'geometrical symmetry' – surely a construct of that powerful tendency of the modern mind to want the Mystery 'impaled and bent/Into an ideological instrument'.

With *Outside Eden* the mythological and the concrete are here united: Muir's 'knowledge of that first pre-industrial order' which he said 'taught me something which is inherent in every good order' is here assimilated to the most fundamental of Western myths. The relationship between the modern world and the order it has displaced is contemplated within the resulting whole. The same may be said of *The Horses* which in one way is very directly a poem of the 1950s: it reflects the unprecedented fear of all men that the next war will be the last war. It reflects that fear but it does not express it. For the situation that Muir describes is the occasion for a statement of faith in man's inherent power of recovery, the capacity to make a fresh beginning. The catastrophe of nuclear war would be an undoing, a de-creating of a world that in so many ways has been moulded after humanity's best aspirations. In a period of time no longer than it took God to create the universe, humanity will have answered Him in an ultimate act of self-annihilating destruction. This is the picture that *The Horses* gives us. The speakers are, again, the few; they survive 'the seven days war that put the world to sleep'. The world they are left with is literally the one we can all imagine. The detail is simple and graphic: the failing of the radios, the evidence of millions dead, the surviving aeroplanes robbed of a function. The result is a silence, the tractors lie about the fields and

> We have gone back
> Far past our fathers' land.

These lines, concluding the first section of the poem, signal the resurgence of hope that the coming of the horses embodies:

> And then, that evening
> Late in the summer the strange horses came.
> We heard a distant tapping on the road,
> A deepening drumming; it stopped, went on again
> And at the corner changed to hollow thunder.
> We saw the heads
> Like a wild wave charging and were afraid.

> We had sold our horses in our fathers' time
> To buy new tractors. Now they were strange to us
> As fabulous steeds set on an ancient shield
> Or illustrations in a book of knights.

It is a real embodiment. These horses are farm horses but they are charged with the mute glory of a world 'far past our fathers' land' that the warships and the aeroplanes cannot obliterate. They are here described in a way that confirms them as simultaneously within and outside our ken. These are the horses of Muir's boyhood, those he described in that unforgettable passage of *An Autobiography* as inspiring the love and dread that the explorer knows before 'a strange country which he has not yet entered'. This last phrase is directly to the point of their significance in this poem. For these horses come, unbidden, from who knows where? They are a physical presence; their sound and changing effect on the distant ear is precisely given in the description of their approach – the tapping followed by the drumming turning to hollow thunder. But their full impact is known only when they appear, when the eye too can know them, can read their meaning.

These, then, are plough horses; but they are, too, 'strange', of immemorial antiquity, a sign of that 'long-lost archaic companionship' of which Muir says 'our dreams and ancestral memories speak even if our rational selves deny it'. The men of the poem are moderns, far removed from the meaning of such companionship. But the terrible fracture with the past of man's creation has opened them to a new awareness of what it meant, so that

> In the first moment we had never a thought
> That they were creatures to be owned and used.

And in these wholly new circumstances, freed of all the trappings and distractions of the old world, they know 'that free servitude' that 'still can pierce our hearts':

> Our life is changed; their coming our beginning.

In *The Horses* the ordinary world of appearances and the timeless world of symbol and vision interpenetrate with complete conviction. We can believe in the picture of nuclear destruction and, equally, accept that root springing clean from Eden 'as on the starting day'. This is Muir's testimony to the claim to have 'one foot in Eden' and the surest proof that it is no mere form of words but a reality to be re-imagined and lived: in every end is a new beginning. And the new beginning lies around and within us. Frequently we are blind to it through self-absorption, but there will come those moments when the fabulous is revealed in the ordinary and 'All is new and near/In the unchanging Here/Of the fifth great day of God' (*The Animals*). Such a moment is recorded in Muir's wartime diary. It sounds like a prose version of his early poem *Horses* but we may see it as linking the 1924 to the 1955 poem and as a further confirmation of the visionary power of which both speak:

As the train lay at the country station I sat watching a tractor in a field and two horses in a plough. Then really too glorious, really too much, four horses abreast dragging something that looked like a great harrow. They looked wild and legendary, as if they had just risen full-grown from the mould. As I watched their necks arching and leaping, like four waves overtopping one another, I felt that these creatures had been fed in fields of inalienable strangeness, in quite another world from the world we know. I reflected a little while afterwards that this was really so; that this statement was strictly accurate, the horse's world being a different world from ours. But we centre everything in ourselves so almost automatically that we hardly ever realise it.[15]

Muir's use of the myth of Eden is natural and unselfconscious, but it does not commit him to a theology. Eden is not mentioned in the 1924 poem, but it is there nonetheless. It enters Muir's poetry explicitly when, imaginatively, the time is ripe for it, when it can be seen as an emblem for a condition of the spirit whose truth he has come to in his own, various ways. These ways have included myths from other, non-biblical traditions which have enabled him to test and reaffirm a faith in man's capacity for self-renewal. The entry of Eden into the late poetry is a sign of the slowly gathered confidence in the truth of its story. That truth has not been adopted; it has been discovered.

The Horses is a story. 'And a story which is thinking of nothing but the story will move us most when we forget or do not know who is telling it.'[16] That sentence comes from one of the late essays (originally lectures) reprinted in *The Estate of Poetry*, but it could have come from a much earlier period in Muir's writing. For it describes a view of art at its most human and mature that he returned to many times. It represents his own aspiration and indeed his instinct. In the sentence preceding the one already quoted he writes: 'A folk song that sings for its own pleasure will give back to us for centuries the emotion out of which it is born.' He had, many years before, spoken of the ballads in the same way: they were 'sure of themselves' as art can be only when, for a time at least, we lose our consciousness of the mind that produced it. Muir is much concerned in *The Estate of Poetry* with what he sees as our declining demand for and capacity to understand the 'story'. He does not by this mean the novel which, though 'it also tells a story in time ... is almost as concerned with the relations which space imposes on us'. 'The old story was quite simple. It followed some figure – Odysseus, or Ruth, or King David – through time, and it remains the most pure image that we have of the temporal life, tracing the journey which we shall take.'[17] Memorably, elsewhere in the same book, having again invoked Hugo von Hofmannsthal's 'true imagination is always conservative', he says, 'we become human by repetition; in the imagination that repetition becomes an object of delighted contemplation, with all that is good and evil in it, so that we can almost understand the saying that Hector died and Troy fell that they might turn into a song'.[18] Muir remained true to these insights throughout his mature poetic life. It is the strength of many of the late poems that the myths upon which they are based have been turned into very distinctive song. When we read such works as *The Annunciation, Orpheus' Dream, Telemachos Remembers* and *The Grave of Prometheus*, we are in touch with the intriguing paradox of which these quotations show Muir to have been so aware: that while each comes from and expresses the resolution of some conflict on the personal level, the surest sign of that resolution is the impersonality of the story each tells. Earlier I gave examples from *An Autobiography* of Muir's unusual responsiveness to the concrete, to his power of rendering the inward meaning of ordinary physical scenes. It was a power that had declared itself in childhood. Then it conveyed to the boy's imagination the mystery of the real world, but of course he could do nothing with it. The additional power of rendering the picture intelligible belongs to the adult. In *An Autobiography* the intelligibility is thus retrospective. In the poetry the picture is often purely imaginary but its clarity derives from a similar power of imaginative penetration, as in *Telemachos Remembers*:

> Twenty years, every day,
> The figures in the web she wove
> Came and stood and went away.
> Her fingers in their pitiless play
> Beat downward as the shuttle drove.
>
> Slowly, slowly did they come,
> With horse and chariot, spear and bow,
> Half-finished heroes sad and mum,
> Came slowly to the shuttle's hum.
> Time itself was not so slow.

Telemachos Remembers is one of Muir's purest pictures. It is a picture of active remembrance. Tireless and patient, Penelope is recalled at the loom, endlessly weaving figures in the web as, in a parallel endeavour,

> Far away Odysseus trod
> The treadmill of the turning road
> That did not bring him to his house.

The essence of Penelope's goodness is that the task is never done, that despite the weariness and the monotony she will not allow it to be done. But to what end?

> And what at last was there to see?
> A horse's head, a trunkless man,
> Mere odds and ends about to be,
> And the thin line of augury
> Where through the web the shuttle ran.

The answer was not clear to Telemachos the boy. But to the man, remembering, those poor 'odds and ends', 'that jumble of heads and spears/Forlorn scraps of her treasure trove' *are* 'pride and fidelity and love' and the ceaseless weaving an image of their essence: 'pride and fidelity and love' are not given; they must be endlessly created and recreated. Otherwise life is null, memory dead, 'the thin line of augury' cut and humanity disnatured. Unlike *The Return of Odysseus* which tells much the same story, *Telemachos Remembers* comments on the sufficiency of the myth it retells. For while Telemachos remembers, we modern readers remember in our turn. We are invited to contemplate the act of remembrance itself as it is embodied in a scene that connects Telemachos with the 'treasure trove' and him with ourselves.

'Simplicity' does not seem an adequate word to apply to such a poem; and yet, if one recalls that early definition of Muir's – 'I don't mean simplicity of mind, but of spirit, singleness, sureness' – then it is seen to fit these poems well. In *The Annunciation* there is an almost childlike elation:

> See, they have come together, see,
> While the destroying minutes flow,

But the elation belongs not to the poet but to the poem.

'I remember stopping', Mum writes in *An Autobiography* 'for a long time one day to look at a little plaque on the wall of a house in the Via degli Artisti, representing the Annunciation. An angel and a young girl, their bodies inclined towards each other, their knees bent as if they were overcome by love, 'tutto tremante', gazed upon each other like Dante's pair; and that representation of a human love so intense that it could not reach farther seemed the perfect earthly symbol of the love that passes understanding. A religion that dared to show forth such a mystery for everyone to see would have shocked the congregations of the north, would have seemed a sort of blasphemy, perhaps even an indecency. But here it was publicly shown, as Christ showed himself on the earth (p. 278).

In the poem we too look at that picture, are taken into its innermost meaning, unconscious of its origins in the incident that Muir describes in prose. This is perhaps his finest approach to the 'high and difficult theme' of incarnation. It perfectly represents his feeling that incarnation is not a possession of the specifically Christian imagination. Still less is it limited to *the* Incarnation. The source of the poem is in part the Christian story, and we cannot and are not meant to forget that. But the major departure from the Gospels and the focus of *The Annunciation* is that the 'increasing rapture' is the angel's as well as the girl's. There is awe at the penetration of the timeless into time but the persuasion of the poem is that the deepening trance is not supernatural: this love is human too. The triumph of the poem is that there is no incongruity in passing from this:

Yet the increasing rapture brings
So great a wonder that it makes
Each feather tremble on his wings

to this:

Outside the window footsteps fall
Into the ordinary day
And with the sun along the wall
Pursue their unreturning way.

'The end of all our exploring will be to arrive where we started . . . and know the place for the first time.'[19] The simplicity of spirit in *The Annunciation* is a complex achievement. It goes without saying that the maturity of this art has been hard won. The arrival at this simplicity in complexity has been made possible by something in Muir's imagination that never altogether lost touch with an earlier simplicity – one that belonged to the race and that he knew intimately:

The old ballads were the poetry of those who could not read. They are in the same world as those medieval churches where the frescoed walls are a picture book of the Bible story, intended for everyone, the lettered and the unlettered, designed to delight the one and to delight and instruct the other. We step into the picture book when we enter a church with frescoes picturing the Creation, the history of the patriarchs and the Judaean kings and prophets, the Annunciation, the birth, life and death of Christ, and the wanderings of the apostles.[20]

Simplifying matters, we might say that his early acquaintance with the world of the ballads guaranteed that he would later be able to see how it overlapped with that of other mythologies. His imagination was thus naturally at home in the full Western inheritance of myth and image. In *The Annunciation* the possible reach of human love is described through the Christian imagery that extends the implications of the poem but does not bind it to a mere repetition of what we can read in the Gospels. There is a similar freedom in the use of Greek myth in *Orpheus' Dream*. In the commonest classical version of the myth, Orpheus goes down into the underworld in search of Eurydice. Under the enchantment of his music Pluto and Persephone agree that Eurydice should return to life with him, but only on condition that in the journey back he does not look round. He cannot resist the temptation and loses her forever. This best known version of the myth is implicit in Muir's poem but its implications are there to be overcome. When at last Orpheus dares to turn round it is not to enter the despair of her eclipse but to see

The poor ghost of Eurydice
Still sitting in her silver chair,
Alone in Hades' empty hall.

Orpheus here is not in the hands of the Gods; he has not simply yielded to an overwhelming temptation. He dares to turn round because he has already recovered Eurydice. The nature of the recovery is the subject of the poem. One cannot paraphrase it; its integrity is that of an image in which the reality of spiritual love is made known to us. In his essay on Muir, John Holloway finds himself talking, with reference to *The Annunciation*, of 'the innermost feel of the poem'[21] and that is an indication of how little either that poem or *Orpheus' Dream* yields to 'interpretation'. The ecstasy is a creative force, protecting the lovers from the ordinary assaults of time, building a virtue that is its own protection. It is there in the 'innermost feel' of the first two stanzas:

> And she was there. The little boat
> Coasting the perilous isles of sleep,
> Zones of oblivion and despair,
> Stopped, for Eurydice was there.
> The foundering skiff could scarcely keep
> All that felicity afloat.

> As if we had left earth's frontier wood
> Long since and from this sea had won
> The lost original of the soul,
> The moment gave us pure and whole
> Each back to each, and swept us on
> Past every choice to boundless good.

In thinking of *The Annunciation* and *Orpheus' Dream* one is reminded of Willa Muir's statement that Muir's art aspired to ecstasy rather than domination. Both poems enable us to share his inspired conviction that time is conquerable within time, that 'deep in the diamond of the day' (*Merlin*) is not an area quite closed off. Always there is the promise of entry to a precious unity of body and soul, an intimation of immortality, a submergence within the ideal pattern that we can mostly only guess at. These poems are among 'those transformations of reality which the imagination itself creates' and of which Muir felt that the Transfiguration was perhaps the most powerful symbol. Blackmur, we remember, cautiously attempting to define Muir's spiritual province, likens him to George Herbert but 'without a parish, or a doctrine, or any one temple to construct'. What occupies Muir and gives his poems their various direction is 'a particular feeling for that transmutation of life which is found occasionally in poetry, and in the literature of prophecy, and sometimes in one's own thoughts when they are still' (23 July 1948). The provenance of those transmutations is always mysterious; the last few poems of the volume *One Foot in Eden* both acknowledge the mystery and express the peace that they bring with them.

Perhaps of all Muir's religious poems the sonnet *My Own* is the one where he attains something of that ease in tribulation, that calm amidst self-criticism that is the mark of Herbert's poetry. In *The Labyrinth*, the deceits were 'strong almost as life'. Here on the other hand, he has come through to a self-knowledge from which he can say of 'the confident roads that at their ease beguile me' – 'never did their lies deceive me'. The language of course has to dispense with the regular emblems of the Christian faith that Herbert could take for granted. The only word Muir allows himself that links him with the traditional dialogue of the Christian with his soul is that very word, 'soul'. The poem speaks, in the familiar spare style, of the division in man that, though it is never mentioned, is consequent on the Fall. On the one hand there is the clearsighted understanding of where 'true knowledge and real power' lie; on the other, the persistence – even by the hour – of aberration and self-deception. Muir speaks with that beguiling ease, that familiarity, with which the seventeenth-century poet addresses the soul:

> And when, lost in the dreaming route, I say
> I seek my soul, my soul does not believe me,
> But from these transports turns displeased away.

To speak with such ease when the subject is his imperfection is a sign not of complacency but of faith. For the imperfection is known through an understanding of the 'true knowledge', just as for Herbert it is known in his love of Christ. The self-criticism and confessional tone are confidently related to a feeling that the endeavour, the aspiration, are in search of an imperishable reality. The determined imaginings of *The Letter* and *The Good Man in Hell* are no more. Now, as with Herbert, the poem is pure affirmation even though its subject is the constant failure of the poet to live that affirmation through his own life:

> But then, but then, why should I so behave me,
> Willingly duped ten, twenty times an hour,
> But that even at my dearest cost I'd save me
> From the true knowledge and the real power?
> In which through all time's changeable seasons grown,
> I might have stayed, unshaken, with my own.

We may say the same of *If I Could Know*, which follows *My Own* in *Collected Poems*. It is – we might say in the secular terms appropriate to a poem that avoids mention of God – a plea for release from subjectivity, from the relativity of his own point of view. However, to use these colourless words is to deny the character of the feeling that moves the poem. Muir is in a tradition of supplication, self-abasement and submission. He does without the Christian language within which for him, as for us, the tradition is most familiar. But it is active throughout the poem, the submission in the final brief lines of the first three stanzas – 'If I could know', 'If I could see', 'If I could hear' – culminating naturally in the simple supplication, 'Teach me to know' of the fourth. Consciousness, time, the tumult of the world: these are obstacles to that ultimate knowledge, which is union with the Creator. But they are also the ambience within which we may learn of the Creator and of our dependence on grace:

> Make me to see and hear that I may know
> This journey and the place towards which I go;
> For a beginning and an end are mine
> Surely, and have their sign
> Which I and all in the earth and the heavens show.
> Teach me to know.

On Muir's tombstone there are these words from his sonnet, *Milton*:

> his unblinded eyes
> Saw far and near the fields of Paradise.

It is the most fitting of epitaphs. Muir's own 'blindness' had been a terrible abeyance of the spirit. But he had won through to a vision in which the 'weary weight of all this unintelligible world' found its natural and understood place. In the poems of his later years there is no trace of that melancholy regret that we might expect with age and declining power. There is, on the contrary, a sense of expansion and enrichment of feeling. 'And now that time grows shorter', he wrote, in one of the poems discovered in manuscript after his death,

> I perceive
> That Plato's is the truest poetry,
> And that these shadows
> Are cast by the true.

The nature of that truth and the consoling purity of vision that its acceptance brings are nowhere more beautifully realized than in the lyric *Song* ('*This will not pass so soon*'). Persephone – in the myth condemned to spend half the year below and half upon the earth – becomes the centre of the gentlest meditation on life and death, the transient and the eternal:

> This will not pass so soon,
> Dear friend, this will not pass,
> Though time is out of tune
> With all beneath the moon,
> Man and woman and flower and grass.
> These will not pass.

It has the simplicity of Muir's best: a simplicity of imaginative power exercised from a basis of faith, of an intuitive knowledge deepened over the years through the discovery of its previous embodiments and transformations in the culture of word, myth and image. The life that we see most immediately, the life of growth and decay, of beginnings and

ends, of darkness and light, is the shadow play of a drama we can
glimpse but never understand:

> Persephone,
> Surely all this can only be
> A light exchange and amorous interplay
> In your strange twofold immortality;
> And a diversion for a summer day
> The death and resurrection of the rose.

Notes

All page references given in brackets in the text refer to *An Autobiography*: see Introduction, n.2 and the Bibliography for full details. All substantial references to this source are given with a page number.

Introduction
1. 17 March 1925. All quotations from Muir's letters are from P. H. Butter's *Selected Letters of Edwin Muir* (1974); dates are given in parentheses after each quotation. In Butter's edition the letters are in chronological order.
2. For convenience I have in the body of the book used this title for a work that consists of two parts written during widely separate periods of Muir's life. The first six chapters were published in 1940 under the title of *The Story and the Fable*. In the 1950s, at the suggestion of his publisher, he added a further seven chapters and the whole appeared in 1954 as *An Autobiography*. It seems best to refer to the work under that title since it is now the only one to which the reader is likely to have access.
3. Hamburger, 'Edwin Muir', p. 50. (Full details of books and articles referred to in the text will be found in the Bibliography.)
4. *The Story and the Fable*, p. 261. The quotation is taken from chapter VII, 'Extracts from a Diary', which was not included in the 1954 edition.
5. *The Story and the Fable*, p. 263.
6. Traherne, *Centuries*, p. 113.
7. The Eliot quotations are from *Four Quartets*. They are, respectively, from *Burnt Norton, East Coker* and *The Dry Salvages*.
8. Traherne, p. 109.
9. *The Estate of Poetry*, p. 64.
10. *Ibid*, p. 62.
11. *Scott and Scotland*, pp. 19–20.
12. *Ibid*, p. 161.
13. Eliot, *Little Gidding (Four Quartets)*.

Chapter 1 *The Story and the Fable*
1. Wordsworth, *The Prelude*, Book 2, lines 346–352.
2. Traherne, p. 110.
3. W. Muir, *Belonging*, p. 166.
4. Blackmur, 'Between the Tiger's Paws', p. 428.
5. The phrase is, of course, John Stuart Mill's and is used of Wordsworth's poems. What I have in mind here can be indicated most straightforwardly

in a sentence of F. R. Leavis's: 'The debasement of the language is not merely a matter of words; it is a debasement of emotional life and the quality of living' (*Culture and Environment*, 1933). That the abuses to which I refer are well-documented is in no small degree due to Leavis' advocacy – particularly through the example of his literary criticism. The best recent examination of the relations between language, thought and feeling in such areas as politics, journalism and sexuality is Ian Robinson's *The Survival of English*, 1973.

6. Holloway, 'The poetry of Edwin Muir', p. 563.
7. Blackmur, 'Between the Tiger's Paws', p. 425.
8. Coleridge, *Dejection*, lines 51–52.
9. *Scottish Journey*, pp. 108 and 112.
10. *Ibid*, p. 114.
11. *The Estate of Poetry*, pp. 8–9.
12. *Transition*, p. 184.
13. W. Muir, *Belonging*, p. 23.
14. *Ibid*, p. 70.
15. 'Yesterday's mirror', p. 405.
16. *Essays on Literature and Society*, p. 218.
17. 'Yesterday's Mirror', p. 407.
18. *Essays on Literature and Society*, p. 155.

Chapter 2   *Beginnings*
1. An age of mysteries! which he
    Must live twice that would God's face see.

(Henry Vaughan, *Childhood*)

2. W. B. Yeats, 'Symbolism in painting' (1898), in *Essays and Introductions*, p. 151.
3. W. Muir, *Belonging*, p. 69.
4. Jung, *Modern Man in Search of a Soul*, p. 280 (Ch. XI, 'Psychotherapy or the Clergy').
5. *Ibid*, p. 186 (Ch. VIII, 'Psychology and Literature').
6. Jung, *Memories, Dreams, Reflections*, p. 17.
7. *Latitudes*, p. 17.
8. *Ibid*, p. 18.
9. *Ibid*, p. 16.
10. *Ibid*, p. 24.
11. *Ibid*, p. 23.
12. Quoted by P. H. Butter in *Edwin Muir, Man and Poet*, p. 83.
13. 'Yesterday's Mirror', p. 407.

Chapter 3   *The Enchanted Knight*
1. Butter, (1966), p. 95.
2. Murphy, *The Modern Poet*, pp. 168–70.
3. *Ibid*.
4. Matthew Arnold, *The Grande Chartreuse*, lines 85–86.
5. Quoted by Butter, p. 136.
6. *Transition*, p. 6.
7. *Belonging*, p. 245.
8. *Latitudes*, p. 175.
9. *Ibid*, pp. 183–4.
10. *Ibid*, p. 44.

11. Blackmur, 'Between the Tiger's Paws', p. 430.
12. *Scottish Journey*, pp. 83–4.
13. 'Yesterday's Mirror', p. 404.
14. Quoted by Butter, (1966), p. 136.
15. *Essays on Literature and Society*, p. 20.

Chapter 4   *The Narrow Place*
1. William Blake, *There is No Natural Religion*, 2nd series, 1788.
2. *Essays on Literature and Society*, p. 230.
3. Day Lewis, *A Hope for Poetry*, p. 54.
4. *Transition*, pp. 12–14.
5. W. Muir, *Belonging*, p. 275.
6. *Transition*, p. 180.
7. Jung, *Memories, Dreams, Reflections*, p. 391.
8. *Ibid*, p. 65.
9. *Ibid*, p. 185.
10. *Ibid*, p. 17.
11. *Ibid*, p. 33.
12. Eliot, *Notes Towards the Definition of Culture*, p. 117.
13. 'Hymn', in *Poetry of the Thirties*, ed. Robin Skelton.
14. *Left Review*, Number 2, November 1934.
15. *Essays on Literature and Society*, p. 34.
16. Quoted by Symons, p. 76.
17. *Ibid*, p. 142.
18. Symons, p. 142.
19. Hynes, *The Auden Generation*, p. 41.
20. *The London Mercury*, vol. XXXI, no. 181 (November 1934), 34–9.
21. Eliot, *Notes Towards the Definition of Culture*, p. 111.
22. *New Statesman*, 21 December 1940.
23. W. Muir, *Belonging*, p. 205.
24. Jung, *Modern Man in Search of a Soul*, p. 194.
25. C. Day Lewis, 'The road these times must take'.
26. C. Day Lewis, *The Magnetic Mountain*.
27. 'Yet we are all responsible for it – I mean all peoples and probably almost all individuals in Europe – by turning away from the soul and pursuing our private ambitions and greeds and personalities, and behaving as if they alone existed. Fifty or a hundred years of that, combined with an immense development of inventive processes, was bound to lead to this' (letter to Alec Aitken, 28 May 1940).
28. Jung, *Modern Man in Search of a Soul*, p. 169.

Chapter 5   *The Solid Foundation*
1. Jung, *Modern Man in Search of a Soul*, p. 278.
2. Yeats, *Essays and Introductions*, p. 119.
3. *The Story and the Fable*, p. 241.
4. Quoted by Butter, (1966), p. 162.
5. *Essays on Literature and Society*, p. 86.
6. *Ibid*, p. 49.
7. Quoted in part in *An Autobiography*, p. 246 and fully in Butter, (1966) pp. 167–8.
8. Noted by Butter in *Selected Letters of Edwin Muir*, p. 65.
9. *The Cloud of Unknowing*, trans. P. Wolters, pp. 65–6.

10. *Ibid,* p. 95. In his diary, Muir wrote at this time: 'There is surely no writing about the soul more wonderful than some of the Upanishads.' He quotes a long passage which includes these words: 'The Self is not known through discourse, splitting of hairs, learning however great' (*The Story and the Fable*, p. 262).

11. *Latitudes*, p. 67.

12. Blackmur, p. 426.

13. *Latitudes*, p. 67.

14. Such an insight might come involuntarily. Towards the end of his life, Muir had a dream that provided the basis for one of his most beautiful poems, *The Brothers*. In the dream he knew what in life, fifty years before, had been obscured in the everyday passions of childhood. Then

> A darkness covered every head,
> Frowns twisted the original face,
> And through that mask we could not see,
> The beauty and the buried grace.

Of the dream Muir wrote, 'I'm sure Blake could have told me everything about it' (24 January 1957).

15. 'The suffering which is reflected in (the contemporary poet's) poetry is, therefore, the suffering of uncertainty, which, unlike all other kinds of suffering, has no power to distil its own alleviation' (*Transition*, p. 189).

16. Yeats, *Essays and Introductions*, p. 41.

Chapter 6   *The Three Mirrors*

1. 'Yesterday's mirror', p. 406.

2. *Ibid*, p. 407.

3. As has often been noted, Muir is fascinated by heraldry and emblem. I have already drawn attention to the powerful contribution they make in *The Combat*. But it has to be said that the 'heraldic mode' is not consistently successful. A religious sensibility must use such metaphor and symbol as is available to it. Cut off for much of his poetic life from the traditional sources of such imagery, Muir reasonably and naturally enough goes to a source that *An Autobiography* shows for him to be natural to his imagination. Muir invented no mythology, but a poem like *The Covenant* illustrates the difficulties that arise when a symbolism is insufficiently familiar to a poet's readers. It is easy enough to read the poem at an abstract level; we have no difficulty in relating the covenant, the frieze of fabulous creatures, the fall, the long journey back, the heraldic crest, to the central statement that it is only in 'sleep-walled night' that they come meaningfully together. But I think it is a poem to which one needs to bring a more than usually deep awareness of what these things have come to signify for Muir. Their familiarity as emblems is not enough to give them poetic life. Certainly, the notion of the 'weariless wave' of temporality that

> Roofs with its sliding horror all that realm

is arresting, but too much depends on it: it isn't easy to share the outrage and sorrow of the final stanza quoted since we have not been helped by the poems to feel the relationship between 'innocence' and 'the heraldic crest of

nature'. The emblems remain almost as cold and fixed as they literally are on the shield.
4. W. Muir, *Belonging*, p. 211.

Chapter 7 *The Journey Back*

1. Quoted by Butter, (1966), p. 229.
2. T. S. Eliot, 'The frontiers of criticism', in *On Poetry and Poets* (1957), p. 106.
3. D. H. Lawrence, 'John Galsworthy', in *Phoenix*, Heinemann (1961), p. 539.
4. *Essays on Literature and Society*, p. 147.
5. *Ibid*, p. 153.
6. *Ibid*, p. 138.
7. *Ibid*, pp. 151–4.
8. Hamburger, 'Edwin Muir', p. 51.
9. *Essays on Literature and Society*, 10.
10. *Ibid*, pp. 120–4.
11. Raine, *Defending Ancient Springs*, p. 107.
12. *Essays on Literature and Society*, p. 121.
13. *Ibid*, p. 164.
14. Jung, *Modern Man in Search of a Soul*, p. 191.
15. Quoted by Butter, (1966), p. 216.
16. Gross, *Sound and Form in Modern Poetry*, p. 70.
17. *Essays on Literature and Society*, p. 103.
18. *Ibid*, p. 225.
19. *The Upanishads*, trans. Prabhavananda and Manchester, p. 30.
20. *The Prelude*, Book 2, lines 315–322.

Chapter 8 *Something to Pursue*

1. Eliot, *The Dry Salvages*, lines 200–16, from *Four Quartets*.
2. *Transition* (1926), p. 195.
3. Butter, (1966), p. 218.
4. Quoted by Butter, (1966), p. 222.
5. *Latitudes*, p. 28.
6. Heller, *The Artist's Journey into the Interior*, p. 112.
7. *Scottish Journey*, p. 72.
8. Raine, *Defending Ancient Springs*, p. 10.
9. *Scotland's Winter* (first published in 1935 but did not appear in a collection until *One Foot in Eden*).
10. Raine, *op. cit.*, p. 5.
11. *The Estate of Poetry*, p. 17.
12. Jung, *Memories, Dreams, Reflections*, pp. 106–7.
13. Raine, *op. cit.*, p. 8.
14. 'Yesterday's mirror', 408–9.
15. Quoted by Butter, (1966), p. 261.
16. *The Estate of Poetry*, p. 80.
17. *Ibid*, p. 29.
18. *Ibid*, p. 87.
19. Eliot, *Little Gidding* lines 240–2, in *Four Quartets*.
20. *The Estate of Poetry*, p. 102.
21. J. Holloway, 'The poetry of Edwin Muir', p. 567.

Bibliography

1 Works by Edwin Muir referred to in the text

Collected Poems, second edition (1963) Faber, London. (All quotations are from this edition).

We Moderns (under the pseudonym of Edward Moore), (1918) Allen & Unwin, London; Knopf, New York (1920).

Latitudes (1924) Melrose, London; Heubsch, New York (1926).

Transition (1926) Hogarth, London; Viking, New York (1926).

John Knox – portrait of a Calvinist (1929) Cape, London; Viking, New York (1929).

The Three Brothers (1931) Heinemann, London; Doubleday, New York (1931).

Poor Tom (1932) Dent, London.

'The present language of poetry' (1934), *The London Mercury* xxxi, no. 181, 34–9.

Scottish Journey (1935) Heinemann, London.

Scott and Scotland (1936) Routledge, London; Speller, New York (1938).

The Story and the Fable (1940) Harrap, London.

'Yesterday's mirror: afterthoughts to an Autobiography' (1940), *Scots Magazine* (New Series) xxxiii, pp. 404–10.

Essays on Literature and Society (1949) Hogarth, London; second edition (1965), revised and with the addition of six previously uncollected essays, Hogarth, London; Harvard U.P., Cambridge, Mass. (1965).

An Autobiography (1954) Hogarth, London; Sloane, New York. This is a reprint of *The Story and the Fable* with a few revisions and some added chapters.

The Estate of Poetry (1962) Hogarth, London; Harvard U.P., Cambridge, Mass, (1962).

Selected Letters of Edwin Muir, edited and with an introduction by P. H. Butter (1974) Hogarth, London.

Full bibliographical details of all Muir's writings will be found in Mellown, Elgin W. *Bibliography of the Writings of Edwin Muir* (1964)

University of Alabama, Alabama; revised edition, Nicholas Vane, London (1966).

2 Books and articles about Muir

Listed here are writings that I have found particularly useful in this study. A more comprehensive list will be found in Huberman (1971) (see below).

BLACKMUR, R. P. (1959) Edwin Muir: between the Tiger's Paws, *Kenyon Review*, xxi, 419–36.

BUTTER, P.H. (1962) *Edwin Muir*, Oliver & Boyd, Edinburgh; Grove, New York.

BUTTER, P. H. (1966) *Edwin Muir: Man and Poet*, Oliver & Boyd, Edinburgh; New York (1967).

ELIOT, T. S. (1964) Edwin Muir, *The Listener*, 28 May 1964, p. 872; reprinted as Preface to *Selected Poems of Edwin Muir* (1965) Faber, London; New York.

GARBER, F. (1966) 'Edwin Muir's heraldic mode', *Twentieth-Century Literature*, xii, 96–103.

GARDNER, HELEN (1961) Edwin Muir (W. D. Thomas Memorial Lecture), University of Wales, Cardiff.

GROSS, HARVEY (1964) *Sound and Form in Modern Poetry*, Ann Arbor, Michigan.

HALL, J. C. (1956) *Edwin Muir*. British Council Series, Writers and their Work: no. 71. London.

HAMBURGER, MICHAEL (1960) Edwin Muir, *Encounter*, xv, 46–53.

HOFFMAN, DANIEL (1967) *Barbarous Knowledge*, Oxford University Press, New York.

HOLLOWAY, JOHN (1960) 'The poetry of Edwin Muir', *Hudson Review*, pp. 550–67.

HUBERMAN, ELIZABETH (1971) *The Poetry of Edwin Muir*, Oxford University Press, New York.

JENNINGS, ELIZABETH (1960) 'The Living Dead – VII: Edwin Muir as poet and allegorist, *London Magazine*, vii, 43–56.

JOSELYN, SISTER M. (1963) 'Herbert and Muir: pilgrims of their age', *Renascence*, xv, 127–32.

MUIR, WILLA (1968) *Belonging*, Hogarth, London.

RAINE, KATHLEEN (1967) 'Edwin Muir', in *Defending Ancient Springs*, pp. 1–16. Oxford University Press, London.

SUMMERS, JOSEPH H. (1961) 'The achievement of Edwin Muir', *The Massachusetts Review*, ii 240–61.

3 Other books cited in the text and notes

DAY LEWIS, C. (1934) *A Hope for Poetry*, Basil Blackwell, Oxford.

ELIOT, T. S. (1943) *Four Quartets*, Faber, London.

ELIOT, T. S. (1948) *Notes Towards the Definition of Culture*, Faber, London; Harcourt Brace, New York.

ELIOT, T. S. (1957) *On Poetry and Poets*, Faber, London; Octagon, New York.

HELLER, ERICH (1965) *The Artist's Journey into the Interior*, Random House., New York; Secker & Warburg, London (1966).

HYNES, SAMUEL (1976) *The Auden Generation*, Bodley Head, London; Viking, New York (1977).

JUNG, C. G. (1967) *Memories, Dreams, Reflections*, Random House, New York; Collins, London, (1967).

JUNG, C. G. (1933) *Modern Man in Search of a Soul*, Kegan Paul, Trubner & Co., London; Harcourt Brace, New York (1976).

LAWRENCE, D. H. (1963) *Phoenix*, Heinemann, London; Viking, New York (1968).

MURPHY, GWENDOLEN (1938) *The Modern Poet*, Sidgwick & Jackson, London.

SKELTON, ROBIN, ed. (1964) *Poetry of the Thirties*, Penguin Books, London.

SWAMI, PRABHAVANANDA and MANCHESTER, FREDERICK *The Upanishads*, Mentor Books, New York and London (1957).

SYMONS, JULIAN (1960) *The Thirties: a dream revolved*, Cresset Press, London.

TRAHERNE, THOMAS (1960) *Centuries*, Faith Press, London.

WOLTERS, CLIFTON (1961) trans. *The Cloud of Unknowing and other Works*, Penguin Books, London.

YEATS, W. B. (1961) *Essays and Introductions*, Macmillan, London; Macmillan, New York (1968).

Index

(Note: all Muir's works are entered here under Muir, Edwin)